Criminal Defence at Police Stations

Criminal defence at the investigative stage has attracted growing attention due to the shifting focus of the criminal process onto pre-trial stages, and the recent European regulations adopted in this area. Increasingly, justice practitioners and legislators across the EU have begun to realise that 'the trial takes place at the police station'. This book provides a comprehensive legal, empirical and contextual analysis of criminal defence at the investigative stage from a comparative perspective. It is a socio-legal study of criminal defence practice, which draws upon original empirical material from England and Wales and the Netherlands. Based on extensive interviews with lawyers, and extended periods of observation, the book contrasts the encountered reality of criminal defence with the model role of a lawyer at the investigative stage derived from European norms. It places the practice of criminal defence within the broader context of procedural traditions, contemporary criminal justice policies and lawyers' occupational cultures. *Criminal Defence at Police Stations* questions the determinative role of procedural traditions in shaping criminal defence practice at the investigative stage.

The book will be of interest for criminal law and justice practitioners, as well as for academics focusing on criminal justice, criminology, socio-legal studies, legal psychology and human rights.

Anna Pivaty is postdoctorate researcher at the Faculty of Law, University of Maastricht, The Netherlands.

Criminal Defence at Police Stations
A Comparative and Empirical Study

Anna Pivaty

LONDON AND NEW YORK

First published 2020
by Routledge
2 Park Square, Milton Park, Abingdon, Oxon OX14 4RN

and by Routledge
52 Vanderbilt Avenue, New York, NY 10017

Routledge is an imprint of the Taylor & Francis Group, an informa business

© 2020 Anna Pivaty

The right of Anna Pivaty to be identified as author of this work has been asserted by her in accordance with sections 77 and 78 of the Copyright, Designs and Patents Act 1988.

All rights reserved. No part of this book may be reprinted or reproduced or utilised in any form or by any electronic, mechanical, or other means, now known or hereafter invented, including photocopying and recording, or in any information storage or retrieval system, without permission in writing from the publishers.

Trademark notice: Product or corporate names may be trademarks or registered trademarks, and are used only for identification and explanation without intent to infringe.

British Library Cataloguing-in-Publication Data
A catalogue record for this book is available from the British Library

Library of Congress Cataloging-in-Publication Data
A catalog record has been requested for this book

ISBN: 978-0-367-17805-5 (hbk)
ISBN: 978-0-367-17807-9 (ebk)

Typeset in Galliard
by SPi Technologies India Private Limited

Contents

List of abbreviations x
List of cases xi
Acknowledgments xiv

1 **Introduction** 1
  1 *Criminal defence practice: the centrality of the investigative stage* 1
  2 *Rationale for the research* 2
  3 *Shifting focus from the trial to pre-trial proceedings* 4
  4 *Research approach* 5
  5 *Outline of the book* 6
  Notes 7

2 **The role of a defence lawyer at the investigative stage: the view from Europe** 9
  1 *Introduction* 9
  2 *From defence rights to the role of a lawyer: an inferential approach* 10
  3 *Sources: the interplay of the ECtHR case law and the EU law* 11
    3.1 The ECtHR approach to the right of early access to a lawyer: a double U-Turn 11
    3.2 The EU Directives and their interpretation 14
  4 *The role of a lawyer at the investigative stage: basic definitions* 16
  5 *The lawyers' role vis-à-vis their clients* 17
    5.1 The lawyer–client relationship 17
    5.2 Advising client 18
    5.3 Protecting welfare and emotional support of detained clients 20
  6 *The lawyers' role vis-à-vis the authorities* 21
    6.1 Obtaining disclosure 21
    6.2 Assisting suspects during the interrogation 21

vi *Contents*

  6.3 Arguing against procedural breaches 25
  6.4 Arguing for the suspect's release from detention 26
  6.5 Participation in the fact-finding process 27
   6.5.1 Participating in the investigations conducted by the authorities 27
   6.5.2 Conducting one's own enquiries or requesting authorities to undertake investigations 29
  6.6 The role of a lawyer with regard to out-of-court disposals 30
 7 Conclusion 31
  Notes 32

3 The Netherlands: lawyer as 'trusted person' and provider of information   35
 1 Introduction 35
 2 Setting the scene 36
  2.1 The role of defence lawyers 36
  2.2 Lawyers at suspect interrogations: decades of opposition 37
  2.3 Positioning the Dutch fieldwork 39
 3 The lawyer and the client: brief and superficial encounters 40
  3.1 The importance of 'trust' and the lack of trust in police station encounters 40
   3.1.1 'Trust' in the professional discourse of lawyers 40
   3.1.2 Lack of trust in observations 41
  3.2 Advising suspects: generic advice in an informational vacuum 43
   3.2.1 Gathering information from clients 43
   3.2.2 Advising clients 46
  3.3 Supporting clients in detention: limitations of the 'trusted person' role 48
   3.3.1 Lawyers' professional discourse on their role as 'trusted person' 48
   3.3.2 Supporting clients in detention in practice 49
 4 Lawyers and the authorities: the lack of participatory role 50
  4.1 Obtaining disclosure from police 50
  4.2 Role at interrogations: lawyers' passivity and police resistance 52
   4.2.1 The use of persuasion in interrogations 53
   4.2.2 Lawyers' reaction to persuasion tactics 56

    4.3 Outside of the interrogation 58
        4.3.1 Challenging procedural breaches and the use of procedural remedies 58
        4.3.2 Participation in the fact-finding process at the investigative stage 59
  5 *Conclusions 61*
    Notes 61

4 England and Wales: lawyer as advisor and provider of 'active defence'   **63**
  1 *Introduction 63*
  2 *Setting the scene 64*
    2.1 The role of defence lawyers 64
    2.2 The history of the right to legal assistance for suspects in police custody 66
    2.3 Arrangements and practices at the time of the fieldwork 66
  3 *Lawyers and their clients: the lawyer as 'legal expert' 67*
    3.1 The discourse on the lawyer–client relationship: lawyers 'simply advise' 68
    3.2 The lawyer–client relationship in observations 69
        3.2.1 The client's 'truthfulness' and dealing with 'non-credible' accounts 70
        3.2.2 Explaining the right to silence 'caution' 72
        3.2.3 Presenting strategy options 73
    3.3 Supporting suspects in detention: limited obligations in the law and in practice 75
        3.3.1 PACE and lawyers' professional discourse: the lawyer's role as mostly 'legal' 75
        3.3.2 The role of providing emotional support in practice 76
  4 *Lawyers and the authorities: the limits of the 'active defence' role 77*
    4.1 Obtaining police disclosure: a negotiated practice 80
    4.2 The role at the interrogation: lawyers avoid being 'confrontational' 81
    4.3 Challenging procedural irregularities 84
    4.4 Negotiating out-of-court disposals and bail 87
    4.5 Participation in the fact-finding process at the investigative stage 89
  5 *Conclusions 91*
    Notes 91

5 The influence of legal procedural traditions: observations from the field 93

1 Introduction 93
2 Procedural traditions, legal regulations and practices 95
  2.1 Legal cultures and legal (procedural) traditions 95
  2.2 The 'inquisitorial' and 'adversarial' procedural traditions 97
    2.2.1 Multiple purposes, multiple meanings 97
    2.2.2 The contours of the two procedural traditions 98
3 Procedural traditions and legal assistance at the investigative stage in practice 101
  3.1 The lawyer–client relationship 101
  3.2 Active or passive role and power in the interrogation room 104
  3.3 Participation in the fact-finding 109
  3.4 Obtaining early disclosure of case-related information 111
4 Conclusions 114
Notes 116

6 The influence of contemporary criminal justice policies 118

1 Introduction 118
2 Contemporary criminal justice policies and the criminal process 119
3 The impact on the role and position of defence lawyers 122
4 Managerialism, austerity and legal assistance at the investigative stage 124
  4.1 The penalisation of silence at the investigative stage 125
  4.2 Lawyers' duties to cooperate with the administration of justice 130
  4.3 Courts' attitudes to defence arguments 132
  4.4 Out-of-court disposals and the role of defence lawyers 135
  4.5 The bureaucratisation of the investigative stage 138
  4.6 Fixed fees and legal assistance at the investigative stage 141
5 Conclusions 145
Notes 146

7 The influence of occupational cultures of lawyers 148

1 Introduction 148
2 Occupational cultures of criminal justice actors 149
  2.1 Police occupational cultures 149
  2.2 Defence lawyers' occupational cultures: the state of knowledge 152
3 Lawyers' occupational cultures and procedural traditions 154

    4 Observations from the fieldwork 155
        4.1 Mistrust of clients and assumptions of their guilt 155
        4.2 Risk avoidance: silence as the 'safest' strategy 159
        4.3 Emotional distancing from clients 162
        4.4 The non-confrontational stance with the authorities 165
    5 Conclusions 168
       Notes 169

8 Concluding remarks   171
    1 Introduction 171
    2 The normative model of the role of lawyers at the investigative stage: between aspiration and rhetoric 172
    3 England and Wales and the Netherlands compared 174
    4 The interplay of procedural traditions, criminal justice policies and occupational cultures 176
    5 Reforming the practice of criminal defence at the investigative stage 177
       Notes 181

Appendix: notes on the research methodology   182
    1 Critical realism and constructivist grounded theory 182
    2 Data collection 184
    3 Being in the field 185
    4 Ethical issues 188
    5 Limitations of the chosen methodology 188
       Notes 189

Bibliography   191
Index   206

Abbreviations

CCP	Code of Criminal Procedure
CIPA	Criminal Investigations and Procedure Act (England and Wales)
CJPOA	Criminal Justice and Public Order Act (England and Wales)
CoE	Council of Europe
CPS	Crown Prosecution Service (England and Wales)
ECHR	European Convention of Human Rights
EComHR	European Commission of Human Rights
ECtHR	European Court of Human Rights
EU	European Union
PACE	Police and Criminal Evidence Act (England and Wales)
SRA	Solicitors Regulation Authority (England and Wales)

Cases

Alchagin v. Russia, 17 January 2012, No. 20212/05
Arthur J.S. Hall and Co. v. Simons [2002] 1 AC 615
Beuze v. Belgium (Grand Chamber), 9 November 2018, No. 71409/10
Blokhin v. Russia, 14 November 2013, No. 47152/06
Brusco v. France, 14 October 2010, No. 1466/77
Campbell and Fell v. United Kingdom, 28 June 1984, Nos 7819/77, 7878/77
Can v. Austria (EComHR), 12 July 1984, No. 11/1984/83/130
Castravet v. Moldova, 13 March 2007, No. 23393/05
Chopenko v. Ukraine, 15 January 2015, No. 17735/06
Croissant v. Germany, 25 September 1992, No. 13611/88
Daud v. Portugal, 21 April 1998, No. 22600/93
Dayanan v. Turkey, 13 October 2009, No. 7377/03
Dev Sol, HR 7 May 1996, ECLI:NL:PHR:1996:AB9820, *NJ* 1996, 687 m.nt. Schalken
Deweer v. Belgium, 27 February 1980, No. 6903/75
Dvorski v. Croatia (Grand Chamber), 20 October 2015, No. 25703/11
Dzhulay v. Ukraine, 3 April 2014, No. 24439/06
Eraslan and others v. Turkey, 6 October 2009, No. 59653/00
EWCA R. v. Paris, Miller and Abdullahi, 97 Cr App LR 99
Fazli Kaya v. Turkey, 17 December 2015, No. 24280/05
Galip Doğru v. Turkey, 28 April 2015, No. 36001/06
Garcia Alva v. Germany, 13 February 2001, No. 23541/94
Gennadiy Medvedev v. Russia, 24 April 2012, No. 34184/03
HR 12 November 1974, *NJ* 1975/41
HR 3 July 1989, ECLI:NL:HR:1989:ZC8175, *NJ* 1990/122
HR 14 September 1992, ECLI:NL:HR:1992:AC3716, *NJ* 1993/54
HR 13 May 1997, ECLI:NL:HR:1997:ZD0705, *NJ* 1998/152 m.nt. Schalken
HR 3 June 1997, ECLI:NL:HR:1997:ZD0733, *NJ* 1997/584
HR 22 September 1998, ECLI:NL:HR:1998:ZD1277, *NJ* 1999/104
HR 18 May 1999, ECLI:NL:PHR:1999:ZD1332, NJ 2000/104
HR 8 May 2001, ECLI:NL:HR:2001:AB1473, *NJB* 2001/105, 1090
HR 8 May 2001, ECLI:NL:HR:2001:AB1566, *NJ* 2001/587

xii *Cases*

HR 23 September 2003, ECLI:NL:HR:2003:AI0032
HR 15 June 2004, ECLI:NL:HR:2004: AO9639, *NJ* 2004/464
HR 30 June 2009, ECLI:NL:HR:2009:BH3079, *NJ* 2009/349
HR 9 November 2010, ECLI:NL:HR:2010:BN7727, *NJ* 2010/615
HR 13 September 2011, ECLI:NL:HR:2011:BQ8907, *NJ* 2011/556
HR 5 June 2012, ECLI:NL:HR:2012:BW7372, *NJ* 2012/369
HR 3 July 2012, ECLI:NL:HR:2012:BW9968, *NJ* 2012/466
HR 1 April 2014, ECLI:NL:HR:2014: 770, *NJ* 2014/268
HR 16 September 2014, ECLI:NL:HR:2014:2764, *NJ* 2014/246
HR 22 December 2015, ECLI: NL:HR:2015:3608
HR 20 February 2018, ECLI:NL:HR:2018:228
Hurtado v. Switzerland, 28 January 1994, No. 17549/90
Huseyn and others v. Azerbaijan, 26 July 2011, Nos 35485/05, 45553/05, 35680/05 and 36085/05
Ibrahim and others v. United Kingdom (Grand Chamber), 13 September 2016, Nos 50541/08, 50571/08, 50573/08 and 40351/09
Imbrioscia v. Switzerland, 24 November 1993, No. 13972/88
İrmak v. Turkey, 12 January 2016, No. 20564/10
Kalashnikov v. Russia, 15 July 2002, No. 47095/99
Keenan v. United Kingdom, 3 April 2001, No. 27229/95
Kovalchuk v. Ukraine, 4 November 2010, No. 21958/05
Laska and Lika v. Albania, 20 April 2010, Nos 12315/04, 17605/04
Lietzow v. Germany, 13 February 2001, No. 24479/94
Mader v. Croatia, 21 June 2011, No. 56185/07
Magee v. United Kingdom, 6 June 2000, No. 50356/08
Mehmet Serif Öner v. Turkey, 13 September 2011, No. 50356/08
Melnikov v. Russia, 14 January 2010, No. 23610/03
Mihai Moldoveanu v. Romania, 19 June 2012, No. 4238/03
Mooren v. Germany, 9 July 2009, No. 11364/03
Natsvlishvili and Togonidze v. Georgia, 29 April 2014, No. 9043/05
Navone and others v. Monaco, 24 October 2013, Nos 62880/11, 62892/11 and 62899/11
Niemietz v. Germany, 16 December 1992, No. 13710/88
Nikula v. Finland, 21 March 2002, No. 31611/96
Öcalan v. Turkey (Grand Chamber), 12 May 2005, No. 46221/99
Özcan Çolak v. Turkey, 6 October 2009, No. 30235/03
Petri Sallinen and others v. Finland, 27 September 2005, No. 50882/99
Pishchalnikov v. Russia, 24 September 2009, No. 7025/04
R. v. Argent [1997] 2 All ER 27; [1997] Crim LR 685
R. v. Bryant and Dickson (1946) 31 Cr App R 146
R. v. DPP, ex p. Lee [1992] 2 Cr App R 304
R. v. Dunn (1990) 91 Cr App R 237; [1990] Crim LR 572
R. v. Gleeson [2004] 1 Cr. App. R. 29
R. v. Lewis [2003] EWCA Crim 223
R. v. McGarry [1998] 3 All ER 805

Rechtbank Gelderland 28 January 2014, *NbSr* 2014/134
Ribitsch v. Austria, 4 December 1995, No. 18896/91
S. v. Switzerland, 28 November 1991, Nos 12629/87 and 13965/88
Salduz v. Turkey (Grand Chamber), 27 November 2008, No. 36391/02
Şaman v. Turkey, 5 April 2011, No. 35292/05
Sapan v. Turkey, 20 September 2011, No. 17252/09
Savas v. Turkey, December 2009, No. 9762/03
Schöpfer v. Switzerland, 20 May 1998, 56/1997/840/1046
Schöps v. Germany, 13 February 2001, No. 25116/94
Simeonovi v. Bulgaria (Grand Chamber), 12 May 2017, No. 21980/04
Smolik v. Ukraine, 19 January 2012, No. 11778/05
Sobko v. Ukraine, 17 December 2015, No. 15120/10
Süzer v. Turkey, 23 April 2013, No. 13885/05
Taïs v. France, 1 June 2006, No. 17969/09
Tikhonov v. Ukraine, 10 December 2015, No. 17969/09
Trymbach v. Ukraine, 12 January 2912, No. 44385/02
Varnava and Others v. Turkey (Grand Chamber), 18 September 2009, Nos 16064/90, 16065/90, 16066/90, 16068/90, 16069/90, 16070/90, 16071/90, 16072/90 and 16073/90
Yunus Aktaş and others v. Turkey, 20 October 2009, No. 24744/03
Zachar and Čierny v. Slovakia, 21 July 2015, Nos 29376/12 and 29384/12

Acknowledgments

This book originates from my PhD dissertation, which I defended at Maastricht University (the Netherlands) on 3 May 2019. I am deeply indebted to my PhD supervisors Taru Spronken and Ed Cape, who encouraged me to embark on a PhD journey, and who gave me ample support and opportunities to grow. I am grateful to the Department of Criminal Law and Criminology at Maastricht University for providing such a stimulating research environment, and giving me the space to finalise my PhD and this manuscript. I wish to thank my departmental colleagues for their friendship, positive energy and for lending me a supportive ear when it was really necessary. I also wish to thank John Jackson, Petra van Kampen, Hans Nelen, Dian Brouwer and Dorris de Vocht for assessing and reviewing the initial PhD manuscript.

My gratitude goes to all (senior) colleagues, with whom I was blessed to collaborate throughout all these years, and who have generously shared with me their knowledge and wisdom: Jackie Hodgson, Jodie Blackstock, Yvonne Daly, Vicky Conway, Miet Vanderhallen, Michele Panzavolta and Anneli Soo. I also wish to thank Violet Mols for her valuable research assistance. A special thanks to Alison Kirk and Emily Summers at Routledge for believing in the potential of my research, and for their incredible editorial support.

I am extremely grateful to all lawyers, police officers and other persons I met while conducting the fieldwork for this study in England and Wales and in the Netherlands. They have allowed me to gain insight into their working lives, shared their insider knowledge and were so willing to accommodate and help me along the way. This research would not have been possible without their generous collaboration.

A final word of thanks goes to my family: Bertrand, Leo and Elise. You have always believed in me, supported me, and you dealt so patiently with my frequent 'absence' while I was finalising this manuscript. I promise to make up for our precious family time very soon.

1 Introduction

1 Criminal defence practice: the centrality of the investigative stage

The traditional image of the work of a criminal defence lawyer is trial-centred. Activities performed by lawyers at the pre-trial stages are viewed as the preparation for the trial. This image, however, is changing. The traditional view that the decisive and most important action happens in court has been brought into question. Pursuant to contemporary reforms aimed at improving procedural 'efficiency', the centre of gravity of the criminal proceedings is increasingly shifting to the pre-trial or investigative stages (Crijns, 2017; Healy et al., 2015). Consequently, the statement that 'effective criminal defence' takes place in court is being challenged. Arguably, nowadays, the work performed by defence lawyers during the investigative stage is equally important, if not more important, than their actions during the trial. These developments are also echoed in European and national legal regulations. European defence lawyers are now expected to enter the proceedings earlier, and to play an increasingly active role during the investigative stage (Jackson, 2016a). This expectation was made even more explicit in the recent EU Directive on the right of access to a lawyer (hereinafter – *Directive 2013/48/EU*).[1]

As from 1 March 2017, anyone suspected of a criminal offence in the EU[2] is entitled to the assistance of a lawyer,[3] free of charge under certain conditions. When someone is arrested, legal assistance must be provided to them 'without undue delay'. If the arrested person wishes to benefit from legal advice, they have the right to meet with the lawyer in private before any questioning takes place. In principle, the lawyer should be present during all interrogations to assist the client in exercising their rights. They should furthermore take part in other investigative actions such as confrontations or identity parades. The lawyer must also attempt to argue against their client's further detention, if being envisaged. In addition, they must discuss the allegations with the client, inform and advise them on relevant legal issues, and determine, together with the client, the procedural strategy during interrogation(s), and during other procedural actions. Sometimes, to determine the strategy, the lawyer needs to seek additional information from third parties. They must also oversee the well-being of their detained client, such as whether they are treated well by the police, or whether they have received the necessary medical assistance. More generally, the lawyer must ensure that the rights and entitlements of the client are being respected, and that the established procedures are duly followed.

The aforementioned tasks represent just a few of the numerous responsibilities of defence lawyers – corresponding to the respective rights of their clients in relation to the investigative stage of criminal proceedings,[4] which follow from European legal norms. The investigative stage, however, is often remarkably short: ranging from several hours in the simplest cases, to several days in the greatest number of 'ordinary' criminal cases. Consequently, for defence lawyers, this stage is arguably the most fast-paced and challenging period of the entire proceedings. The difficulties are exacerbated by the fact that the work often has to be done outside regular office hours – for example, when suspects are arrested and interrogated at night-time or over weekends. Occasionally, police officers' or clients' behaviour towards lawyers can be uncooperative or even hostile. The environment of police custody is far from pleasant, with the lack of light, space, basic comfort, and other oppressive manifestations of confinement and human suffering (Skinns, 2010). One English lawyer interviewed for this study, for instance, compared assisting suspects detained by police to 'working on the production line in a slaughterhouse' (INTEng2).[5] The metaphor referred not only to the unpleasant working conditions, but also to the time pressures under which lawyers often find themselves. Lawyers may need to assist several clients on their 'duty day', or police might wish to proceed to interrogation, putting pressure on the lawyer to end the consultation with the client as quickly as possible.

How do lawyers deal with the various tasks and responsibilities at the investigative stage allotted to them in their day-to-day practice? Do they conceive of their role at this stage in the same way as envisaged in the respective normative pronouncements? How is the role of lawyers at the investigative stage of the criminal proceedings influenced by the broader context, such as the existing procedural traditions, criminal justice policies, or lawyers' occupational cultures? These were the central questions that guided the research presented in this book.

2 Rationale for the research

The focus on legal assistance at the investigative stage of the criminal proceedings was inspired by the numerous legal writings on this topic. Access to a lawyer before and during the (first) suspect interrogations by police has been the object of heated debates in several European countries for as long as 40 years.[6] Proponents of early access to legal assistance, mostly among academics and defence lawyers, argued that it was necessary to subject police interrogations to external scrutiny, with the aim of preventing miscarriages of justice triggered by false confessions.[7] Its opponents, mostly among law enforcement and government institutions, claimed that extending access to a lawyer to the investigative stage would hinder crime investigations, precluding criminals from receiving deserved punishment, and from victims receiving deserved justice.[8] In England and Wales, the proponents of early access to legal assistance eventually prevailed, which led to the adoption of respective provisions in the 1985 Police and Criminal Evidence Act (PACE). In other European jurisdictions, such as the Netherlands, but also France, Belgium, Scotland or Ireland, the debates about appropriate legal regulation of early access to a lawyer have continued until the present day. Most of these jurisdictions, including the Netherlands, reviewed their legislation to incorporate the right of early access. These processes were often triggered by the ECtHR case law, most notably *Salduz v. Turkey (2008)*, and most recently, the EU procedural rights' Directives, including *Directive 2013/48/EU*. However, these states have also resisted the incorporation of the right of early access to legal assistance in their national laws, often opting for minimalist interpretation of the *Salduz* principles and the *Directive 2013/48/EU* (Giannoulopoulos, 2016; Jackson, 2016b; Pivaty, 2018).

This research originally aimed to provide empirical arguments to shed light on the above-mentioned debate: namely, does early access to a lawyer indeed help prevent false confessions? Does it interfere with effective investigations? Do crime clearance rates drop when lawyers enter the interrogation room? However, it became clear quite early on that such a study would not be feasible due to the methodological complexity. Instead, the focus of the research shifted from ascertaining the impact or consequences of lawyers' actions to zooming into the *role* that defence lawyers play at the investigative stage of the proceedings.

Indeed, once the right of early access to a lawyer has been recognised in the law (this is currently the reality in all EU countries – members of *Directive 2013/48/EU*), the next question should be: What *role* should lawyers (be entitled to) play at the investigative stage? Whilst *Directive 2013/48/EU* and other European pronouncements clearly define the *scope* of the right of early access to a lawyer, the provisions concerning the *role* of the lawyer at the investigative stage are rather vague. This allows for great diversity among Member States: for example, some states, like the Netherlands, Belgium or France, have introduced restrictions on the role of lawyers during suspect interrogations, which do not exist in other states (Blackstock et al., 2013; Giannoulopoulos, 2016; Jackson, 2016b). Are these restrictions in line with *Directive 2013/48/EU*? To respond to this question, it is necessary to understand the implicit meanings of the role of the lawyer at the investigative stage embedded in *Directive 2013/48/EU* and other European regulations.

This study, however, is concerned not (only) with the 'law on the books', but mostly with the 'law in action'. Thus, once the normative view on the role of lawyers at the investigative stage is formulated, the following step is to ascertain whether – and to what extent – this view is reflected in the daily working practices of defence lawyers. Two European jurisdictions are chosen for this exercise: England and Wales and the Netherlands (the choice is explained in Section 4). The day-to-day professional practices of defence lawyers are examined by means of extensive naturalistic observations and in-depth qualitative interviewing.

4 *Introduction*

However, the ultimate goal of this research is to provide insight into whether – and how – the professional practices and 'working cultures' (see Chapter 7) of criminal defence lawyers could be aligned with the contemporary normative view of their role at the investigative stage. Thus, this study also engages with the following questions: Why have the observed professional practices of legal assistance at the investigative stage developed in a certain way? What are the (comparative) factors underlying this development? Can the influence of these factors in shaping lawyers' professional practices be documented? How can the knowledge regarding the role of the different factors inform our 'theory of change'?

This study was furthermore inspired by the relative scarcity of comparative research on the 'working cultures' of criminal defence lawyers, as compared, for instance, to similar research on prosecutors[9] and police.[10] Most existing empirical literature on criminal defence lawyering originates from England and Wales. The most comprehensive account of criminal defence lawyers' working practices in England and Wales, and possibly worldwide, is the seminal work of Mike McConville, Jacqueline Hodgson, Lee Bridges and Anita Pavlovic entitled *Standing Accused: The Organisation and Practices of Criminal Defence Lawyers in Britain* (1994). Similar research from other European jurisdictions (published in English) is largely lacking. Notable exceptions are the works of Jackie Hodgson (2005), and Stewart Field and Andrew West (2003) focusing on French criminal defence lawyers. However, these accounts, as well as the research of Mike McConville and colleagues date back 15–25 years. In the last decade, in England and Wales there has been growing interest in research on the professional practices of criminal defence. Authors like Daniel Newman, Tom Smith, Ed Johnston, Lucy Welsh and Vicky Kemp have explored various aspects of these practices, often in the context of the recent 'managerialist' reforms of criminal justice and legal aid budget cuts. Although these works raise important theoretical questions, they are not comparative; it therefore remains to be seen whether lawyers in other (European) jurisdictions than England and Wales experience the same pressures and influences. Thus, this research fills a gap in the international (European) literature on criminal defence lawyering, and in the literature on the criminal process more generally.

3 Shifting focus from the trial to pre-trial proceedings

The pre-trial phase of criminal proceedings, and particularly the investigative stage, was chosen as the focal point of this study for the following reasons. Traditionally, comparative criminal justice literature (as well as judicial bodies such as the ECtHR: Jackson and Summers, 2018b) has focused on the trial as the determinative stage: the 'apex' of criminal proceedings. However, recent research highlights the declining importance of the trial, and the growing significance of the pre-trial investigation phase across the European jurisdictions (Cape et al., 2007). This can be attributed, firstly, to the increasing sophistication of investigation techniques and methods, and the increasing number of requisite procedural and case management rules. Thus, the preparation to the trial often takes longer, and requires greater effort, than the trial itself. This makes it less likely that evidence, especially forensic evidence, is gathered or examined for the first time at the trial stage. As a result, the focus of the fact-finding process inevitably shifts towards the pre-trial stages.

Another development that results in pre-trial proceedings acquiring more weight is the increased use of coercive investigative measures, or other measures interfering with individual rights, often employed in a preventative manner. The last decades witnessed a growth in the use of both the traditional coercive investigation methods such as stops, arrests and searches,[11] and the new so-called 'proactive' or 'covert' methods of investigation, such as the use of informants, infiltration or video and telephone surveillance.[12] Thirdly and most importantly, trials in Europe have become less frequent as a result of increased pressure for procedural efficiency. A growing number of European jurisdictions have increasingly resorted to alternative methods of dealing with criminal cases in order to avoid an expensive and time-consuming trial.[13] As a result, many criminal cases are terminated at the pre-trial stages of the proceedings, meaning that for many criminal suspects, pre-trial proceedings constitute their only experience of the criminal justice system (Cape et al., 2007: 8).

4 Research approach

This study empirically explores the role of criminal defence lawyers at the investigative stage in England and Wales and the Netherlands. The rationale for a comparative approach is the methodological assumption that researching similar social phenomena operating in different, but comparable contexts, would enrich the understanding of the underlying contextual factors that shape these phenomena (Creutzfeldt et al., 2016). The chosen jurisdictions reflect certain differences relevant to the subject-matter of this research. First, the two jurisdictions represent two leading European criminal procedural traditions: the adversarial tradition (England and Wales) and the inquisitorial tradition (the Netherlands). This differentiation was assumed to be relevant for this study (see Chapter 5).

Another difference is the relative length of experience with legal assistance at the investigative stage, and particularly in the context of first police interrogation(s) of suspects: at the time that the fieldwork for this study was conducted, England and Wales had had more than 30 years of experience with legal advice before and during suspect interrogations, whilst in the Netherlands, it had been in place for only 2–3 years. Other reasons for choosing these two jurisdictions were the ease of practical and linguistic access, as well as the availability of empirical information on the operation of the criminal process. Whilst England and Wales probably has the richest history of such research out of all European jurisdictions, the Netherlands has a stronger tradition of empirical research in criminal law and procedure, than other continental European countries.[14]

A major challenge of this study was to identify and select the theories or 'causal mechanisms' (a methodological term adopted in this work: see Appendix) to compare and explain the empirical results. The methodological premise of this research, as explained in the Appendix, is that any social process is influenced by an infinite number of causal mechanisms or explanatory factors. Therefore, researchers are inevitably selective when deciding to focus on certain factors, but not others. This research zooms into the factors derived from comparative literature examining the criminal process 'in context'. These are, most notably, the works of Christje Brants, Stewart Field, Jacqueline Hodgson, Maximo Langer, Mike McConville, David Nelken, and the 'founding father' of contextual inquiry into criminal procedure, Mirjan Damaška. These scholars have pioneered in situating various criminal procedural institutions and practices within broader contexts, most notably: the relationship between the state and the individual, and the societal attitudes towards the state – lying in the heart of the notion of 'legal procedural tradition', the prevailing criminal justice policies, and the professional or occupational cultures of criminal justice actors. Therefore, this research situates the practice of criminal defence at the investigative stage within the broader context of the (adversarial and inquisitorial) procedural traditions, contemporary criminal justice policies (managerialism, crime control and austerity) and the occupational cultures of defence lawyers.[15]

5 Outline of the book

This book comprises eight chapters. Chapter 1 is the Introduction. Chapter 2 describes what is called the 'normative view' of the role of criminal defence lawyers at the investigative stage of criminal proceedings implied in the European regulations. It defines the 'model' role of the defence lawyer at the investigative stage. It is based on the premise that the main task of lawyers at this stage is to facilitate 'effective participation' of the accused in the pre-trial proceedings, including by mounting an effective defence against the accusation. This view of the role of lawyers is in line with the contemporary understanding of the centrality of the pre-trial proceedings as described in Section 2. The model role is built around two 'pillars': the lawyer's role vis-à-vis the client and the lawyer's role vis-à-vis the investigative authorities. Chapters 3 and 4 describe the findings of the empirical inquiry in England and Wales and the Netherlands organised around the two aforementioned 'pillars' of the role of lawyers at the investigative stage of the criminal proceedings. They aim to assess whether – and to what extent – the role of criminal defence lawyers *in practice* corresponded to the 'model' role implied in the European regulations.

Chapters 5–7 are devoted to comparative analysis. They engage with the various contextual factors, which shaped the practical realisation of the role of the lawyer at the investigative stage in the Netherlands and in England and Wales, as experienced during the fieldwork. Chapter 5 discusses the influence of the prevailing procedural traditions, 'inquisitorial' or 'adversarial', on the lawyer's role at the investigative stage in the two jurisdictions. Chapter 6 describes the impact of contemporary criminal justice policies, and Chapter 7 examines lawyers' occupational cultures shaping the role of lawyers at the investigative stage of the proceedings. Chapter 8 (Concluding Remarks) synthesises the findings concerning the influence of the various factors identified in Chapters 5–7 on the professional practice of criminal defence at the investigative stage. The study concludes that changing the law alone would not bring this practice closer to the normative view of the role of a lawyer at the investigative stage. To achieve change, action should be taken on all levels, including lawyers' occupational cultures.

Note that the state of the relevant legislation, case law and other regulations reported in this manuscript is up-to-date until 1 January 2018. Any subsequent changes have not been systematically incorporated.

Notes

1 *Directive 2013/48/EU* of the European Parliament and of the Council of 22 October 2013 on the right of access to a lawyer in criminal proceedings and in European arrest warrant proceedings, and on the right to have a third party informed upon deprivation of liberty and to communicate with third persons and with consular authorities while deprived of liberty, OJ L 294, 6.11.2013, 1–12.
2 These rights are derived from *Directive 2013/48/EU* (articles 3(2) and 3(3)) and the ECtHR case law discussed in Chapter 2.
3 'Lawyer' is used as the general term referring to persons who are entitled to provide legal advice and assistance in criminal proceedings, or during certain phases of criminal proceedings. Note that in England and Wales, for instance, so-called 'accredited representatives', who might not be lawyers *stricto sensu* (they may not possess a law degree), are entitled to provide legal assistance at the investigative stage. See Chapter 4.
4 The 'investigative stage (or phase) of criminal proceedings' is understood in this work as preliminary police investigation into a criminal offence, including police interrogation(s) of a suspect, which usually involves the latter's arrest and detention by police (police custody).
5 For an explanation of the system of referencing the empirical material, see Appendix.
6 In the Netherlands, the political debate about the right of custodial legal assistance started in late 1960s. This debate led to an experiment with legal assistance before the first police interrogation organised in 1982, but in 1988 the Minister of Justice refused to support a respective legislative amendment (Spronken, 2001: 107–111). In France, the right to custodial legal advice had been originally planned to be introduced in 1993, but these plans were dropped by the subsequent government; so the right was introduced only in 2000 (Hodgson, 2005: 118–119).
7 In the Netherlands, for example, the Dutch Bar Association and the Dutch Criminal Lawyers' Association (NVSA) formed in 1992 have regularly brought attention to the subject of early access to legal assistance (for an overview, see Spronken, 2001: 108–112). The reform, which led to the introduction of the right of early access to a lawyer (following the *Salduz* judgment) was triggered by a series of notorious miscarriage of justice cases, which revealed dubious interrogation practices of the police (Blackstock et al., 2013).
8 These arguments were used, for instance, in the Netherlands to block proposals to introduce the right of early access to a lawyer (Spronken, 2001). In 2011, five Member States (Belgium, France, Ireland, the Netherlands and the United Kingdom) submitted a letter to the Council of the EU (2011/0154 (COD), No. 14495/11) expressing reservations to the draft Directive on the right of access to a lawyer proposed by the European Commission, inter alia, because it would seriously hamper the effectiveness of criminal proceedings.
9 See e.g. McConville et al., 1991; Hodgson, 2005; Montana and Nelken, 2011; Montana, 2016; Lindeman, 2017; Soubise, 2017; Soubise, 2018.

8 *Introduction*

10 Some of this research is summarised in Chapter 7.
11 For example, in England and Wales the number of arrests performed annually rose from 1.27 million in 1981 (cited in Hillyard and Gordon, 1999: 509) to 1.46 million in 2008/2009 (see Police Powers and Procedures 2008/09, Home Office Statistical Bulletin, 4 April 2010, 11). The number of stops and searches increased from 110.000 in 1986 to approximately 1.500.000 in 2008/2009. See Table 2.1 in Sanders et al. (2010: 78).
12 On the rise of 'proactive' or 'covert' policing in Europe, see Field and Pelser, 1998.
13 Such as, for example, guilty plea agreements or out-of-court (pre-trial) settlements.
14 Recently, for instance, several evaluation studies had been undertaken in the Netherlands into the practical operation of the legal regulations relevant to this study. See Stevens and Verhoeven, 2010; Vanderhallen et al., 2014; Thomas et al., 2016; van Kampen et al., 2018.
15 The occupational cultures of the police, although relevant as a possible factor influencing the role of lawyers at the investigative stage in practice, were omitted due to the methodological difficulties of observing and interpreting such influence.

2 The role of a defence lawyer at the investigative stage
The view from Europe

1 Introduction

Traditionally, criminal law and adjudication had been regarded as the exclusive competence of European nation-states. This view began to change with the establishment of the Council of Europe and the European Union. Within the CoE, the main instruments exercising influence over the national criminal justice systems are the European Convention of Human Rights and the case law of the European Court of Human Rights (the ECHR system). Although the implementation of the standards generated by the ECHR system has been imperfect (Spronken, 2012), possibly not one national system of criminal procedure of the CoE Contracting States has been entirely immune from their influence (Keller and Stone-Sweet, 2008; Motoc and Ziemele, 2016).

In recent years, the impact of the ECHR system on domestic criminal procedures has been felt particularly strongly with respect to the right of early access to legal assistance. In its famous *Salduz v. Turkey* (2008) judgment, followed by about 300 'progeny' rulings, the ECtHR held that criminal suspects had the right to confer with a lawyer already prior to their first questioning by law enforcement authorities. This ruling, however, was met with strong resistance in those European countries which did not envisage this right in domestic law, such as Belgium, France and the Netherlands (Giannoulopoulos, 2016; Jackson, 2016b). Yet, they were forced to amend their laws to implement the *Salduz* case law, inter alia under pressure from highest domestic courts (Blackstock et al., 2013; Giannoulopoulos, 2016).

The momentum created by *Salduz* was maintained by the EU. At the time of the *Salduz* judgment, the EU had been drafting its own legislation on fair trial rights in criminal proceedings. This move was inspired inter alia by the individual rights deficit in the EU policies on judicial cooperation in criminal matters (Hodgson, 2011). It has led to the adoption of the so-called 'procedural rights Directives' package' set out in the *Roadmap for Strengthening Procedural Rights of Suspected or Accused Persons in Criminal Proceedings (Council Resolution 2009/C 295/01)*,[1] binding on those States that opted into the Directives. The provisions concerning the right to legal assistance in the early stages of the criminal proceedings were negotiated as part of the Directive on the right of access to a lawyer (*Directive 2013/48/EU*), the most controversial of the 'procedural rights' package' (Spronken and de Vocht, 2011). Although its initially proposed provisions were diluted during the negotiations (Jackson, 2016b; Pivaty, 2018), *Directive 2013/48/EU* has clarified and expanded the standards derived from the ECtHR *Salduz* case law (Ogorodova and Spronken, 2014).

Directive 2013/48/EU therefore strengthens the legal protection of the right to legal assistance in criminal proceedings in the EU. However, it was argued that in order to advance the normative understanding of 'procedural fairness', particularly at the pre-trial stages, attention must be paid to the institutional roles and procedural forms, rather than, or in addition to, the individual fair trial rights (see Section 2 of this chapter). Strong defence role is central to achieving procedural fairness, because it allows to build a counterargument to test the prosecution case, and thus to guarantee the necessary institutional balance in the criminal proceedings (Jackson and Summers, 2018a).

This chapter develops the normative view of the *role* of a defence lawyer at the investigative stage of the criminal proceedings implied in the European regulations. The chosen focus is on the lawyer, and not on the defence party as such, which includes the defendant and their lawyer. Therefore, the chapter omits the question of whether and to what extent the defendant has the respective participatory rights independently from their lawyer. The following sections first explain the chosen approach to the development of the normative view of the lawyer's role and the choice of the sources. Subsequently, the chapter proposes the general definition of the role of a defence lawyer at the investigative stage of the proceedings, and describes the various tasks or functions of defence lawyers, derived from the relevant European norms. These tasks are divided into those directed primarily at the client, and those oriented towards the (investigative) authorities. A more general discussion on the nature of the lawyer–client relationship, as envisaged in European regulations, precedes the description of the lawyer's tasks vis-à-vis the client.

2 From defence rights to the role of a lawyer: an inferential approach

As argued by Jackson and Summers (2018a: 7 onwards), the existing international fair trial rights' frameworks, centred upon the individual rights of the accused, have important limitations. Protection of the accused's rights is insufficient to ensure procedural fairness from a systemic viewpoint, because the latter requires attention to procedural settings and institutional roles. Fair trial rights were designed to be applied during the trial. Thus, they address the institutional roles with regard to the trial (for instance, through the principles of judicial impartiality and independence), but not in respect of the pre-trial proceedings. In fact, the regulatory focus upon the trial was aimed at diverting attention from the unfairness of the crucial stage of the proceedings, namely the investigative stage (Jackson and Summers, 2012: 100). Although the ECtHR and, importantly, the EU legislator have extended the application of fair trial rights to the pre-trial stages, it is unclear how these rights would play out in a procedural setting, which lacks the guarantees of the 'equality of arms' embedded in the trial.

The right to legal assistance is not an exception in this regard. Although traditionally a trial right, the right of access to a lawyer was extended to the investigative stage by the relevant ECtHR case law, most notably *Salduz*, and the EU procedural rights' legislation (*Directive 2013/48/EU*, article 3 (2)). Arguably, the rationale of the right to legal assistance is to provide a counterbalance to the prosecution in defending the suspect against the criminal accusation (Jackson and Summers, 2018b). This signifies that if the right is expanded to the investigative stage of the proceedings, the suspect's lawyer must be able to mount an effective defence against the criminal accusation already at this procedural stage (Pivaty, 2018). Yet, the existing fair trial rights framework does not give clarity concerning how this objective can be realised in the procedural context of the investigative stage, characterised inter alia by secretive nature, and the absence of an impartial and neutral decision-maker.

The following paragraphs of this chapter develop a normative framework which would allow to give life to the above-mentioned rationale for the right to legal assistance at the investigative stage of the proceedings. Concretely, it establishes which objectives and functions a lawyer must be able to fulfil and how they can be achieved within the procedural setting of the investigative stage.[2] To develop this normative framework, an 'inferential approach' to formulating the role of a lawyer at the investigative stage is adopted. Namely, the definition of this role is deduced from the various rationales for the right to custodial legal advice embedded in the European normative frameworks (ibid.). These include: protecting suspects against torture, ill-treatment and other forms of compulsion, and more generally, safeguarding their right to silence, as well as preventing false confessions; ensuring effective participation of a suspect in the criminal proceedings and contributing to procedural justice; protecting the suspect against arbitrary deprivation of liberty; and against breaches of procedural rules by the authorities. These rationales contain certain assumptions about the role of a defence lawyer. In other words, the objectives implied in these rationales would not be achieved unless lawyers (are allowed to) exercise a certain specific role at the investigative stage of the criminal proceedings. Implicit and explicit assumptions concerning the lawyer's role at the investigative stage may also be found in the ECtHR case law, and in the EU regulations on suspects' procedural rights. The following section describes the approach used in this chapter to incorporating the ECtHR and EU pronouncements in the proposed normative framework.

3 Sources: the interplay of the ECtHR case law and the EU law

3.1 *The ECtHR approach to the right of early access to a lawyer: a double U-Turn*

Historically, the supra-national right of early access to a lawyer in criminal proceedings was derived from the ECtHR case law. In the early days, however, the

12 Role of a defence lawyer

Court operated on a presumption that any pre-trial restrictions, including of the right of access to a lawyer, would be cured, if the suspect enjoyed the full panoply of defence rights during an adversarial trial. *Imbrioscia v. Switzerland* (1993), the first ECtHR case involving legal assistance in the context of pre-trial interrogations, is a good illustration of this early approach. In *Imbrioscia*, the applicant's lawyer was not present during interrogations conducted by the public prosecutor and the police, and his chosen lawyer was not informed of the interrogations. The ECtHR concluded that the fairness of the proceedings taken 'as a whole' was not violated, because the applicant's trial was attended with all necessary safeguards. In its early approach, the ECtHR did not scrutinise the reasons for the denial of the right to legal assistance at the pre-trial stages, relying instead on the general wording that it could be restricted 'for good cause'. This approach allowed for 'broad if not structural limitations of the right' (Ölcer, 2013: 390).

The ECtHR approach to the right of early access to a lawyer has drastically changed following the Grand Chamber judgment in *Salduz*. *Salduz* was questioned by police in the absence of a lawyer and confessed, and later retracted his statements alleging that they were made under duress, but was nonetheless convicted. The ECtHR found a violation of Article 6, stating that 'the rights of the defence will in principle be irretrievably prejudiced when incriminating statements made during police interrogation without access to a lawyer are used for a conviction' (paragraph 55). Since then (and before the judgment in *Ibrahim and others v. UK* [2016] discussed further in this section), the *Salduz* principle was fairly consistently applied by the Court. Namely, it found a violation of a fair trial, where the suspect's right of access to a lawyer in police custody was restricted, and where this resulted in evidence which was later used for his conviction.[3] In *Salduz*, the ECtHR has also changed its appreciation of the legitimate reasons for the restrictions of pre-trial access to a lawyer. The new standard relied on a very narrow wording of the possible restrictions of the right: first, it must be 'demonstrated in the light of the particular circumstances of each case that there are compelling reasons to restrict the right', and that 'such restriction should not unduly prejudice the rights of the accused', such as when 'incriminating statements made during police interrogation without access to a lawyer are used for a conviction' (paragraph 55). In contrast to its earlier approach, the Court also proclaimed an intention to closely scrutinise the justifications for restricting access to a lawyer in police custody advanced by government authorities.

In the post-*Salduz* case law, the ECtHR has also effectively disposed of the requirement to examine whether the restriction of pre-trial access to a lawyer, resulting in evidentiary information that had a bearing on the conviction, affected the 'overall fairness of the proceedings' (*Sobko v. Ukraine* [2015]; *Chopenko v. Ukraine* [2015]; *Tikhonov v. Ukraine* [2016]; *İrmak v. Turkey* [2016]). Rather, this link had been automatically assumed, which was explicitly stated by the Court in *Pishchalnikov v. Russia* (2009) (paragraph 81). As the Court observed in *Huseyn and others v. Azerbaijan* (2001), 'the Court cannot speculate on the exact impact which the applicants' access to a lawyer during [police custody] would have had on the ensuing proceedings', insofar as the applicants made statements without the benefit of legal advice, which were attached to the case file (paragraph 172). This approach signified a move towards greater recognition by the Court of the importance, and indeed the determinative nature, of the pre-trial proceedings, and consequently the need to devise stronger procedural protections of suspects' rights in such proceedings (Pivaty, 2018).

Some voices, including several concurring judges in *Salduz*, called on the Court to further expand the *Salduz* standard (*Concurring Opinion of Judge Bratza*; *Concurring Opinion of Judge Zagrebelsky, joined by Judges Casadevall and Türmen*). They demanded the acknowledgment that a fair trial may be violated by the denial of access to a lawyer at the outset of police detention, even it did not affect the suspect's evidentiary position. This was effectively the stance taken by the Court in *Dayanan v. Turkey* (2009) and several post-*Dayanan* cases (*Eraslan and others v. Turkey* [2009]; *Fazli Kaya v. Turkey* [2013]). In these cases, the Court found a violation of a fair trial, even though the applicants made no prejudicial statements while in police detention, and invoked no other 'concrete prejudice' to their defence rights. The ECtHR argued that restrictions on access to a lawyer during the entire period of police custody deprive the suspect of the benefits associated with early access to legal advice, including 'the fundamental aspects of that person's defence: discussion of the case, organisation of the defence, collection of evidence favourable to the accused, preparation for questioning, support of an accused in distress and checking of the conditions of detention' (*Dayanan*, paragraph 32).

The *Dayanan* stance reflected a broad view on the lawyer's role at the investigative stage of criminal proceedings, not limited to protecting suspects from self-incrimination, but also embracing other elements, which are no less important for the exercise of 'active defence' at the early procedural stages (Pivaty, 2018). This approach, as argued in the following section, was endorsed in *Directive 2013/48/EU*. Yet, the Court itself did not pursue the *Dayanan* approach, and was careful to limit its potential reach by stating that it applied only to those situations, where deprivation of access to a lawyer in police detention was mandatory and systematic, for example because of legislative restrictions (*Smolik v. Ukraine* [2012]; *Ibrahim*; confirmed in *Beuze v. Belgium* [2018]).

Despite the step backwards with regard to the *Dayanan* finding, the Court's approach in the *Salduz* and early post-*Salduz* case law signified a true revolution in its stance on the right of pre-trial access to legal assistance. The extremely narrow wording of the possible restrictions of the right (along with the high level of scrutiny of such restrictions) calls for the conclusion that, following *Salduz*, the ECtHR had treated the right of access to a lawyer in police custody as nearly absolute. This is especially remarkable because the Court generally approaches the procedural rights provided by Article 6 as qualified rights (Vitkauskas and Dikov, 2002).

Recently, however, the ECtHR has recently taken a turn in quite the opposite direction. This turn reflected the general trend within the Court towards greater restraint and deference of the Contracting Parties (Stiansen and Voeten, 2018), also reflected in the recent (post-2011) case law on a fair trial (Füglistaler, 2016). The move towards restricting the reach of *Salduz* jurisprudence has become apparent following the *Ibrahim and others v. UK* judgment. In *Ibrahim*, the Court held that even where no compelling reasons existed to restrict pre-trial access to a lawyer, the use of statements made without access to a lawyer could be compatible with a fair trial. In that case, the Grand Chamber continued, a whole range of factors should be considered, such as: whether the suspect had an opportunity to challenge the use of evidence; whether there was other incriminating evidence; whether the national proceedings complied with national law; as well as the public interest in bringing the perpetrators to justice (paragraph 274).

Ibrahim constituted a radical departure from the ECtHR (post-)*Salduz* approach. Goss argued the intention behind the *Ibrahim* ruling was to 'convert Article 6 into a simple, two-word "fair trial" guarantee, under which the assessment of every alleged violation boils down to whether or not the overall proceedings were fair' (Goss, 2017: 1150). It also departs from the earlier recognition by the Court of the importance of devising stronger fairness standards applicable at the pre-trial procedural stages. The post-*Ibrahim* jurisprudence confirmed the trend towards lowering the level of protection of the right of early access to a lawyer in the ECtHR case law. In *Simeonovi v. Bulgaria* (2017), the ECtHR found no violation of a fair trial where the suspect has not enjoyed access to a lawyer, despite numerous requests, for the first three days of police detention without any apparent reason for this restriction. The Court reconfirmed its *Ibrahim* finding that the absence of compelling reasons for restricting pre-trial access to a lawyer did not automatically lead to a finding of violation, but still necessitated the 'overall fairness' analysis. This conclusion was taken one step further by the Court in *Beuze* (even though it found a violation of Article 6 in the given circumstances). In *Beuze*, the ECtHR ruled that the 'overall fairness' must (still) be assessed – and therefore no violation of Article 6 might be found – not only where restrictions on the right to pre-trial access to a lawyer are not duly justified in the particular case, but also when they resulted from 'statutory restrictions of a general and mandatory nature' (paragraph 165).

3.2 The EU Directives and their interpretation

In parallel with the developments in the ECtHR case law, the EU, in its turn, has been drafting its own legislation on the right to legal assistance in criminal proceedings, alongside other procedural rights of the accused. The drafting of the EU procedural rights Directives coincided with the 'revolutionary' turn taken by the ECtHR in the *Salduz* and post-*Salduz* case law. The intention behind the Directives was to expand on and 'give life' to the ECHR and ECtHR case law (van Puyenbroeck and Vermeulen, 2011). Thus, the Directives' drafters relied on the-then existing ECtHR standards as their departure point (Pivaty, 2018).

This explains the numerous references to the ECHR and ECtHR case law in the Directives' text. For instance, Recital 6 of *Directive 2013/48/EU* mentions the goal to advance 'further development within the Union of the minimum standards set out in the Charter [of Fundamental Rights of the European Union] and ECHR'.

The EU procedural rights' Directives unequivocally expand the reach of the fair trial rights, including the right of access to a lawyer, to the investigative stage of the criminal proceedings. Thus, Directive *2013/48/EU* states that the right to legal assistance begins to apply to suspects 'from the time when they are made aware by the competent authorities of a Member State, by official notification or otherwise, that they are suspected or accused of having committed a criminal offence' (article 2). In fact, the Directive on the right to information (*Directive 2012/13/EU*)[4] and *Directive 2013/48/EU* were designed primarily to address the problems with the non-compliance with these rights at the pre-trial procedural stages (Spronken and Vocht, 2011; Ruggeri, 2017). Thus, *Directive 2013/48/EU* has expanded and strengthened the existing ECtHR standards on the right of early access to legal assistance by clarifying the moments from which the right applies, the obligations of investigative authorities to facilitate access, the conditions for waiver of the right, as well as the right to 'effective participation' of the lawyer during an interrogation (Ogorodova and Spronken, 2014). It may be therefore be concluded that *Directive 2013/48/EU* (along with other procedural rights' Directives) reflects the idea of the centrality of pre-trial stages of the proceedings, and of the pressing need to improve fairness at these stages.

Most provisions of *Directive 2013/48/EU*, however, require further interpretation (namely, by CJEU), particularly because they were rendered more ambiguous or vague during the negotiations (Soo, 2017; Pivaty, 2018). The ECtHR case law constitutes one source for such interpretation, although CJEU is not mandated to follow it (Ogorodova and Spronken, 2014). It appears that in respect of the right of early access to a lawyer, the Directive provisions should be interpreted in line with the *Salduz* and post-*Salduz* case law, rather than with the *Ibrahim* judgment and its progeny. This is based on the following considerations. First, as mentioned earlier, similarly to *Directive 2013/48/EU*, *Salduz* is based on the notion of centrality of pre-trial proceedings, which as argued earlier, was abandoned in *Ibrahim*.

Second, the (post-)*Ibrahim* approach is arguably based on an erroneous understanding of the rationales behind the right of early access to a lawyer (Pivaty, 2018). Namely, *Ibrahim*, *Simeonovi* and *Beuze* endorse a limited understanding of the value and rationales behind this right, effectively viewing it as part of the right not to incriminate oneself. Yet, although the protection of the privilege against self-incrimination is an important source of the right of early access to a lawyer, the latter is a self-standing right derived from various rationales, including the need to ensure effective suspect participation in the proceedings, the equality of arms and the protection of other procedural rights, such as the right to liberty or the right to information. All these rationales were clearly enunciated in *Salduz* and other related (pre-*Ibrahim*) ECtHR jurisprudence. For these reasons, the following sections, which articulate the normative view of the role of a lawyer at the investigative stage of the criminal proceedings, rely on the expansionist interpretation of *Directive 2013/48/EU*, drawing inspiration from the *Salduz* and post-*Salduz* (pre-*Ibrahim*) case law of the ECtHR.

4 The role of a lawyer at the investigative stage: basic definitions

The most general definition of the lawyer's role in criminal proceedings may be found in the *Havana Declaration on the Basic Principles of the Role of Lawyers*. It describes this role as 'advising clients as to their legal rights and obligations, and as to the working of the legal system in so far as it is relevant to the legal rights and obligations of the clients' (advisory function), and 'assisting clients in every appropriate way, and taking legal action to protect their interests' (assistance function) (paragraphs 13 (a) and (b)). The essence of the lawyer's role at the investigative stage can be derived from the various rationales for the right of early legal assistance implied in the respective ECtHR case law (particularly *Salduz* and the post-*Salduz* case law) and the EU procedural rights' Directives (Pivaty, 2018). These rationales may be divided into 'protective' and 'participatory'. The protective rationale concerns the protection of suspects against abuses of their rights and procedural breaches by state authorities. The participatory rationale implies the facilitation of defendants' effective participation in the criminal proceedings. It entails, most importantly, that lawyers must be able to take action to *defend* their clients against the accusation put forward by the authorities. Such action may consist of assisting clients to exercise procedural rights, but it also implies the lawyer's participation in the evidentiary (fact-finding) process.

The respective lawyer's tasks may include: advising (informing) suspects on their rights and legal procedures, and advising them with respect to the questioning; protecting clients from breaches of rights and procedures; arguing for their release from custody (when they are detained); and participating in the evidence-gathering process. This list, however, is not exhaustive. One of the lawyer's duties is '[a]ssisting [clients] in every appropriate way, and taking legal action to protect their interests' (paragraph 13 (b), *Havana Declaration*). This implies that lawyers are expected to defend and uphold the rights and interests of their clients whenever necessary, and when it does not run contrary to the law and lawyers' professional ethics (paragraph 14).

Finally, according to the ECtHR case law (described in the next section), the lawyer–client relationship based on confidence and trust is the foundation for the effective exercise of the lawyer's role, including at the investigative stage. Additionally to the traditional 'legal' tasks, it was suggested that criminal defence lawyers (should) also provide moral and social support to their clients. Such support is especially relevant at the investigative stage, where suspects are often deprived of liberty, and are 'removed from [their] normal environment' (*Can v. Austria* [1984]).

5 The lawyers' role vis-à-vis their clients

5.1 *The lawyer–client relationship*

An effective lawyer–client relationship is, in the ECtHR's view, of paramount importance for the effective exercise of defence rights (*Gennadiy Medvedev v. Russia* [2012], paragraph 35). Confidence and trust of the client in the lawyer are necessary for an effective lawyer–client relationship (*Croissant v. Germany* [1992], paragraph 29). The trust relationship is important, because the lawyer's effectiveness depends, inter alia, on whether the client is willing to share information that is important for the conduct of the defence.[5]

According to the ECtHR, the foundation of an effective lawyer–client relationship lies in the lawyer's commitment to their client's interest and dedication to the client's case (*Medvedev*). A suspect, who is usually not a legal expert, must have confidence that their lawyer will do their utmost to defend their interest.[6] In *Nikula v. Finland* (2002), the ECtHR stated that 'the threat of an *ex post facto* review of counsel's criticism of another party to criminal procedure [the prosecutor] is difficult to reconcile with defence counsel's duty to defend their clients' interests zealously' (paragraph 54). Therefore, lawyers have the ethical duty to defend their client's rights zealously, and to act in their best interest.[7] The ECtHR asserts the principle of independence of the legal profession, and states that 'the conduct of the case is essentially a matter between the defendant and his or her counsel' (*Daud v. Portugal* [1998], paragraph 38). The independence of the legal profession, similarly to the avoidance of the conflict of interest and the lawyer's duty of professional secrecy are meant to guarantee the lawyer's loyalty to their client's interest (*Mihai Moldoveanu v. Romania* [2012]; *Petri Sallinen and others v. Finland* [2005]; *Niemietz v. Germany* [1992]).[8]

The lawyer's *only* loyalty lies with their client, and the lawyer's *only* role (including at the investigative stage) consists of advancing their client's interest and rights. The Havana Declaration, for instance, defines the role of the criminal defence lawyer as 'to protect and establish [clients'] rights and to defend them in all stages of criminal proceedings' (paragraph 1). Similarly, the Recommendation of the CoE on the freedom of the exercise of the profession of lawyer defines the role of a lawyer as 'defending the legitimate rights and interests of their clients' (principle III.1). Neither of these two documents, nor the ECtHR case law, implies at any point that the defence lawyer may be expected to advance any other interests than those of their client, or to do anything that is not related to the protection of their client's interest.[9] Lawyers may not be required to contribute to procedural efficiency or other broader societal objectives, unless it coincides, or does not interfere with, the client's best interest. Furthermore, the principle of loyalty implies that lawyers should prioritise their clients' interests over any other possibly conflicting interests, including their own (paragraph 15, *Havana Declaration*). At the same time, the lawyer may not do, and may not be required to do, anything that is dishonest, immoral or that would otherwise put the public image of the administration of justice into disrepute, to advance the client's interest (paragraph 12, *Havana Declaration*). This follows, inter alia, from the ECtHR case law on the lawyer's freedom of expression, where the Court has stated that lawyers, who have a special status in the justice system as intermediaries between the public and the courts, may be expected to contribute to maintaining public confidence in the administration of justice (*Schöpfer v. Switzerland* [1998]). Thus, the ECtHR implicitly defines an effective lawyer–client relationship as a relationship where the client has confidence and trust in their lawyer, based on the lawyer's undivided loyalty and dedication to the client's interest.

Lawyer–client confidentiality and privacy of lawyer–client communications are explicitly mentioned in various sources, including the ECtHR case law, as another precondition for an effective lawyer–client relationship (*S. v. Switzerland* [1991], paragraph 48). It seems evident that, to be willing to communicate with their lawyer in a free and uninhibited manner, the client must have confidence that the information shared will not become known to the authorities or other parties (*Campbell and Fell v. United Kingdom* [1984], paragraph 46). The objective of ensuring privacy and confidentiality of lawyer–client communications is also reflected in *Directive 2013/48/EU* (article 4) and other EU instruments.[10] The lawyer–client relationship may be threatened not only by visible surveillance of lawyer–client communications, but also where there are reasons to believe that such surveillance may occur (Pattenden and Skinns, 2010). In the words of the ECtHR (*Castravet v. Moldova* [2007], paragraph 51),

> An interference with the lawyer–client privilege ... does not necessarily require an actual interception or eavesdropping to have taken place. A genuine belief held on reasonable grounds that their discussion was being listened to might be sufficient, in the Court's view, to limit the effectiveness of the assistance which the lawyer could provide. Such a belief would inevitably inhibit a free discussion between lawyer and client and hamper the detained person's right effectively to challenge the lawfulness of his detention.

5.2 Advising client

The lawyer's role of advising clients at the investigative stage consists of informing them about procedural rights, the respective laws and procedures, and, importantly, providing advice concerning the upcoming interrogations and other procedural actions. Similarly, gathering information from the client and the authorities may be seen as part of the lawyer's advisory role, because the lawyer cannot effectively advise in the absence of the relevant information (Blackstock et al., 2013: 355). However, there are no specific legal provisions on how lawyers should gather information from their clients.

Providing information about the rights, procedures and relevant law is the most 'traditional' task of a lawyer. Indeed, the lawyer's role is most commonly associated with *legal* advice, which distinguishes it from the role of other persons providing support to suspects at the investigative stage.[11] Being properly informed about procedural rights is necessary for the 'practical and effective exercise of these rights' (*Directive 2012/13/EU*, recital 19). The right to silence is a central procedural right at the investigative stage. In *Brusco v. France* (2010), the Court held that the lack of access to legal assistance during the first 20 hours of police custody meant that 'the lawyer was unable ... to inform the applicant about his right to remain silent and not to incriminate himself before the first interrogation ...' (paragraph 54). Legal assistance is necessary to enable suspects to understand the consequences of waiving their procedural rights such as the right to silence (*Directive 2013/48/EU*, article 9 (1) (a); *Şaman v. Turkey* [2011], paragraph 33). Thus, it is the task of a lawyer to explain these consequences to suspects, and ensure that they understand them.

What other legal knowledge is necessary to ensure suspect's effective participation at the investigative stage? Suspects must be informed about their procedural status and the relevant procedural rules, such as the police detention regulations. Suspects also need to know about the possible (interim) procedural outcomes[12] and the conditions for their application. Suspects must also be informed about the law establishing the conditions under which their behaviour may be sanctioned (the 'elements of the offence'), and the relevant rules governing the evidentiary process. Some of this information may be provided by the authorities, but their duties in this respect are quite limited. As an illustration, *Directive 2012/13/EU* contains the obligation to inform suspects about the suspicion (article 6 (2)) and the reasons for their arrest (article 6 (3)), but not about the elements of the impugned offence(s), which therefore must be given by a lawyer. The Directive imposes a duty to provide information concerning the maximum duration of police custody, and the rights while in custody (article 4), but not about the detention and interrogation procedures.[13]

Another element of the lawyer's informational role at the investigative stage, according to the ECtHR, is to assist clients in choosing the stance to be adopted during interrogations. As the Court stated in *Pishchalnikov*, 'the applicant may not have had sufficient knowledge, experience, or even sufficient self-confidence to make the best choice without the advice and support of a lawyer' (paragraph 80). Without the professional assistance of a lawyer in making this strategic choice the suspect would, in the Court's view, be deprived of the opportunity to exercise procedural rights effectively (ibid., paragraph 85). The decision about the procedural strategy is not limited to whether to respond to questions or to remain silent. A suspect may, for instance, decide to respond to some, but not all questions. When responding to questions, they may choose to provide a (fully or partially) exculpatory explanation. The suspect may also decide to confess, or to admit to certain allegations. If the suspect chooses to confess or make admissions, they might admit to a lesser or more serious offence, or decide not to volunteer information, which is not known to the authorities.

The respective normative sources do not provide much guidance about the allocation of decision-making in the lawyer–client relationship. In *Pishchalnikov*, the Court implies that it is up to the client to choose the strategy at the interrogation, but the lawyer *assists* the client in making this decision. This means that the lawyer should, as the minimum, give a clear explanation of the possible consequences of choosing this or that option with respect to the particular client's circumstances, as well as, oftentimes, recommend a particular option to the client.[14]

5.3 Protecting welfare and emotional support of detained clients

Although the primary responsibility for ensuring suspects' welfare in detention lies with the authorities, EU law suggests that lawyers have a complementary role in this regard. For example, recital 29 of *Directive 2013/48/EU* suggests that lawyers should be able to raise the question of compliance with European standards with regard to the condition of their clients' detention before the relevant authorities. These standards especially concern the duty to ensure that the persons in detention are not subjected to inhuman and degrading treatment, and to protect their life and personal integrity, formulated in the ECtHR case law, including the obligation to provide medical assistance (*Ribitsch v. Austria* [2012]; *Kalashnikov v. Russia* [2002]; *Keenan v. United Kingdom* [2001]; *Taïs v. France* [2006]; *Hurtado v. Switzerland* [1994]). The lawyer's task of ensuring the client's well-being in detention was mentioned by the Commission in *Can* (paragraph 55). Later, in *Dayanan*, the Court stated that one of the lawyer's tasks at the investigative stage is the 'support of an accused in distress and checking of the conditions of detention' (paragraph 32).

Lawyers may need to monitor their clients' detention conditions, identify the risks for their health and their special needs, and act upon any relevant welfare concerns, for instance, by informing the authorities about them. Furthermore, suspects' welfare in police custody may be influenced by issues like the possibility to receive visits, make telephone calls, eat or drink, exercise, smoke, or make arrangements for their absence from work, home or school. The satisfaction of these needs falls within the discretion of the police, when suspects are detained. Research on police custody has shown that sometimes police fail to respond, or are insufficiently sensitised to this kind of suspects' needs (Skinns, 2010: 90). The lawyer's role may thus be to identify these needs and bring them to the authorities' attention.

Providing emotional support to clients in detention enables lawyers to exercise their other functions. Suspects who are deprived of liberty might only be able to effectively cooperate with the lawyer after their anxiety and immediate preoccupations have been addressed. Suspects who are in a poor physical or mental state, as discussed further in this chapter, are more susceptible to interrogative pressure, and more prone to (false) self-incrimination (which lawyers are meant to prevent). Finally, as demonstrated by research, clients' satisfaction with lawyers and trust towards them are premised as much on lawyers showing empathy and concern for clients' welfare as on their perceived legal expertise (Peterson-Badali et al., 2007; Sommerlad and Wall, 1999; Tata et al., 2002; Feldman and Wilson, 1981).Thus, the lawyer's attention to the client's well-being and other needs in detention is likely to foster an effective lawyer–client relationship.

6 The lawyers' role vis-à-vis the authorities

The following sections describe those functions of the lawyer at the investigative stage, which are primarily oriented at interacting with the authorities on the suspect's behalf. These functions include: gathering information from the authorities, defending clients in the course of interrogation, and reacting to the (alleged) procedural breaches and irregularities. The following paragraphs also describe the lawyer's tasks related to the participation in the fact-finding process at the investigative stage, and the lawyer's role vis-à-vis out-of-court disposals at this stage, which are increasingly used across European jurisdictions.

6.1 Obtaining disclosure

The lawyer's function of gathering case-related information from the authorities, or obtaining 'disclosure', is implied in the obligation to provide effective legal advice at the investigative stage. The usefulness of the lawyer's advice depends on the amount of information the lawyer has about the details of the accusation, the existing evidence, the circumstances of the arrest and the suspect's personal situation (Blackstock et al., 2013; Toney, 2001). This was acknowledged by the ECtHR in *Sapan v. Turkey* (2011), where it noted in paragraph 31:

> ... [T]he Court observes from the documents in the case file that the applicant indeed saw a lawyer on 13 March 2003 for a short period of time, between 10.30 and 10.55 a.m. ... [T]he applicant's lawyer had not been allowed to examine the investigation file at that point ..., which would seriously hamper her ability to provide any sort of meaningful legal advice to the applicant.

The right of the defence to access material evidence is recognised in article 7 of *Directive 2012/13/EU*. It does not, however, define the earliest moment of the proceedings when such access must be provided (Pivaty and Soo, 2019). In any case, under article 7 (1), access to documents, which are essential to effectively challenge the lawfulness of arrest or detention, must be provided in due time before the respective judicial hearing, which usually takes place at the end of the police detention period. In addition, the duty to provide certain case-related information to the suspect and the lawyer at the investigative stage may be read into article 7 (3) of *Directive 2012/13/EU*, which requires that access to such information should be granted 'in due time to allow the effective exercise of the rights of the defence'. Because the interrogations of the suspect at the investigative stage are crucial for the conduct of the defence, article 7 (3) arguably requires that access to material evidence should be granted already before such interrogations take place to enable the effective exercise of defence rights (Pivaty and Soo, 2019).

6.2 Assisting suspects during the interrogation

The right of every suspect to have a lawyer present during pre-trial interrogations is now firmly established in the ECtHR jurisprudence (*Navone v. Monaco* [2014]) and article 3 (3) (b) of *Directive 2013/48/EU*.[15] The Directive provides that the lawyer should be able to 'participate effectively' in the interrogation, but that such participation shall be in accordance with the procedures under national law. However, such procedures must not 'prejudice the effective exercise and essence of the right'. This is further explained in recital 25 of *Directive 2013/48/EU*, stating that 'the lawyer may, inter alia, in accordance with such rules, ask questions, request clarification and make statements'.

The following tasks of a defence lawyer in respect of a suspect's interrogation may be derived from the various rationales for the right of early access to a lawyer mentioned in the beginning of this chapter. First, even before the interrogation starts, the lawyer may need to assess whether the suspect is 'fit for interview'. Namely, the lawyer must ensure that the interrogation is not coercive in view of the suspect's health state. This specific task follows from the rationale of protecting suspects from torture, ill-treatment and illegal coercion. For example, questioning someone who is undergoing intense physical pain or psychological suffering is coercive, and may violate Article 3 of the ECHR, even if no physical force is being used.[16] This might also apply to questioning someone who suffers from drug or alcohol withdrawal. In *Kovalchuk v. Ukraine* (2010), the applicant was questioned and confessed to murder while suffering from 'psychotic and behavioural disorders, [a] state of delirious withdrawal from alcohol, [and] hallucinations' (paragraph 13). The ECtHR found that Article 3 was violated, because 'police ... took advantage of his vulnerable emotional state and pressured the applicant into giving a false confession' (paragraph 60). He was also questioned without a lawyer, who could have stopped the questioning and ensured that the applicant had received medical assistance. Suspects suffering from mental disorders or very young suspects, might be unable to cope with the interrogation due to their vulnerable state. A vast body of psychological literature suggests that suspects with certain characteristics, e.g. young age, intellectual disabilities, and certain mental disorders, are especially susceptible to interrogative pressure (Follette et al., 2007; Drizin and Leo, 2004; Kassin et al., 2010). The respective European regulations require to undertake medical examination of children (article 8 (1), *Directive 2016/800*) and adults considered 'vulnerable' in criminal proceedings (recital 12 and paragraph 12, *Recommendation 2013/C 378/02*), inter alia to determine their capacity to undergo questioning. The lawyer's role is to oversee that such assessment is carried out properly, and, if necessary, argue that the suspect is not fit to be interviewed.[17]

Second, lawyers have a continuous obligation to advise clients throughout the interrogation. As mentioned earlier, the choice of procedural strategy might need to be revised in the course of the questioning. A suspect may also need advice concerning the potential legal implications of (not) responding to the particular questions. With the exception of brief explanations, legal advice would often need to be given confidentially. This means that the interrogation would need be stopped to provide the suspect with an opportunity to speak with the lawyer in private.

Third, lawyers are expected to protect clients from unfair questioning. The rationale of effective participation requires that the suspect should have a fair chance to mount a defence, including the possibility to present evidence under fair conditions vis-à-vis the opposing party. This principle also applies at the investigative stage, and it is manifested, inter alia, in the requirement that the interrogation must be conducted fairly. 'Fairness' requires, first, that no improper pressure should be applied to induce self-incrimination, and, second, that suspects, if they wish to speak, should be given a fair opportunity to present their case. Furthermore, the requirement of informed participation implies that the suspect must understand the questioning, be aware of the implications of responding to questions, and that they must not inadvertently (meaning: unknowingly or involuntarily) incriminate himself. Access to a lawyer during police questioning is meant to ensure that the effective participation requirement is implemented in practice. It is thus the lawyer's role to anticipate and prevent the damaging effects of questions that are possibly unfair.

Questioning of the suspect is unfair when it involves improper compulsion or other psychologically coercive or manipulative tactics. Questioning can also be unfair, where a suspect is not given a fair opportunity to present their case. This may happen, for instance, where interrogators ask leading questions (that suggest a certain answer) or questions containing hidden or explicit assumptions, instead of obtaining an account emanating from the suspect (McConville et al., 1994: 117).[18] This may also happen where interrogating officers dismiss the suspect's responses as untrue or illogical, or insist on a certain line of inquiry, but fail to pursue others, including those suggested by the suspect. Finally, questioning may be unfair where the suspect is not given an opportunity to respond to questions on an informed basis, meaning fully understanding the question(s), and the implications of responding to them. This may include confusing questioning: for instance, questions containing flawed logic, are ambiguous, impossible for the suspect to respond (Cape, 2017: 294, 297). Another type of 'uninformed' unfair questions are those that are not related to the impugned offence(s), which may cause the suspect to inadvertently incriminate themselves or other persons of other offences (Cape, 2017: 292–293; McConville et al., 1994: 123). Likewise, questions containing intellectual 'traps' – for instance, asking the same or a similar, question at different points of interrogation, or questions aimed to 'catch' suspects on the apparent inconsistencies in their responses, or contradictions with other evidence[19] – may be confusing to (some) suspects.[20]

Fourth, lawyers are expected to assist clients in enforcing their procedural strategy during interrogation. It is commonly known that most suspects respond to questions, and only a small minority remain silent.[21] In many European countries, police are likely to use at least some degree of persuasion to obtain self-incriminating accounts from suspects, and in a minority of cases they may resort to improper compulsion. As a result of such persuasion or pressure, suspects may fail to adhere to their initial decision concerning whether to remain silent or to respond to questioning, and whether or not to confess. The lawyer's role in this respect would be to counteract the coercion exercised by the authorities. This was expressed in *Magee v. United Kingdom* (2000), where the ECtHR stated that in a situation where the suspect was held *incommunicado* and was interrogated at length, access to legal assistance would have served as 'a counterweight to the intimidating atmosphere specifically devised to sap his will and make him confess to his interrogators' (paragraph 43). The lawyer's support during the interrogation to enable the suspect to persevere with their decision to remain silent, or to deny guilt, may be particularly important in cases involving juveniles and vulnerable suspects. This aspect of the lawyer's role was stressed by the ECtHR in paragraph 160 of *Blokhin v. Russia* (2013):

> Given [the applicant's] very young age, the Court does not doubt that he felt vulnerable and intimidated when facing the police officers alone. In the Court's opinion, the circumstances surrounding the interview were psychologically coercive and conducive to breaking down any resolve the applicant might have had to remain silent. Having regard to these considerations, the Court considers that the applicant, as a matter of procedural fairness, should have been given access to a lawyer as a counterweight to the intimidating atmosphere capable of sapping his will and making him confess to his interrogators.

Fifth, lawyers are expected to assist suspects in providing their accounts during the interrogation (where the latter decide to do so). This duty derives in particular from the rationale of effective participation of the defence in criminal proceedings and the equality of arms principle. Based on the principle of ensuring informed suspect's participation, the lawyer's objective would be to prevent the client from inadvertently incriminating themselves when providing an account. Thus, where a client wishes to admit responsibility or guilt, the lawyer must ensure that they understand the consequences, for instance, in terms of strengthening the police case. Where a suspect wishes to deny, the lawyer must inform them about the respective advantages and disadvantages.

Furthermore, as it follows from the rationale of enabling the suspect to mount an effective criminal defence, the lawyer must ensure that the interrogation yields the best possible outcome for the suspect in terms of the legal and evidentiary position. This may include an array of responsibilities, depending on the nature of the suspect's account. For instance, where the suspect decides to admit responsibility or guilt, the lawyer may need to ensure that all relevant mitigating circumstances are duly covered (and, if relevant, recorded). If the suspect decides to provide a defence, the lawyer's duty could be, for example, to ensure that the client's account is clear and coherent, and that any eventual inconsistencies or discrepancies with the evidence, if possible, are explained in the suspect's favour. Finally, the lawyer may be required to verify the accuracy of the interrogation record. In *Mader*, the ECtHR has indirectly acknowledged the need for the lawyer's presence during suspect interrogation, inter alia, to verify the accuracy of the (written) recording (paragraphs 150–158). In this case, the applicant complained that his confession was fabricated by police officers, and that he was forced to sign the written interrogation record in the absence of his lawyer (the lawyer came in to sign the record several days after the interrogation took place) (paragraphs 142–143). Research conducted across European jurisdictions has documented systematic occurrence of inaccuracies in written records of interrogations, and the accompanying risks of false self-incrimination and fabricated confessions (McConville et al., 1991; Hodgson, 2005: 188–189, 191–195; Blackstock et al., 2013: 371–372).

6.3 Arguing against procedural breaches

The lawyer has the duty to ensure lawfulness of police actions vis-à-vis their clients at the investigative stage (*Can*, paragraph 55; *Süzer v. Turkey* [2013], paragraph 83). The lawyer's role is not to control the compliance of police with procedural rules in general, but only to protect their clients against the possible harm caused by such non-compliance. Therefore, lawyers must only react to those procedural breaches and irregularities which adversely impact their clients' position. Indeed, it appears logical that lawyers should not challenge those procedural mistakes or breaches which resulted in more favourable treatment of their client. This should be distinguished from cooperating with any 'deals' offered by the authorities, which involve promises of circumventing the law in exchange for a confession or specific information. Cooperating with such a deal would be contrary to the requirement that lawyers should not do anything that might bring into disrepute the public image of the legal profession and the administration of justice, as described in Section 5.1.

The respective ECtHR case law implies that the lawyer should react to procedural breaches irrespective of whether national law assigns a clear or automatic remedy,[22] or whether the breach is considered 'formal' or 'minor'. Furthermore, the reaction should be immediate, meaning at the moment when they occur, and not at a later stage, such as the trial.

This is based on the following considerations. First, at the investigative stage (and during detention), almost any procedural breach is potentially harmful to suspects, because most respective procedural rules are designed to protect them from unfairness or arbitrariness.[23] Second, it is often difficult at this stage to predict the effect of certain procedural breaches, however 'minor' they may seem, on the subsequent proceedings. Even those procedural breaches that appear only remotely connected to (one of) the fundamental rights of a suspect may constitute an infringement of a fundamental right, in combination with other procedural violations (Pivaty, 2018). For example, the failure of the police to accurately record the time of the arrest may lead to excessively long detention, which, in addition to being an infringement on the suspect's right to liberty, might also be a factor causing involuntary self-incrimination, as well as false confessions (Kassin et al., 2010). The lawyer's failure to react immediately to an alleged procedural violation may render the courts reluctant to acknowledge such a breach, and to afford an appropriate remedy (Pivaty, 2018).

6.4 Arguing for the suspect's release from detention

The lawyer's function of arguing in favour of their client's release from detention follows, inter alia, from the rationale of protection of the right to liberty behind the right to legal assistance. This function was mentioned by the EComHR in *Can*. It also follows from the ECtHR case law concerning judicial review of deprivation of liberty, which requires that suspects should benefit from access to legal assistance in the course of such review (Pivaty, 2018). In *Öcalan v. Turkey* (2005), for instance, the Court has specifically recognised the suspect's right to legal assistance at the earliest stages of criminal proceedings to prepare to the judicial review of the initial detention. The input of a lawyer may prove essential, because suspects, who are often not legal experts, are unlikely to be able to effectively argue that the deprivation of liberty was unlawful, unnecessary or devoid of sufficient grounds.

The role of protecting the suspect's right to liberty at the investigative stage consists of, for instance: making representations to the authorities concerning the lawfulness of the (continued) deprivation of liberty, the existence of sufficient grounds for the arrest or continued detention or the (conditions of) the suspect's release following the custody period.[24] If the suspect is brought before the judge, the lawyer's role consists of building and presenting arguments against further detention at the respective judicial hearing. And lastly, in exceptional circumstances, lawyers might need to challenge the lawfulness of the deprivation of liberty, or exercise the right to *habeas corpus*, already before the regular judicial review of detention.[25]

An important precondition for the effective exercise of this function is that the lawyer must have access to the evidence, which is 'essential to challenging effectively the lawfulness of an arrest or detention' (*Directive 2012/13/EU*, article 7 (1) and recital 30). *Directive 2012/13/EU* provides that such evidence must be given to suspects and their lawyers promptly, 'at the latest before a competent judicial authority is called to decide upon the lawfulness of the arrest or detention', and 'in due time to allow the effective exercise of the right to challenge the lawfulness of the arrest or detention' (article 7 (1)). The ECtHR considers the requirement of access to the case file in connection with the judicial review of detention an essential element of the equality of arms (*Schöps v. Germany* [2001]; *Lietzow v. Germany* [2001]; *Garcia Alva v. Germany* [2001]; *Mooren v. Germany* [2009]). This requirement relates, at the minimum, to all evidence used to substantiate the existence of the 'reasonable suspicion' that the suspect has committed an offence, and of the grounds for (continued) detention (article 5 (1) (c) ECHR), such as witness statements, search and seizure records, or records of surveillance measures undertaken against the suspect (see the ECtHR case law cited previously). In addition, it appears that the information necessary to assess whether the relevant procedures were duly followed (arrest warrant, official records of arrest and detention) must be disclosed.

6.5 Participation in the fact-finding process

An important aspect of effective suspect's participation in criminal proceedings is the right to know and challenge the existing evidence, as well as to contribute to the information, which is used as the basis for important procedural decisions. It would hardly be possible to imagine an effective defence in a criminal case which would not involve reacting to the existing body of evidence, or presenting one's own evidence. Furthermore, bearing in mind the crucial importance of pre-trial procedural stages for the gathering and evaluation of evidence, it may be suggested that it is becoming increasingly impossible to imagine an 'effective defence' without the involvement of the defence with the evidentiary issues (already) at the investigative stage. This tendency is also reflected in the ECtHR case law and in *Directive 2013/48/EU*. Several ECtHR judgments established a violation of a fair trial due to the lack of access to legal assistance during various investigative actions conducted by the authorities during the pre-trial stages (*Özcan Çolak v. Turkey* [2006]; *Savas v. Turkey* [2009]; *Yunus Aktas and others v. Turkey* [2009]; *Melnikov v. Russia* [2010]; *Mehmet Serif Öner v. Turkey* [2011]; *Laska and Lika v. Albania* [2010]; *Galip Doğru v. Turkey* [2015]). In these cases, the Court has stated that 'the investigation stage is of crucial importance in criminal proceedings, as the evidence obtained at this stage determines the framework in which the offence charged will be considered' (*Mehmet Serif Öner*, paragraph 21). Furthermore, based on *Dayanan*, it may be concluded that the Court confers the rights to participate in the evidence-gathering activities of the defence lawyer already at the investigative stage. *Directive 2013/48/EU*, likewise, confers upon the lawyer the right to participate, in accordance with the national law, in investigative actions undertaken during pre-trial proceedings (article 2 (b)).[26]

Participation of the suspect, and consequently of the lawyer, in the fact-finding at the investigative stage, involves two elements: first, participating in the investigative actions conducted by the authorities; and second, initiating or conducting own fact-finding, or requesting the authorities to conduct investigative activities. The remainder of the paragraph addresses these aspects of defence participation separately.

6.5.1 Participating in the investigations conducted by the authorities

At the investigative stage, lawyers may be expected to participate primarily in those investigative acts which are undertaken with the suspect's participation, most typically: identification parades (ID parades), reconstructions of the crime scenes and confrontations with witnesses or alleged victims. The most elaborate ECtHR case law concerns the lawyer's participation in ID parades, therefore this paragraph mostly uses examples related to ID parades to illustrate more general conclusions.

The lawyer's presence may be required, as follows from the ECtHR jurisprudence, to verify whether the investigative action was conducted fairly; whether the results were properly recorded; as well as whether the information obtained was reliable. In *Liska and Lika*, the Court found that without professional legal advice, the applicants were unable to assess or contest the fairness of an ID parade. The applicants' conviction of robbery relied mostly on the results of the ID parade conducted at the investigative stage (paragraph 20). The applicants were made to wear white and blue balaclavas of the kind that were worn by the robbers, while other participants wore black balaclavas (paragraph 13). The Court ruled that a fair trial was violated due to the 'manifest disregard of the rights of the defence', namely because '[t]here was no independent oversight of the fairness of the procedure or opportunity to protest against the blatant irregularities' (paragraph 67).

In *Yunus Aktas and others*, the applicants were not afforded access to legal assistance throughout the entire period of police custody (during which they made self-incriminating statements), including the ID parade. The Court found a violation of the right to a fair trial cumulatively, noting, in respect of the ID parade, that one of the applicants was officially arrested only after the ID parade (paragraph 47), and that the victim in court denied that he had identified the applicant during the ID parade (paragraph 49). Had the lawyer been present at the parade, he could have verified whether its results were recorded correctly. Finally, in *Mehmet Şerif Öner*, the Court implied that the lawyer could verify and contest, already at the investigative stage, the reliability of the ID parade results (paragraphs 21 and 22). In this case, two of the three witnesses, who had positively identified the applicants at the ID parades (conducted nine years after the offence in question had taken place), failed to confirm this in court, stating that too much time had passed since the alleged event. Nevertheless, domestic courts convicted the applicants, relying in part on these witnesses' pre-trial statements.

An interesting conclusion to be drawn from the above-mentioned case law is that, had the lawyer been present during the investigative actions and remained passive, it is unlikely that the ECtHR would have found a violation of a fair trial. Indeed, the Court's findings of unfairness of investigative action soften depending on whether or not the suspect has been afforded access to legal advice: even if there were serious concerns about fairness, the fact that the lawyer was present, and did not (immediately) raise these concerns, is likely to lead to the finding that a fair trial has not been breached (*Melnikov*; *Alchagin v. Russia* [2012]). Thus, the ECtHR case law implies that lawyers must, where necessary, actively intervene in the course of such actions. The active element of the lawyer's role during investigative actions was emphasised in the ECtHR case law concerning witness confrontations. For instance, in *Melnikov* the Court has stated that, in the absence of the lawyer, it was unlikely that the applicant 'was in a position to understand the confrontation procedure and effectively exercise his right to examine a "witness" with a view to casting doubt on the authenticity and credibility of [witnesses'] incriminating statement' (paragraph 79).

6.5.2 Conducting one's own enquiries or requesting authorities to undertake investigations

The right of the defence to contribute to the body of evidence is not specifically granted by the ECHR or the ECtHR case law, although the Strasbourg authorities referred to the possibility of the defence conducting its own inquires, including at the investigative stage (Cape et al., 2010; Jackson and Summers, 2012). In *Can*, the Commission stated that the lawyer's tasks at the pre-trial stages include not only the preparation for the trial, but also 'the identification and presentation of any means of evidence at an early stage where it is still possible to trace new relevant facts and where the witnesses have a fresh memory' (paragraph 55). In *Dayanan*, the Court noted that the suspect, through the assistance of the lawyer, must be afforded the opportunity to investigate facts and collect potentially favourable evidence already at the investigative stage (paragraph 32). Finally, in *Trymbach v. Ukraine (2012)*, the dissenting judges noted that in this particular case, the rationale for affording the applicant early access to a lawyer would have been to assist him in gathering the evidence to substantiate his argument that he should have been prosecuted for a less serious crime (*Joint Dissenting Opinion of Judges Spielmann, Power-Forde and Buromensky*).

The question arises whether both modalities of defence participation in the fact-finding process (conducting one's own inquiries, and requesting authorities to conduct investigations) should be available, or whether granting either of them suffices. Indeed, the mode of participation of the defence in the fact-finding process differs in the adversarial and inquisitorial procedural traditions (see Chapter 7). The tradition of parties undertaking their own inquiries is characteristic of adversarial procedural systems, whilst in inquisitorial systems, the defence could participate only indirectly by requesting the authorities to gather additional evidence (Langer, 2004). However, neither of the two traditions has been capable of ensuring a fully effective role for the lawyer in terms of contributing to the fact-finding. Accounts from the countries following the adversarial tradition point at the lack of resources and formal powers of the defence to conduct its own inquiries (Pizzi, 2000; Young and Wall, 1996).[27] In such systems, the absence of the formal defence's right to request the authorities to undertake inquiries, complementary to the right to undertake its own investigation, prevents the defence from participating in the fact-finding process effectively. This right exists in systems following an inquisitorial tradition such as Germany (Weigend, 2013) or the Netherlands (see Chapter 3). Accounts from countries following the inquisitorial tradition, in their turn, suggest that, likewise, effective defence participation in the fact-finding process is compromised, where the latter is entitled to request the authorities to undertake additional inquiries, but not to conduct its own investigation. In most European criminal procedure systems, the defence is not expressly prohibited from conducting its own inquiries. However, lawyers do not often use these powers, because the evidence presented by the defence may be seen as inferior in strength and reliability than the evidence collected by state authorities (Jackson and Summers, 2012; Hodgson, 2005). At times, requesting the authorities to collect evidence might be inopportune for the defence, for instance where it concerns a reluctant witness who does not trust the authorities.

Therefore, it appears that, irrespective of the legal system, in order to participate effectively in the fact-finding, defence lawyers must have the opportunity both to conduct their own investigation and request the authorities to undertake inquiries. In Italy, for instance, defence lawyers were granted both these rights (Grande, 2008). The rationale for granting the defence the right to participate in the fact-finding process at the early procedural stages is similar to the rationale behind the requirement of 'speediness' to ensure the effectiveness of investigations: namely, the concern that with the passage of time, the quality and amount of available evidence would inevitably deteriorate (*Varnava and Others v. Turkey* [2009]).

6.6 *The role of a lawyer with regard to out-of-court disposals*

An out-of-court disposal presupposes waiver of the right to a court, namely the right to the determination of the case on the merits by an impartial and independent tribunal, as well as, possibly, the right to appeal (*Deweer v. Belgium*[1980], *Natsvlishvili and Togonidze v. Georgia* [2014]). However, it does not imply waiver of all procedural rights. On the contrary, certain procedural rights – such as the right of access to a lawyer and the right to information – acquire additional importance in the context of out-of-court settlements, because they serve as a guarantee of validity of the waiver of the right to a court.

Reviewing the compliance of a plea-bargaining procedure (which, likewise, presupposes a waiver of the right to a court) with Article 6 of the ECHR in *Natsvlishvili and Togonidze*, the ECtHR noted that such a waiver would only be valid if it is 'accepted … in full awareness of the facts of the case and the legal consequences and in a genuinely voluntary manner' (paragraph 93). The first applicant's waiver was found compatible with Article 6, inter alia, because he was 'duly represented by two qualified lawyers of his choice' (paragraph 92), and because he was given the information necessary to enable a valid waiver. He had been given access to the case file in due time, and enjoyed access to the lawyer from the first police interrogation. Therefore, it could be inferred that the applicant had been informed about his procedural rights and the legal consequences of the plea bargaining agreement, and received (individualised and informed) legal advice throughout the negotiations with the prosecutor.

Applying these principles by analogy to out-of-court settlements reached at the investigative stage, the following conclusions can be drawn. To enable an informed decision concerning the offer[28] of an out-of-court disposal, suspects – and their lawyers – must be given at least the following information. They must be granted access to the existing evidence to assess whether it is sufficient to establish the suspect's guilt beyond a reasonable doubt (with or without a confession from the suspect), and whether it was obtained lawfully.[29] Suspects and their lawyers must also be made aware of the (procedural) circumstances of the suspect's arrest and detention (as the defence may argue for a more advantageous outcome in case of certain procedural irregularities). Suspects must also be informed about the proposed sanctions, and other measures included in the out-of-court disposal decision, and their consequences (for example, whether or not they result in a criminal record).

Much of this information – for instance, concerning the sufficiency of the evidence, lawfulness of the arrest and detention procedure, or the consequences of accepting an out-of-court disposal versus opting for a trial – constitutes individualised legal advice, and thus can best be provided by the lawyer (*mutatis mutandis, Zachar and Čierny v. Slovakia* [2015], paragraphs 70–73; *Tikhonov*). Moreover, the lawyer's role in respect of out-of-court disposals at the investigative stage is to ensure that the suspect's acceptance of such disposal is 'genuinely voluntary', meaning that the latter was not subjected to 'undue pressure', 'duress or false promises', 'constraint' or a 'threat of a serious prejudice' (*Natsvlishvili and Togonidze*, paragraph 93; *Deweer*, paragraphs 49 and 50). While the possibility of a higher sanction imposed by a court most probably would not be considered a 'threat of a serious prejudice' (*Deweer*, paragraph 10), it may be argued, for example, that (implied) threats of longer detention, or imprisonment sentence, particularly where the latter is unlikely, might constitute 'undue pressure'. Furthermore, inducements to confess or to waive certain procedural rights as the precondition for the offer of an out-of-court disposal may amount to a 'constraint' incompatible with Article 6 of the ECHR.[30] Thus, the lawyer's role is to ensure that admissions, confessions or waivers of any other procedural rights by the suspect in the context of an out-of-court disposal are truly voluntary.

Finally, the principles of the adversarial proceedings and the equality of arms imply that the lawyer must have a fair opportunity to influence the fact-finding to the client's advantage. In the context of out-of-court disposals, this implies, at the minimum, the right of the defence to comment on the evidence, for instance, with a view to arguing that the prosecution should be dropped altogether; and such matters as the appropriateness of the legal qualification of the alleged offence, and the suitability of the proposed sanction. This, in turn, implies the lawyer's duty, where appropriate, to build and raise such arguments before the respective authorities.

7 Conclusion

This chapter has provided a dynamic normative account of the criminal defence lawyer's role at the investigative stage, taking into consideration the contemporary (legal) developments on the national and European level, namely the growing emphasis on the pre-trial procedural stages. It may be concluded that the modern-day lawyer's role at the investigative stage is multifaceted, and it cannot be boiled down to one 'most important' function or task, such as, for instance, 'providing legal advice', 'influencing the evidence-building' or 'assisting suspects in the context of police interrogation(s)'.

32 *Role of a defence lawyer*

The most recent European legislation endorses an 'active' and 'participatory' role of the defence lawyer at the investigative stage of the proceedings. This role entails active participation during suspect interrogations and engagement with the evidentiary issues already from the earliest moments of the criminal proceedings. The participatory approach, furthermore, requires that lawyers should provide individualised legal advice to their clients already during the early procedural stages – meaning, such advice that is tailored to the specific circumstances of the client's case and their procedural position. It encompasses the various types of roles – 'advice', 'protective' and 'advice defence' (Jackson, 2016a: 194) – which are interrelated and interdependent (Pivaty, 2018).

This chapter demonstrates that the EU procedural rights' Directives and particularly *Directive 2013/48/EU* imply that European criminal defence lawyers are expected to exercise a wide range of functions at the investigative stage. This expectation, however, comes with a commensurate obligation of the state authorities to provide sufficient space, time and resources for lawyers to enable them to exercise these functions. (Although it is also the lawyers' responsibility to demand or ensure that these facilities are provided to them, and take appropriate action if this is not the case.) Furthermore, as follows from the sources described in Section 3.1, the lawyer's obligation to provide 'active' and 'participatory' defence at the pre-trial stages exists only towards the client, but not vis-à-vis the authorities. Thus, for instance, legal provisions, which 'force' the lawyer – or the defence party in general – to submit their requests for investigative actions as early as possible, under the threat that such requests might be rejected if brought during the trial, are not compatible with the normative framework described in this chapter.[31]

The empirical findings presented in the following chapters aim at ascertaining whether and to what extent the normative requirements and expectations related to the lawyer's role at the investigative stage of the criminal proceedings were met in the two researched jurisdictions: England and Wales and the Netherlands.

Notes

1 Resolution of the Council of 30 November 2009 on a roadmap for strengthening procedural rights of suspected or accused persons in criminal proceedings, OJ C 295, 4.12.2009, 1–3.
2 Note that the purpose of this normative view is to describe what a 'practical and effective' right to legal assistance at the investigative stage should look like in the existing institutional setting, and not to assess whether this setting meets the requirements of procedural fairness. Arguably, to guarantee procedural fairness at the investigative stage, the detention and interrogation powers of the police must be substantially reviewed. See also Jackson and Summers, 2012: 101.
3 The ECtHR appeared to depart from this principle (finding no violation of a fair trial in these circumstances) in several post-Salduz judgments, such as *Dvorski v. Croatia* (2013) (treated by the Court as the case concerning the right to a lawyer of one's choice) and *Dzhulay v. Ukraine* (2014), where the Court seemingly overlooked the suspect's confession, focusing instead on the circumstances around the ID parade (see *Dissenting Opinion of Power–Forde*).
4 *Directive 2012/13/EU* of the European Parliament and of the Council of 22 May 2012 on the right to information in criminal proceedings OJ 2012, L 142.

5 Cf. Court of Appeal for Ontario 27 January 1999, *R. v. McCallen*, OJ L 202, para. 34: 'The solicitor–client relationship is anchored on the premise that clients should be able to have complete trust and confidence in the counsel who represent their interests. Clients must feel free to disclose the most personal, intimate and sometimes damaging information to their counsel, secure in the understanding that the information will be treated in confidence and will be used or not used, within the boundaries of counsel's ethical constraints, in the clients' best interests.'
6 *R. v. McCallen*: 'The relationship of counsel and client requires clients, typically, untrained in the law and lacking the skills of advocates, to entrust the management and conduct of their cases to the counsel who act on their behalf. There should be no room for doubt about counsel's loyalty and dedication to the client's case.'
7 Cf. Principle III.1 of the Recommendation No. R (2000)21 of the Committee of Ministers to the member states on the freedom of the exercise of the profession of lawyer of 25 October 2000: 'in defending the legitimate rights and interests of their clients, lawyers have a duty to act independently, diligently and fairly'.
8 Cf. Recommendation on the freedom of the exercise of the profession of lawyer, Principle III.2; Principle e) of the Charter of Core Principles of the European legal profession, Council of Bars and Legal Societies in Europe.
9 In some European jurisdictions, such as England and Wales, the lawyer's obligation to act as 'officer of the court', recognised by the professional regulations, is increasingly interpreted as the duty to contribute to the effective administration of justice (Cape, 2006).
10 See e.g. Recital 33 and Articles 4. 4 (a) and 4.5 of the *Directive 2016/800* of the European Parliament and of the Council of 11 May 2016 on procedural safeguards for children who are suspects or accused persons in criminal proceedings, OJ L 132, 21.5.2016, 1–20.
11 For instance, parents, guardians or other support persons with respect to children and vulnerable suspects in police custody. See Article 3, *Directive 2016/800*; Articles 9 and 10, Commission Recommendation 2013/c 378/02 of 27 November 2013 on procedural safeguards for vulnerable persons suspected or accused in criminal proceedings, OJ C 378, 24.12.2013, 8–10 (*Recommendation 2013/C 378/02*).
12 In England and Wales, for instance, the following decisions may be taken following police custody: to charge the suspect with the offence; to caution the suspect; to release the suspect on bail (with a charge, or pending the decision to charge); to take no further action (where there is not (yet) sufficient evidence to charge) or to release the suspect without charge (i.e. to fully exonerate the suspect from the suspicion).
13 Cf. Guideline 4 (e), UN Guidelines and Principles on Access to Legal Aid in Criminal Justice Systems suggesting that the authorities should 'provide every person, on admission to a place of detention, with information on his or her rights in law, the rules of the place of detention and the initial stages of the pre-trial process'.
14 In England and Wales, for instance, the Standards of Competence for the accreditation of solicitors and representatives advising at the police station provide that 'reasoned and considered advice' should be given to suspects in police custody 'concerning the answering of questions, the right to silence, the making of a written statement under caution … etc.' See Unit 3 Element 2 paragraph 3.8.3. See also Cape, 2012: 472, 480.
15 See also Article 6 (4) (b) *Directive 2016/800*.
16 Examples of such situations may be found in US case law. In *Beecher v. Alabama*, the suspect was interrogated and confessed while feverish, under the effect of morphine and suffering from intense pain in his leg, which was eventually amputated. The Supreme Court found that confession was given under coercion and has overturned the conviction. 389 US Supreme Court 35 1967, *Beecher v. Alabama*. In *Mincey v. Arizona*, a suspect was interrogated in intensive care department of a hospital, was unable to talk because of the tube in his mouth, and had to respond to questioning in writing. The Supreme Court has overturned his confession, inter alia, because he was

34 *Role of a defence lawyer*

'weakened by pain and shock' and 'barely conscious', so that his 'will was simply overborne'. 437 US Supreme Court 385 1978, *Mincey v. Arizona*, paragraphs 401–402.
17 See, by analogy, the description of the lawyer's role in respect of the assessment of the 'fitness for interview' in England and Wales in: Cape, 2017: 162–165.
18 Posing leading and suggestive questions to vulnerable suspects may increase the risk of false confessions (Oberlander et al., 2013: 351).
19 The leading interrogation manual for the Dutch police suggests the tactic of 'building cognitive pressure' by gradually exposing contradictions and inconsistencies in the suspect's account, to persuade deceitful suspects to tell the truth. See van Amelsvort et al., 2017.
20 With regard to vulnerable suspects, it was argued that questioning aimed at confronting such suspects with contradictions in their statements may be linguistically and/or cognitively too complex for them to understand, and to give an adequate response (Mahony et al., 2012).
21 For an overview of the research, see Pivaty, 2018: 71–72.
22 Two types of procedural breaches exist: those for which a clear or automatic remedy exists in domestic (case) law (e.g. annulment of the respective procedural action and exclusion of the resulting evidence), and other procedural breaches, which may be remedied if domestic courts find that, as the consequence of such breaches, the proceedings against the defendant were unfair. In France, for example, this distinction is reflected in the concepts of *nullite textuelle*, i.e. inadmissibility of evidence based on the text of the law, and *nullite substantielle*, i.e. a nullity which is not envisaged in the law, but may be declared if the respective breach affects the essential elements of criminal procedure (e.g. the rights of the defence). Delmas-Marty and Spencer, 2004: 269–270.
23 See, for instance, PACE and the accompanying Codes of Practice in England and Wales.
24 See, for instance, in respect of England and Wales, PACE, Section 47 (1A), Bail Act 1976 Sections 3(6) and 3A(2).
25 The need to raise a *habeas corpus* at the investigative stage would be rare, given its relatively short duration. See, e.g., in respect of England and Wales, Bradley and Ewig, 2007: 502.
26 See also Article 6 (4) (c), *Directive 2016/800*.
27 Because of this disparity of resources, police in England and Wales have the duty to pursue all lines of enquiry, including those that exculpate the suspect. Paragraph 3.4, Criminal Procedure and Investigations Act 1996 (Section 23 (1)) Code of Practice).
28 In some jurisdictions such as the Netherlands, the suspect's consent to the out-of-court disposal (in the form of 'penal order') is not formally required. The Dutch penal order is rendered unilaterally by the prosecutor, but it may be opposed by the suspect in court within a certain time limit. In practice, however, Dutch prosecutors increasingly seek the suspect's consent to the penal order to ensure that the latter would not challenge it in court. See Chapter 3.
29 In England and Wales, for instance, the Ministry of Justice Guidance Simple *Cautions for Adult Offenders* (applicable to the police) states that the suspect must be informed of the evidence against them before they are asked to accept a caution. See paragraph 78.
30 For a discussion of whether admissions or confessions are always truly 'voluntary', where an out-of-court disposal is proposed (in respect of England and Wales), see Sanders et al., 2010: 398.
31 This is effectively what is proposed in the new draft of the Dutch Code of Criminal Procedure (see Chapter 3). See also van Kampen et al., 2018.

3 The Netherlands
Lawyer as 'trusted person' and provider of information

1 Introduction

The Dutch criminal process is commonly described as consisting of an 'inquisitorial' investigation and an 'accusatorial' trial (Keulen and Knigge, 2016: 35–41). Although the 1926 Code of Criminal Procedure (hereinafter – CCP) has undergone modifications that have expanded the participatory defence rights (Reijntjes, 2017: 11), Dutch scholars characterise it as strongly influenced by the inquisitorial tradition (Spronken, 2001: 101–105; Brants, 2013). It is described as being focused on the pre-trial stage, the purpose of the trial being to review the results of the pre-trial investigation (Prakken and Spronken, 2007: 155). For most suspects, criminal proceedings begin with arrest and, subsequently, interrogation: in 2014, 286.132 suspects and 251.900 arrests were registered by the police.[1] Suspects may be kept in custody for interviewing for up to three days (*incommunicado* in certain cases) and in exceptional cases six days, although most are released within six to nine hours (article 56a (2) CCP). Police records of suspect interrogations are included in the case file (dossier) and admissible in evidence (Corstens, 2018: 238–239). The prosecutor is an important player in the Dutch criminal process (ibid.: 109). Prosecutors initiate the proceedings, oversee pre-trial investigations, compile the dossier and support charges in court. Recently, the role of prosecutors has grown in importance due to, inter alia, their increasing power to issue penal orders (discussed in Section 1.2).

Judges in the Netherlands are professionals appointed for life. There is no system of a jury or lay participation in criminal adjudication. At the pre-trial stages, examining magistrates review the lawfulness of the arrest and authorise pre-trial detention and the use of intrusive investigative measures. Magistrates may also conduct investigative actions, such as, in particular, hearing witnesses at the request of the defence (Corstens, 2018: 361–362). At the trial, a judge, or a panel of judges, leads the questioning of the suspect and witnesses (if present) based on the dossier, which they (the judges) study thoroughly in advance. Trials in the Netherlands, particularly those conducted by one judge, are known to be short (Brants, 2013: 1086). Witnesses are often not heard in court, but their pre-trial statements are used in evidence (Blackstock et al., 2013: 101).

36 *The Netherlands*

This chapter describes the practices of legal assistance at the investigative stage in what is considered a strongly 'inquisitorial' procedural setting. It begins by describing the role of a lawyer in the Dutch criminal process, and the developments concerning early access to legal assistance. It continues by summarising the findings of the fieldwork in the Netherlands. In the concluding part, these findings are contrasted with the view embedded in the respective European regulations described in Chapter 2.

2 Setting the scene

2.1 *The role of defence lawyers*

The lawyer's role in the criminal proceedings is to act as the suspect's 'advisor, trusted person and representative' (Corstens, 2018: 96–97; Statuut Raadsman, Rule 1).[2] Defence lawyers have several participatory rights, including the right to request the hearing of witnesses, to request a complementary investigation, to direct questions to witnesses, and, as of recently, to participate in suspect interrogations (HR 30 June 2009, ECLI: NL: HR:2009: BH3079; Wet Implementatie Richtlijn 2013/48/EU). Lawyers are not precluded from conducting investigations (this right is 'read into' article 28 CCP) (Statuut Raadsman, Rule 28; Spronken, 2001: 235–237), but their results need to be added to the dossier to count as 'evidence'. Thus, at the pre-trial stages, lawyers must request the prosecutor to attach evidence to the dossier (Brants, 2013: 1086), so they can introduce it at the trial (Boksem et al., 2011: 95–96). The defence may bring witnesses to the trial (articles 260 (4) and 287 (2) CCP),[3] but – unlike prosecutors or judges – they have no independent powers to summon witnesses. Suspects and their lawyers may also pose questions to witnesses at the trial, subsequent to the judge and the prosecutor, unless the witness is introduced by the defence (article 292 CCP).

At the pre-trial stages, most participatory defence rights can be limited by the police or prosecutor in the interests of the investigation (Prakken and Spronken, 2007: 174). This concerns, for instance, the right of access to the dossier (article 30 (3) CCP), to conduct investigations, to effective participation in the interrogation (Besluit inrichting en orde politieverhoor), and, exceptionally, of the lawyer's access to the client (article 50 CCP). These provisions remain unchanged in the revised CCP. At the pre-trial stage, the defence may obtain access to the dossier through the prosecutor (article 30 (1) and 51 CCP). The prosecutor may limit access, for example, by deciding that certain information must remain confidential, or that certain materials are irrelevant (articles 30 (3), 34 (4), 149b CCP). Although the case law requires that that all materials potentially beneficial for the defence must be disclosed (*Dev Sol*, HR 7 May 1996, ECLI:NL:PHR:1996:AB9820, *NJ* 1996, 687 m.nt. Schalken), this is difficult to effectuate in practice. Thus, although the defence may request the prosecutor to complete the dossier (article 34 CCP), they would often not know about the existence of non-disclosed materials in the first place.

The Dutch criminal lawyers' professional ethics describes lawyers as unequivocally partisan, and having no duty as 'officer of the court' (Statuut Raadsman, Rule 5; Rule 2 (2) Gedragsregels). The defendant is the *dominis litis* in criminal proceedings, and the lawyer's rights generally follow from those of the defendant (Spronken, 2001: 639). Lawyers must seek clients' input into strategic decisions, and may not knowingly act against clients' will. The principle of independence from one's client (article 10a (1a) Advocatenwet), in principle derived from the inquisitorial tradition, does not grant Dutch lawyers the power to unilaterally define the defence strategy. Rather, it absolves them from the duty to follow clients' instructions involving illegal or unethical activities, or legally futile lines of defence (Gedragsregels, Rule 1 (1); Spronken, 2001: 505–506). An irreconcilable difference of opinion may lead to termination of the lawyer–client relationship by either party (Statuut Raadsman, Rule 16).

Ethically, Dutch lawyers have considerable freedom in conducting the defence, provided that their actions are endorsed by the client. This freedom is limited only by the requirements to act lawfully (Statuut Raadsman, Rule 6), and to refrain from actions 'unworthy of the proper exercise of the lawyers' function' or compromising lawyers' integrity (article 10a (d) Advocatenwet). With regard to criminal defence, this translates into the obligation to consider the need to protect privacy and refrain from defamation of third parties (Statuut Raadsman, Rules 19 and 27). The general rule of professional ethics, according to which Dutch lawyers may not deceive the court (Gedragsregels, Rule 6), is interpreted less restrictively with regard to criminal defence professionals. They may not *actively* deceive the court, for example by fabricating evidence, but they may rely on the facts or evidence as relayed to the court by the client, even if they know them to be untrue (Spronken, 2001: 638). Thus, Dutch lawyers, unlike English lawyers (as described in Chapter 4), are not constrained in the choice of procedural strategy, where they know that their client wishes to deceive the authorities.

Traditionally, Dutch criminal defence lawyers have not been actively involved in the fact-finding process. This is partly because evidence is rarely gathered or presented anew at the trial (this practice, which was developed on the basis of the 1924 *de auditu* judgment of the Supreme Court (Reijntjes, 2017: 29–31), will be legitimised in the revised CCP). Although the defence may submit reasoned requests to undertake certain investigative actions to the examining magistrate (articles 182–184 CCP), doubts were raised by commentators about whether they can always take practical advantage of this provision. This is due to, inter alia, the magistrates' heavy workloads, and the lack of knowledge of the dossier by the defence, often necessary to justify the request (van der Meij, 2010; Franken, 2012).

2.2 Lawyers at suspect interrogations: decades of opposition

The right to legal assistance in the context of custodial suspect interrogations was first introduced by the landmark 2009 post-*Salduz* judgment of the Dutch Supreme Court. The history of the debate about legal assistance in the context of police interrogations was narrated in detail by Spronken and Brants (Spronken, 2001: 108–125; Brants, 2011). Suffice to say that the Dutch government had been extremely reluctant to extend the right of access to a lawyer at police interrogations, fearing that this would interfere with effective investigations. It took 40 years after the first deliberations in the Parliament (Spronken, 2001: 108), and several coinciding political influences, namely several 'miscarriage of justice' cases that came to light in 2005–2010 and the *Salduz* jurisprudence of the ECtHR, for this right to become recognised in the Dutch law.

The 2009 Supreme Court judgment, however, did not acknowledge the right to the lawyer's presence during interrogations for all categories of suspects, but only for juveniles. The public prosecutor issued a directive based on this judgment effective 1 April 2010 (Aanwijzing Rechtsbijstand Politieverhoor). This included the right for all suspects to a prior consultation with the lawyer for a maximum of 30 minutes, and additionally the right of juveniles to have their lawyer or 'trusted person' (parent or relative) present during interrogations. The already-existing duty lawyer scheme, which covered the period after the first interrogation, was extended to the period before the first interrogation. This newly introduced right became commonly known as '*Salduz* assistance'.

In the meantime, the new ECtHR post-*Salduz* case law emerged, referring explicitly to the right of access 'during' or 'in the course of' the interrogation (*Navone and others*). Directive 2013/48/EU, likewise, conferred the right to all criminal suspects. Yet, the Supreme Court, when called to clarify the Dutch legal position on 'interrogation assistance', had initially refused to decide on the matter, stating that defining the general scope of the right was the legislator's task (HR 1 April 2014, ECLI:NL:HR:2014: 770, *NJ* 2014/268). Indeed, the draft legislation implementing the Directive, and covering the right to 'interrogation assistance', had been released for consultation two months prior to this ruling (Wet Implementatie Richtlijn 2013/48/EU). Due to the contentious nature of the subject matter, however, fast progress on the draft was not to be expected. Another Supreme Court judgment, issued in late 2015, was necessary for the universal right to 'interrogation assistance' to become recognised in Dutch law. The Court established the deadline of 1 March 2016 to effectuate the right, which was done through a policy directive of the public prosecutor (HR 22 December 2015, ECLI: NL:HR: 2015:3608).

Effective 1 March 2017, the Dutch legislation implementing *Directive 2013/48/EU* entered into force, granting a statutory footing to the right to interrogation assistance for all criminal suspects (Wet Implementatie Richtlijn 2013/48/EU; Besluit inrichting en orde politieverhoor). Whilst this legislation brings the Dutch law closer to the EU law requirements, certain aspects of it, carried over from the earlier 2010 and 2016 public prosecutor's Directives, remain controversial. These are, namely, the 30-minute limit on the lawyer–client pre-interrogation consultation (article 28c (1) CCP), and the limitations on the lawyer's participation during the interrogation (see Chapter 6).

2.3 Positioning the Dutch fieldwork

The fieldwork in the Netherlands was carried out between 2011 and 2014. (The details of the research methodology are described in the Appendix.) Therefore, it was undertaken when the right to 'interrogation assistance' was conferred only on juvenile suspects.[4] Although the fieldwork was undertaken before this right was extended to adult suspects (in 2016), most of the findings described in this and the following chapters arguably remain valid. This research focuses on cultures, traditions and practices, which take longer to change and adjust than the respective legal regulations.

Besides, most regulations on legal assistance at the investigative stage in the Netherlands have remained unchanged since the time of the fieldwork. Suspects are informed about the right to legal assistance (free of charge, except for minor offences) during the 'presentation before the assistant prosecutor' shortly after arrival to the police station. The 'assistant prosecutor' is a senior police officer, acting under delegated powers, who assesses the legality of arrest and decides whether the prolongation of the initial arrest is necessary, as well as informs the suspect about the charge and the right to legal assistance. The assistant prosecutor also usually questions the suspect, including by requesting a 'short reaction' to the allegation(s). This practice is called 'interrogation (*verhoor*) by the assistant prosecutor', although interestingly it is not considered an 'official' interrogation triggering the application of procedural rights (articles 53–55a, 154–159 CCP; Blackstock et al., 2013: 222). (In practice, this interrogation is often used to gauge whether suspect is likely to remain silent, or even to persuade them to accept an out-of-court settlement or to admit guilt (see ibid.: 226).) If suspects state that they wish to see a lawyer, they are asked whether they have a preferred lawyer. If no preferred lawyer is named, a duty lawyer is assigned. The regulations provide for a consultation of a maximum of 30 minutes, although in practice, longer consultations are often allowed. In most cases though, lawyers utilise the full 30 minutes. Lawyers leave the police station immediately after the consultation, unless they intend to stay on to provide 'interrogation assistance'. At the time of the fieldwork, lawyers could attend interrogations of juvenile suspects, although in practice, they often delegated this task to 'trusted persons'.[5] If the suspect's initial detention is prolonged, the lawyer who provided them with 'consultation assistance' would visit them again.

Each judicial district has its own duty lawyer scheme run by the Legal Aid Board. The Legal Aid Board defines the criteria for inclusion on the duty lawyer list and fees for police station attendance. The on-call arrangements may differ per region, but generally two or more lawyers would be on call each day, covering three or four police stations equipped with detention facilities. The on-call duty begins at 7 a.m. and finishes at 8 p.m., although calls usually come in during office hours, when most interrogations take place.

3 The lawyer and the client: brief and superficial encounters

The fleeting and superficial nature of lawyer–client exchanges at the investigative stage was a striking finding of the Dutch fieldwork. Allusions were regularly made to the practice of '2-minute consultations', where a lawyer 'tells the suspect to keep his mouth shut and walks away'. In the observed cases, lawyers' contact with their clients usually lasted no longer than 10–15 minutes. Lawyers went into the consultation room knowing nothing or almost nothing about the client and the client's case. Clients, in turn, were often either unable to meaningfully communicate with lawyers, or unwilling to confide in them (due to being mistrustful, anxious, agitated, shocked, ashamed or intoxicated); or they were genuinely unaware of the circumstances around the impugned offence.

The Dutch observations were conducted with 'duty' lawyers, whom suspects were meeting for the first time, and not with their 'preferred' lawyers. Thus, the findings described later may not apply to the relationships between suspects and preferred lawyers. Yet, only about one-third of arrested suspects in the Netherlands ask for a particular lawyer (Klein Haarhuis et al., 2018). In addition, preferred lawyers are not always available to attend police stations on short notice: at the time of the fieldwork, only half of suspects asking for a particular lawyer were actually assisted by them (Peters et al., 2014). In observations, it happened regularly that suspects were attended by duty lawyers, because their preferred lawyer was unavailable. These suspects tended to mistrust duty lawyers, especially because they were usually not told why they were being seen by a different lawyer.

The following sections address two major themes related to the lawyer–client interactions at the investigative stage which emerged from the Dutch fieldwork: the lack of 'trust' in police station encounters, and the superficial nature of 'advice' given by lawyers.

3.1 The importance of 'trust' and the lack of trust in police station encounters

3.1.1 'Trust' in the professional discourse of lawyers

Lawyer–client 'trust' (*vertrouwen*) is given much attention in the lawyers' ethical rules and professional discourse (as was also reflected in the interviews). The Dutch Code of lawyers' professional ethics states that the lawyer should aim at the 'mutual relationship that is based on good will and trust' with their client (Gedragsregels, Rule 24). The old Code for Dutch lawyers stated that 'trust' is important because the lawyer 'can only fulfil his function well, where the client provides him with all information that is important for the assessment and handling of his case' (Gegragsregels 1992, paragraph 1.2). When there is no trust, a lawyer is unable to ensure an effective defence of their client (Gegragsregels 1992, Preamble), and therefore if trust is broken, the lawyer–client relationship must end (Statuut Raadsman, Rule 16). It is the lawyer's responsibility to take steps aimed at building trust (Statuut Raadsman, Rule 14), and maintaining a relationship of trust (ibid.). At the investigative stage, the lawyer is a suspect's confidant, often being the only person the suspect may rely on, particularly when in detention (Spronken, 2001: 60).

Similarly, the interviewed Dutch lawyers considered that building the relationship of trust with their clients forms the central part of their role at the investigative stage. One lawyer, for instance, defined his role at this stage as follows:

> It is the role of a trusted person in the first place, vis-à-vis the clients. Because they are locked up in a dark cell and they get to deal with detectives and custody officers. I often notice that when suspects are willing to tell their story [when they trust their lawyer], they really cling to me and are also looking for a bit of emotional support.
>
> (INTNeth7)

Trusting one's client, understood as believing that the client was 'telling the truth', was, likewise, considered important by the interviewed Dutch lawyers, because the client was often the only source of knowledge about the incriminated events. As one lawyer noted:

> [At the investigative stage] ... you don't have the case files and you have to trust the story of your client and that is someone you never met before and he has to trust you and you have to trust him ... , and he has to tell you his story. You really need to create trust, that is very important for the first conversation.
>
> (INTNeth22)

Lawyers wanted to know the client's 'true story' to be more effective in their representations and to avoid professional embarrassment. The 'truth' was preferred, even if it meant a confession or a direct admission.

As one lawyer put it:

> At the starting point I want to hear from my client what happened ... I do explain why it is important, he needs to be truthful towards me. My client is allowed to tell me everything and he is allowed to ask for confidentiality. The reason why I need all the information is because I do not want to be surprised, I want the truth, his truth. And that information I can use in my defence strategy. When he holds back information ... there is a risk that my strategic move can go wrong.
>
> (INTNeth23)

3.1.2 Lack of trust in observations

Despite stressing the importance of trust, the interviewed lawyers doubted whether they should a priori believe their clients' stories. As one of the lawyers quoted in the paragraph previously noted later in the interview, 'often they [clients] give a "random" story and you only see at the presentation before the examining magistrate [i.e. when the case file is accessed] that he just made something up' (INTNeth22). In the words of a lawyer shadowed during the fieldwork, 'most suspects [arrested at a police station] lie to their lawyers, this is a given' (FNNeth13.02.2012). Lawyers also did not expect clients to be fully open with them during their first encounter. They knew that suspects might have reasons not to trust them (yet). In the words of one lawyer: 'I do understand [why clients might lie to duty lawyers], these people think you are part of police' (INTNeth24).

The observations have largely confirmed the lawyers' perceptions that many clients were mistrustful of them. In psychology, the main elements of interpersonal trust are: reliability or competence, or relying on the other person's judgment or promise; emotional trust, or believing that the other will not cause you emotional harm, and being willing to make personal disclosures; and integrity or honesty, or believing that the other person is objective, truthful and sincere (Rotenberg, 2010). Thus, there is no trust (yet) where suspects, for instance, do not appear to seek or rely on their lawyer's advice; to believe what the lawyer tells them; or where they avoid making personal disclosures to the lawyer. Whilst this study did not employ psychological tools to assess suspects' trust in lawyers, it did document the apparent manifestations of mistrust, such as, for instance, suspects telling lawyers that they mistrusted them; suspects being reluctant to give details of their 'story'; or suspects being unwilling to disclose embarrassing facts to lawyers.

In one observed case, for example, a suspect – who told the lawyer that he had not asked for a lawyer and did not need one – spoke with the lawyer very reluctantly; disclosing no more than that he was 'quietly sitting' with his friends in a café when arrested, and responding 'I don't know' to all other questions, including the time of the day that he was arrested, and the people who were with him at that time (FNNeth20.02.2012). In another case, a suspect accused of trading stolen goods refused altogether to speak with the lawyer about the alleged offence, giving evasive answers of the sort, 'I don't know what has happened' and 'Without money you cannot buy anything' (FNNeth21.02.2012). He also did not seem to understand who the lawyer was, and especially that he was not part of the police. At the end of the consultation, when the lawyer told him that he would now be interrogated by the police, the suspect asked: 'What? Interrogated again?' In a third case, a suspect was arrested on a drug-related charge on the stairs leading to an apartment, where marijuana was being grown. The suspect denied fervently to the lawyer that she had any relation to the drugs found in the apartment, although her clothes, as it was evident both for the lawyer and the researcher, smelled strongly of marijuana (FNNeth22.08.2012).

In yet another case, the suspect refused to respond to the lawyer's questions in the first consultation (before the interrogation), saying that he had 'no idea' why he had been arrested (for robbery). He did, however, give a detailed account in the second consultation, after having fully confessed at the interrogation (FNNeth27.02.2012). In a different case observed on the same day, the suspect told the lawyer that he thought he did not need a lawyer, and gave a very contradictory account. He insisted throughout the consultation that the ecstasy pills found in his car were placebos (although the lawyer had already been told by police that they were 'real'), but also that he did not know anything about them, and that they must have been put in the car by someone else (FNNeth27.02.2012). He also told the lawyer, in response to the question about his criminal record, that he had been convicted only once, which the lawyer knew was untrue.

Suspects were sometimes reluctant to disclose their criminal record to duty lawyers. They also appeared unwilling to admit to drug use. Thus, one suspect told the lawyer that he had used drugs 'once', but not anymore. However, he also said that he had been under the influence of 'pills, weed and speed' when the suspected offence was committed (two days earlier) (FNNeth27.02.2012). Another suspect told the lawyer that she was a speed user, although the lawyer believed that she looked more like someone who was heroine-dependent (FNNeth25.08.2012).

Often, it appeared that suspects who requested a preferred lawyer, but instead were seen by a duty lawyer, mistrusted the latter. Sometimes, they openly expressed this sentiment, like in one observed case, where the suspect told the lawyer that he did not wish to talk to him, but only to his preferred lawyer. He only agreed to tell the lawyer about the circumstances of his arrest when the lawyer stated that he would contact the suspect's own lawyer (FNNeth07.03.2012). Duty lawyers were well aware that suspects who already had a preferred lawyer would be less inclined to trust them. Therefore, often they did not try to obtain any disclosure from such suspects, or to give them any advice.

3.2 Advising suspects: generic advice in an informational vacuum

3.2.1 Gathering information from clients

A prominent finding of the Dutch observations was that lawyers gathered very little information from their clients during police station encounters. With a few exceptions, lawyers did not aim to obtain detailed disclosure from clients at this stage. Rather, their expectation was that the client would share the information gradually, following prosecution's disclosure. As one lawyer noted: 'one starts to discuss the case [with one's client] on its merits (*inhoudelijk*) only after the hearing regarding the application for pre-trial detention' (FNNeth03.03.2012). The lack of the client's trust in the lawyer appeared to be one of the reasons why Dutch lawyers obtained so little information. In the words of one lawyer:

> [When taking client's disclosure], the trick is to keep asking questions and not to let go. But often it is difficult, especially with people you just met for the first time, you want them to trust you and you have to have the feeling that you have a connection ... And often you see that in the [first consultation] they don't tell you everything yet, and if you come back [again], then they talk a bit more and that they think a bit more like 'ok, I trust this man'. This is a gradual process ... you should not push too far, like saying 'I really have to know everything now', then people quit.
>
> (INTNeth15)

On the extreme side, lawyers did not gather any case-related information. In one observed case, involving a suspect who was not the lawyer's regular client, the lawyer obtained no disclosures at all during their first encounter. The consultation lasted five minutes and was transcribed almost verbatim:

LAWYER (L): You are suspected of a robbery ...
SUSPECT (S): Yes, at a gas station.
L: Was it a gas station?
S: What are the facts?
L: I don't know. I only know what is on the referral form, and what the officer told me. He said it was a robbery ...
S: I see ...
L: Do you want to make a statement? ... You do not have to make a statement ... We usually advise our clients not to make a statement, because if you do, it may be disadvantageous.
S: And how would it be seen if I say that I do not wish to cooperate?
L: Police would of course try to tell you that they found a lot of evidence. They would try to make you give a statement. But it is to your advantage if you wait ... Or you may of course say that you have nothing to do with it. Because ... Do you have anything to do with it? Indeed, you do not have to tell me ...
S: No. I don't know anything.
L: Good, then you should say: I know nothing ... If your detention is prolonged, I will come to visit you again today and then maybe we will know more. This is my card [Gives him the business card.] ... This is not the first time that you are arrested?
S: No, I was arrested before, but for other things.
L: So you know how it works?
S: Yes ... Police say it was an 'old fact'. It happened in January.
L: (looking at the referral form): It is not mentioned here ...
S: So I will say nothing.
L: It is a right decision. We don't have access to the dossier yet.

(FNNeth11.09.2012)

In this encounter, the lawyer deliberately avoided discussing the allegations with the client. He judged it unnecessary, because in his view, the client's best (and only) option was to remain silent: this was a 'serious' offence (robbery), involving a 'repeat offender' (thus unlikely to be released following the initial detention). The client was going to be presented to the examining magistrate, where the lawyer would learn about the 'facts' and evidence from the dossier.

This was one of only two observed consultations where a lawyer obtained no disclosure at all (the other involved a case where the suspect, presumably a foreigner, did not speak a word either to the police or to the lawyer, and it was impossible to know which language he spoke or indeed what his name was: FNNeth07.03.2012). In most observed cases, however, lawyers took some, but limited, disclosure. For instance, in one case, a lawyer was attending a client suspected of threatening an employee in a social housing company. The lawyer asked the suspect why and when he was arrested, and was asked to describe his relationship with the housing company. He did not, however, ask him whether he had a criminal record, nor did he ask about the circumstances in which the alleged threat was made (FNNeth20.03.2012). After taking disclosure in this manner, the lawyer advised the suspect to tell the police that he did not mean to harm the complainant and to 'write a letter of excuse', hoping that the charges would be dropped. Later, however, I found out that the 'case' had been treated as rather serious by the police (FNNeth23.03.2012). Important details were omitted during the consultation. The suspect had previously been convicted of public violence, which was considered sufficient proof that he could act upon the threat. Moreover, the threat was made in the presence of a witness. Had the lawyer questioned his client more carefully, he could have obtained this information, and might have given different advice.

Where suspects presented a defence to the lawyer – for example, by alleging that the complainant was falsely accusing them, or asserting self-defence – the latter rarely 'probed' their account. In one example, a suspect, who had previous convictions for domestic violence, was accused of physical assault on his partner. He told the lawyer that he and his partner 'had a word exchange' that had 'escalated', and that subsequently she attacked him with pepper spray. He alluded that there had been a fight, but that 'he had walked out'. The lawyer did not ask about the circumstances of the fight, nor about any injuries suffered by the parties. He simply went on to advise the client to deny responsibility: 'You must say: I did not do anything' (FNNeth16.02.2012).

Possibly, lawyers avoided probing clients' defences because they were concerned about coming across as accusatory. Indeed, without access to the dossier, lawyers could not challenge their clients' accounts by referring to concrete facts. They could only pose general questions like: 'Why do you think the complainant accused you?', which might indeed sound like an accusation. Besides, lawyers possibly avoided detailed questioning because they believed their clients to be guilty. One encountered lawyer, for instance, told the researcher that he did not probe client's defences 'for ethical reasons'. That is because if he 'knew too much', and the client decided to lie, he would feel complicit in fabricating a false account, and thus of interfering with truth-finding (FNNeth14.02.2012). Finally, it may be that (some) lawyers did not try to obtain more information, because they considered it unnecessary. This approach seemed typical where, in the lawyer's optic, it was predetermined that the suspect should remain silent: as in the 'robbery at a gas station' case described earlier. Indeed, in interviews, some lawyers said that it was not necessary to obtain a detailed client's account prior to getting access to the dossier.

Most lawyers, when faced with vague, contradictory or non-credible clients' accounts, advised them to remain silent, but others did not give any advice at all. Thus, in one case, a client, suspected of trading stolen goods,[6] told the lawyer that he bought the goods in a large second-hand store, but was given no invoice.

46 *The Netherlands*

He intended to tell this to the police. The lawyer clearly doubted the credibility of his story: if it was a large store, it is unlikely that no invoice was given. He told the client that in his view, without an invoice, it would be difficult to prove that the purchase was legal. The client responded defensively: 'Look, sir, this is a very large enterprise. They sell machines as good as new. How would I know that it was stolen? There was no sign hanging on it, sir …' The lawyer then stopped inquiring into the facts, and did not give any advice (FNNeth27.02.2012).

A minority of the observed lawyers (7 out of 32), however, systematically spent a large part of the consultation gathering information from the client. In one such case, a lawyer thanks to detailed questioning of the client – including by 'reconstructing' the scene of the alleged fight – managed to identify weaknesses in the client's self-defence account, and advised them to remain silent to avoid unnecessary self-incrimination (although the commonly given advice in such cases was to give an account) (FNNeth08.08.2012).

3.2.2 Advising clients

INFORMING ABOUT RIGHTS

About half of interviewed lawyers[7] said that their role at the investigative stage was about providing information: 'it's not about the content, because you don't have anything yet' (INTNeth6; see also Stevens and Verhoeven, 2010: 154). Yet, the information that lawyers provided to clients in the observed consultations was rather limited. Lawyers usually informed suspects about their right to silence and the consequences of exercising it, and about the police detention procedures. Some lawyers also gave general advice about how to handle an interrogation, such as how to resist interrogative pressure or how to verify the written record. Other information, for example, about the right to legal aid, or the right to interpretation, was rarely given, even where it was relevant.[8]

The right to silence was mentioned in most observed consultations, although sometimes it was presented as a possibility, rather than a right: you *can* remain silent.[9] Some lawyers simply told their clients that they 'are not obliged to respond to questions' (in the same way as police inform suspects about this right). The implications of remaining silent, such as the risk of longer detention, were mentioned only in every third consultation. Some lawyers also explained the difference between full silence and responding to certain questions: namely, that the latter might lead to an inference of guilt. However, not once were lawyers observed to verify whether clients understood their rights, for example, by asking them to explain what the use of the right to silence entails.

ADVISING ON PROCEDURAL STRATEGY

Only in every fourth observed pre-interrogation consultation did the lawyer mention that the client may choose between two (or more) options of procedural strategy at the interrogation. The options presented typically were: to 'remain silent' or to 'refuse to respond to questions', and to '(openly) tell your story' or to 'tell the truth'. (Presumably, 'telling the story' implied both making (a) partial admission(s) or a full confession, and denying guilt and presenting a defence; however, these two possibilities were not specified.) In interviews, some lawyers mentioned a third option: to 'tell a lie'. These three options correspond to those mentioned in the professional literature (Prakken and Spronken, 2009: 292–296). After outlining the options, some lawyers proceeded to warn their clients about the dangers of lying or making up a false defence. A fourth option presented by some lawyers was, in essence, to give a denying statement and to remain silent: 'make a *short* statement' or 'do not say what you don't want to say'. This did not (sufficiently) protect clients from inadvertent self-incrimination, because lawyers did not explain what kind of information the clients should or should not disclose in their statement. Some observed Dutch lawyers did not explain the difference between 'remaining silent' ('say nothing') and 'making a short denial statement' ('say that you know nothing'). Denying guilt may have different procedural consequences than remaining silent, because it may be interpreted as 'deliberately false', but some lawyers appeared to imply that they have similar meanings. Thus, one lawyer told the suspect of burglary that he should say: 'I myself know nothing. I want to use my right to silence' (FNNeth16.03.2012).

When explaining the consequences of the various options, most lawyers said to clients that 'if they remain silent, they may stay in detention longer'. Others added, 'however, it is not up to the police to decide', and that 'even if they give an account [to the police], they may stay longer'. Usually this was meaningless advice, because lawyers could not predict whether suspects' behaviour at the interrogation would influence their detention or release. Thus, suspects accused of more 'serious' offences were unlikely to be released even if they had given a full account. However, in the absence of access to the dossier, lawyers often could not accurately gauge the seriousness of the allegations.

In four out of ten observed consultations, lawyers did not clearly recommend a certain strategy at the interrogation. (And in every third consultation the lawyer neither informed the suspect about the existing options nor suggested a particular strategy.) One lawyer, for instance, typically told her clients that 'they have the right to remain silent, but if they use this right, they may need to remain in detention longer', and asked them 'what they thought about it'. When they said, for example, that they were not going to remain silent, she never commented on it (FNNeth23.08.2012). This contradicted the interview findings, in which most lawyers said that they would recommend an option, because 'most people eventually want to hear what they should do' (INTNeth14). This contradiction may be explained in several ways. Almost all interviewed Dutch lawyers specialised in criminal law (32 out of 34), whilst only about half of the observed consultations were given by specialised lawyers. Specialised lawyers may be more confident, and therefore more explicit in their advice. It is also possible that some interviewed lawyers exaggerated their level of compliance with what they considered 'good professional practice'.

The encountered Dutch lawyers were reluctant to help their clients formulate responses to (anticipated) police questions. Such practice was described as 'influencing' the suspect's statement, which must be 'spontaneous' or 'come from the suspect himself' (FNNeth13.08.2012). As one lawyer remarked:

> I believe this is not the role of a lawyer to suggest answers to a suspect. It is a suspect who tells his story, and I tell him what the consequences are. I am not going to help a suspect create a story. Some colleagues try to do that, but I do not think it is proper. I think it is dangerous ...
>
> (INTNeth3)

Yet, sometimes it appeared necessary to assist suspects in formulating their answers, especially where lawyers advised their clients to remain partially silent. In one case, for example, a 14-year-old suspect, accused of stealing a phone (he maintained that he got it from his father), did not seem to understand that he was not obliged to tell the police how the phone came into his possession. He asked the lawyer 'what exactly he should say at the interrogation', to which the lawyer responded that 'he was not there to put words in his mouth'. This advice confused the suspect (FNNEth25.08.2012).

Remarkably, in more than half (39 out of 70) observed consultations taking place before the first interrogation, suspects did not make it clear which strategy they would adopt during the questioning or whether they agreed with the lawyer's recommendation (if given). Many lawyers appeared to believe that it was futile to obtain such an agreement, because suspects might change their minds during an interrogation. In the words of one lawyer,

> ... [N]o matter how convincing you are, and no matter how much the clients agree and tell you they will remain silent, it is always surprising to see afterwards who speaks and who remains silent. Because those who convincingly say 'I'm not going to speak to the police, I won't do what they want from me' often end up giving a complete statement.
>
> (INTNeth1)

3.3 Supporting clients in detention: limitations of the 'trusted person' role

3.3.1 Lawyers' professional discourse on their role as 'trusted person'

The Dutch lawyers' role of a 'trusted person' entails the provision of social and emotional support to (detained) clients. A leading professional guide for criminal lawyers states that the lawyer must 'realise that he [the suspect] is ... cut out from his environment', and that he is often concerned about matters not related to the criminal case, but which are very important for him personally (Prakken and Spronken, 2009: 5). It suggests that the lawyer 'should not act as a social worker', but should, for instance, try to involve social services where possible and necessary (ibid.). Another guide suggests that the lawyer should deal with 'the direct consequences of deprivation of liberty', namely, to address, in cooperation with social services, issues like the need for medication, clean clothes, childcare, pet care, home maintenance and work (Boksem et al., 2011: 62).

Likewise, the interviewed Dutch lawyers emphasised the importance of the 'trusted person' role at the investigative stage. One lawyer, for instance, described it as follows:

> It is a little bit of everything ... Bring clothes, call relatives ... I think at this stage your role is broader [than purely legal questions]. You are the only one who is a real friend of the suspect. You are his only link to the outer world ... I ask clients if I should call someone for them ... [C]all relatives, ensure that your client has got medication, try to reassure the client, this kind of things ...
> (INTNeth6)

Lawyers also said that addressing clients' social needs was essential in securing trust. In the words of one lawyer:

> Creating a trust relationship, I think, works best when you talk about the personal information. So who do we need to inform, do you have pets at home that need to be taken care of, is there an employer, school, you name it.
> (INTNeth1)

3.3.2 *Supporting clients in detention in practice*

In practice, the encountered lawyers tended to limit their engagement with the clients' broader social and emotional needs in detention. These limits were expressed by commonly used phrases like 'I am not a social worker', or 'I am not a postman'. For most lawyers, addressing client's broader needs in detention involved making a call to the suspect's family to 'inform them [about the suspect's arrest], but also to arrange clothes and cigarettes' (INTNeth22). As one lawyer noted:

> The point is that I can inform people [i.e. the suspect's family]. But I won't call five times a day 'can you do this, can you get that'. I limit myself to one call for clean clothes. Later when they are in pre-trial detention, they can arrange for other things themselves.
> (INTNeth21)

Often, lawyers inquired into the suspect's social needs towards the end of the consultation, using a 'standard' set of questions: 'Do you want to have someone informed about your detention?', 'Do you need clothes or medication?' It was doubtful that this approach was aimed at, or contributed to, increasing the client's trust in the lawyer. Rather, it appeared that lawyers were simply going through their usual routines, or posed these questions for the researcher's sake.

The observed lawyers rarely followed up with the authorities on their clients' needs for medical care. Some lawyers, faced with clients who had an obvious medical condition, such as severe alcohol withdrawal, or a mental health issue impeding their ability to communicate with the lawyer, did not raise this during the consultation or to the police. Others suggested to a custody officer that

50   *The Netherlands*

'perhaps the suspect needs to see a doctor', but did not follow up in any way (FNNeth21.02.2012; 12.09.2012). For instance, in one case, a suspect, who was undergoing psychiatric treatment for autism and depression, at some point during the consultation put his head on the table and covered it with his elbows. Alarmed by the suspect's condition – and remarking (to the researcher) that perhaps the suspect was suicidal – the lawyer suggested to the police that 'maybe' they should call a doctor. He did not follow up on whether the client had received any medical attention (FNNeth20.02.2012).

Lawyers also rarely inquired into their clients' conditions or well-being in detention. Where suspects complained about the conditions of their detention – for instance, that they were not given any airing time, or did not get a meal – not once was a lawyer observed to follow up with the police. Typically, lawyers told clients that they should address the police themselves. Yet, sometimes it was doubtful whether suspects were capable of making such demands. In one case, for instance, a Polish suspect told the lawyer that he was not given a possibility to call his family to notify them that he had been arrested in the Netherlands. The lawyer responded that 'he must be able to call his family', and should ask the police to give him access to a phone. It was difficult to imagine how the suspect could have done this, because he did not speak Dutch nor English (FNNeth20.02.2012).

4 Lawyers and the authorities: the lack of participatory role

Traditionally, Dutch lawyers rarely interact with the investigative authorities (police). Prosecutors and judges (examining magistrates) are the lawyers' habitual interlocutors in the criminal proceedings, also with regard to pre-trial investigations. The fieldwork took place in the midst of legislative changes, which necessitated greater lawyers' engagement with the police. The encounters mainly occurred when lawyers attended clients for a consultation at the police station, and during suspect interrogations. The interactions between duty lawyers and police were usually limited to procedural formalities. Lawyers were rarely observed inquiring into the nature of the allegations, or making 'representations' concerning the course of investigation, the use of detention powers or procedural outcomes (see Section 3.3.2 on out-of-court disposals).

The following sections explore the themes related to the various functions of lawyers at the investigative stage; from obtaining disclosure on case-related information, to participating in interrogations (and in the fact-finding process more generally), participating in out-of-court disposals, and challenging procedural breaches.

4.1 Obtaining disclosure from police

In Dutch law, suspects and their lawyers have the formal right of access to the dossier (written case materials) from the outset of the proceedings (Art. 30 (1) CCP). In practice, however, access was usually provided only after several days, when the suspect appeared before the examining magistrate, or much later, if the suspect was not detained (Hermans, 2009; van Kampen and Hein, 2013). In 2013, CCP was amended in an attempt to improve defence access to the dossier at the early stages. According to the amendment, the prosecutor must ensure that the defence is granted access to the dossier no later than the first interrogation (article 4 Besluit Processtukken). However, by the time the fieldwork was concluded, i.e. one year later, the new regulation had not led to a considerable change in practice (nor, at it seems, until now: see van Kampen et al., 2018).

In Site 1, the local prosecutor's office had issued an instruction, according to which lawyers could request the dossier from the prosecutor by email, once they had been notified about a client's arrest at the police station. The prosecutor would then consult the officer in charge, and decide whether or not access should be granted. However, lawyers could rarely, if ever, receive the dossier in the first hours after arrest – when their clients were being interrogated – either because it had not been compiled yet, or because its location was unclear. In the words of one lawyer:

> The prosecutor would say that he had requested the file from the police. And even if you call [the police], they say 'we have forwarded it to that and that department and they will have to take care of that'. And most of the times it takes so long to find it, that the client has already been released, so there is no real urgency anymore.
>
> (INTNeth1)

In Site 2, there was no specific procedure in place for requesting the dossier. Lawyers typically received access to the dossier several days or months after the first consultation at the police station, when the client was presented to the examining magistrate, or shortly before the trial.

Obtaining case-related information from the police was, likewise, problematic. The lawyer referral form typically contained no more than the legal qualification of the impugned offence(s) (often inaccurate or exaggerated), and whether or not there were co-suspects in the case (Blackstock et al., 2013: 293–294). Upon the lawyer's arrival to the police station, a brief description of the suspected offence(s) was given, such as: the client is suspected of 'theft of cosmetic products from shop X in town Y'. Lawyers were not told about the evidence, unless this could serve a strategic purpose, such as to persuade the lawyer to advise the suspect to confess. This occurred in less serious cases, where lawyers were more likely to advise clients to make a statement. As one lawyer noted:

> For example, in a simple shoplifting case ... when I talk to a detective and he says 'Listen, we got camera recordings, we have a charge filed, we have security who saw this guy running away', then that's a different starting point than when you're not told anything ... But if it's an extensive investigation with given ground, my experience is that ... the police are not very keen on sharing information with you.
>
> (INTNeth8)

In observations, lawyers rarely tried to obtain disclosure from the police. Only in a minority of cases (in 32 out of 95 cases) did they request more information from the assistant prosecutor or the custody officer, usually about how long the suspect would be detained or whether there were co-suspects. Remarkably, in none of the observed cases did the lawyers request information from the officer(s) in charge, who would have been the most appropriate source. Officers in charge were difficult for lawyers to access, because they were not permanently present in the custody suite. Besides, lawyers usually did not know which officer(s) were in charge of the investigation. But even in those rare cases where the lawyers did encounter the detective(s) in charge, they did not ask for additional disclosure. Thus, in one such case, a lawyer visited a 12-year-old girl of Roma origin, suspected of shoplifting, who spoke limited Dutch, had hearing difficulties and an alleged learning disability. Because of her particular vulnerability, the detective in charge went to the custody suite to speak with the lawyer about attending the interrogation. This would have been an ideal occasion for the lawyer to try and discuss the client's case. However, the lawyer did not attempt to engage with the officer, telling him instead that the client wished for her brother to attend the interrogation as 'trusted person', and therefore the lawyer would not be present (FNNeth21.03.2002).

4.2 Role at interrogations: lawyers' passivity and police resistance

The Public Prosecutor's guideline in force at the time of the fieldwork defined the Dutch lawyer's role at the interrogation as essentially passive (Aanwijzing Rechtsbijstand Politieverhoor). Lawyers were supposed to intervene only to counter 'unlawful pressure', or to ensure that the suspect understands the questioning and the written interrogation record. The Dutch Bar Association and the Dutch Criminal Lawyers Association, in turn, had envisaged a more active role than described in the Prosecutor's regulation. The guidelines of the Bar Association stated that lawyers should intervene in an interrogation to counter unlawful pressure, but also for other 'justified reasons', by making comments, asking questions, advising the client, and by requesting a break for a private consultation (Protocol Raadsman Politieverhoor[10]; Leidraad Politieverhoor[11]).

In practice, however (as corroborated by other research: Stevens and Verhoeven, 2010; Vanderhallen et al., 2016), Dutch lawyers were passive during interrogations, despite the efforts of the professional associations to encourage a more active stance. This finding should be seen in the context of the (draft) regulations implementing *Directive 2013/48/EU*, envisaging a limited role for the lawyer. The Dutch police have shown strong resistance to active lawyers' participation in interrogations, as documented by this and other observational studies (Stevens and Verhoeven, 2010). Police were also observed to use various tactics, aiming to symbolically exclude lawyers, and to minimise their possible influence on their client's behaviour during the interrogation (Blackstock et al., 2013: 402–405). They have furthermore commonly resorted to persuasive and manipulative tactics to obtain desired statements from suspects.

4.2.1 The use of persuasion in interrogations

The use of persuasion was recorded in at least 34 out of 49 observed interrogations.[12] 'Persuasion' was understood as any psychological tactic used to incite 'non-cooperative' (in the police's view) suspects to speak, confess or provide certain information. The range of persuasive tactics used was wide, and the following are some typical examples.[13]

PROSPECTS OF DETENTION OR RELEASE AS A PRESSURE MECHANISM

The prospect of (longer) detention was often used to motivate 'reluctant' suspects to make admissions. In one observed case, for instance, a 17-year-old suspect, interrogated three times in two days, told the officer that 'he has already told them thousand times that he wasn't there, but they didn't want to believe him, so he can do nothing else than remain silent.' The officer reacted in the following way:

> ... The officer tells S. that 'he can respond what he wishes', but he should understand that in this case he would definitely stay in detention longer. 'I hope you know that you won't go far with this kind of statement?' – he says. He explains that if S. continues to deny guilt or remain silent, police would need more time to investigate, and that his detention would 'definitely' be prolonged. He tells S. that tomorrow he will be presented to the examining magistrate, and then 'immediately' his detention will be prolonged for another 3 days, weekend not included. So he will have to stay at the police station until next Thursday. There is also a chance that the judge would place him directly in pre-trial detention, and this means 14 days and eventually 90 days in prison. He adds that the judge might consider his statement a 'deliberately untrue statement'.

Following this, the suspect became extremely anxious, and asked the officer 'how he should respond to questions so that his detention would not be prolonged' (FNNeth11.05.2002).

On the other hand, the prospect of quick release or case resolution was sometimes used to encourage suspects to cooperate in relatively minor cases. In one such case, for example, police told the suspect that 'if everything goes well' during the interrogation, he would soon go home with a fine (the suspect confessed) (FNNeth22.03.2012). In another, more problematic (and more serious) case, the officer, faced with a suspect who said that he wished to cooperate in order to be released sooner, did not correct the latter's wrong belief that he would be released following the interrogation. The suspect believed he was suspected of *one theft*, but in fact the allegation involved *multiple thefts*, but neither he nor his lawyer were informed about this (FNNeth15.04.2012). The officer did not directly answer the suspect's question about whether he would be presented before the examining magistrate, saying that 'the interrogation was going very well', but the prosecutor needed more time 'to work on the papers', although they were 'doing everything to make sure that he is released as soon as possible'.

BEING FRIENDLY OR 'EMPATHETIC' AS A MEANS TO OVERCOME EMOTIONAL RESISTANCE

The leading Dutch interrogation manual places particular emphasis on developing 'good contact' with (non-cooperative) suspects to overcome their resistance to 'telling the truth' (van Amelsvoort et al., 2017: 341). The manual enumerates different reasons for such resistance, including strategic reasons, internal 'blockages' (such as feelings of guilt or shame), and reasons linked to the interviewer or the interrogation environment. To overcome resistance, interrogator(s) should strive to create a psychologically comfortable atmosphere, implying that it is 'safe' for the suspect to talk about the alleged offence and to make self-revealing admissions. Suspects' cooperation should be rewarded by positive reinforcement, such as verbal praise and encouragement.

The tactic of 'being friendly' was indeed routinely used with suspects who were unwilling to make admissions or respond to questions. Cases involving sexual allegations, where officers were instructed to 'win trust' to overcome suspects' 'resistance', were illustrative of this tactic. These cases usually involved continuous interrogations during three days of detention, aiming to break through the suspect's emotional barriers. This was achieved in various ways, such as: adopting a warm and confidant tone, showing (or simulating) interest in the suspect as a person, posing a lot of questions about the suspect's private and emotional life, as well as offering possible justifications for the alleged behaviour, and other 'minimisation' tactics. In one observed case, for instance, the interrogating officers managed to obtain admissions from a suspect who had presented himself as an 'alternative therapist', and was being accused by several patients of inappropriate touching. He had persisted in remaining silent, but admitted, on the third day of questioning, to performing 'therapeutic' acts on his patients involving genitals. The admissions followed a series of questions, by which the officer sought to demonstrate that he had keen interest in the philosophy of the suspect's therapeutic approach (FNNeth21.05.2002;01.06.2002).

MANIPULATING INFORMATION ABOUT EVIDENCE

'Strategic' disclosure of evidence during the interrogation is considered an important tool in obtaining information from deceitful suspects (Vrij, 2017). The Dutch interrogation manual describes the technique of 'boxing in' allegedly deceitful suspects with the information gathered by the police, by skilfully exposing contradictions between this information and the suspect's account. The goal is to 'catch' suspects in a lie, which should persuade them that continuing to lie is futile (van Amelsvoort et al., 2017: 344–345).

The observed interrogations, however, did not demonstrate much resemblance to the strategic mind games of the type described earlier. The evidence was, indeed, disclosed quite often – although not to set clever intellectual traps, but rather to pressurise 'reluctant' suspects into confessing. Thus, in one case, involving allegations of kidnapping and attempt of murder in co-perpetration, the suspect, who oscillated between denying guilt and remaining silent, was continuously 'confronted' with various pieces of evidence, including passages from victims' statements and crime scene photos. The senior officer in charge of the investigation gave the following directions to the interrogating team:

> You should continue asking: how come the witnesses say that and that? 'You say that you were under the rain and you were not wet, but rain is water, and water is wet, so how can it be that you are not wet?' – explain it to him in this way ... The most important [thing] is not to become emotional. If he becomes emotional, ask him calmly why he reacts in this way ... And vary the pressure: up and down, up and down ...
>
> (FNNeth11.05.2002)

In another observed case, involving allegations of arson and attempted murder, the suspect, who denied being involved, was first 'informed' that his co-suspect had implicated him. He was then put under considerable pressure by being told that 'there is too much evidence against him': his fingerprints were found on the canister allegedly used to set the fire, and 'there are two people who know for sure what happened' (which was misleading, because the witnesses only saw two people in the car near the crime scene, but did not identify the suspect) (FNNeth24.02.2012).

PERSUASION TACTICS AND UNLAWFUL PRESSURE

Although the persuasion tactics described in this section involved considerable psychological pressure, their use was widely accepted in practice. This was probably because, when assessed separately, these tactics were unlikely to amount to 'unlawful pressure' as defined in Dutch law (article 29 CCP). Long, intensive and insistent questioning in the course of three days, while the suspect continuously invoked his right to silence, was not found to breach Article 29 (HR 8 May 2001, ECLI:NL:HR:2001:AB1473, *NJB* 2001/105, 1090). Nor was telling the suspect that it would be better for him to cooperate, because he could then go home, as long as this was true, and as long as it did not constitute an explicit threat of deprivation of liberty (HR 22 September 1998, ECLI:NL:HR:1998:ZD1277, *NJ* 1999/104). Confronting the suspect with evidence and 'informing' them that a long sentence awaited them, where this was likely to be true, was also not considered unlawful pressure (HR 23 September 2003, ECLI:NL:HR:2003:AI0032). As a result, inducements to confess, which did not expressly and intentionally rely on false or fabricated information, were considered acceptable in practice. By contrast, false promises and threats, lying about evidence, the use of physical violence and the threat thereof, the use of authority to intimidate the suspect ('putting a fist on the table') were all found to constitute 'unlawful pressure' (Boksem et al., 2011: 55; HR 3 July 1989, ECLI:NL:HR:1989:ZC8175, *NJ* 1990/122; HR 13 May 1997, ECLI:NL:HR:1997:ZD0705, *NJ* 1998/152 m.nt. Schalken). Indeed, these tactics were described as 'old school' and were not commonly applied.

4.2.2 Lawyers' reaction to persuasion tactics

In most observed interrogations with lawyers present (7 out of 9), they were passive and did not intervene, even when considerable pressure was exercised on the suspect (Blackstock et al., 2013: 398–399). In interviews, most lawyers said that they did not intervene often, and if they did, this was usually to correct something in the interrogation record, or where the suspect did not understand the questioning. In this respect, the following interview excerpt is typical:

INTERVIEWER (I): What are reasons to intervene?
LAWYER (L): If the client doesn't understand the question. And if the police make a record, which you can immediately tell is not correct. Anyway, I try to correct what is put on paper, see if it corresponds. I have to correct typos, but also things that have not been said according to my own notes. And I make sure that whatever I noted but is not recorded in their minutes is added.
I: Does it happen a lot, that you have to intervene?
L: Well ... no. Real interventions during the interrogation, like 'you're way off now and things are going all wrong', I never experienced that. But it has happened that a client didn't understand the question, and it is your job to make sure that they do.

(INTNeth9)

Lawyers acknowledged that another reason for intervening might be when police 'use too much pressure', however, many believed that in their presence, police were not 'crossing the line' (of unlawful pressure, which as explained in the preceding section, covers only rather extreme psychological coercion). As one lawyer described it:

> My reasons to intervene are when my client is struggling because he is vulnerable, sad, or sick, or when an officer goes too far, however if I am present an officer won't easily go too far. I did experience that there was a lot of pressure, but no unlawful pressure.

(INTNeth22)

Some encountered lawyers also said that they would exercise caution when intervening to directly challenge police behaviour. One lawyer, for instance, gave the following example of a case where he had intervened, in an interrogation of a minor suspect:

> It was about a fight in a nightclub, and the detective emphatically suggested that my client had hit and kicked, while he persistently denied [it]. From the way they were asking questions it appeared that [they were saying] 'we are convinced you did it, why don't you just confess'. And so in the end I objected to that.

(INTNeth5)

Likewise, another lawyer noted that he would not intervene immediately after police would commence using tactics aimed at overcoming a suspect's silence:

> If there is any influencing or directing by the interrogators, I won't immediately intervene. If they ask 'why are you using your right to remain silent?', I prepared my client for that and he does fine, then great. But if they keep pushing and say 'I am not happy with that answer, give me another answer', then I will intervene.
>
> (INTNeth13)

In the view of the lawyers, police were wary of those interventions from lawyers which limited the officers' freedom to influence (or manipulate) suspects to obtain a desired statement. These were, for instance, interventions that challenged the questions posed, or that prevented suspects from giving 'spontaneous' answers. Lawyers said that they would make such interventions subtly, rather than openly. As one lawyer has described it:

> Well I'm quite humble during the interrogation. I normally sit at the back, reserved, but when I see that my client starts stating things that he should better not state ... Then I use all tricks, for example, tipping over my coffee, haha. Sometimes you want a break, so you ask if you are allowed to discuss with your client. This question itself is already an intervention. You try to intervene without you having the right to intervene. Of course you think you have the right, but police think that it is not according to the rules. 'May I have a brief moment with my client', you try to convince the police that it is to their advantage, because eventually you have no power.
>
> (INTNeth24)

However, not all Dutch lawyers agreed that they preferred to take a passive stance. Thus, one lawyer described how she managed to intervene during an interrogation, despite having been threatened with exclusion for being 'obstructive':

> Once I almost got excluded from an interrogation in an indecency case involving a minor, that was also a person with a mental handicap, but police were really feeding him the answers, the guy just didn't understand it. Then he was saying yes, and I said 'sorry but I don't think he means yes, you are asking two questions in one sentence can you ask them one at a time?' they said 'you should not interfere, you are an observer, you have to shut your mouth' – 'no I am here to defend'. [E]ventually I said 'well then I want to interrupt for a minute and discuss things with my client'; 'No, only your client can request a break, not you' so I said 'Client, do you want to discuss it with me? Yes? Then you should let him' ...
> When we came back, the police said 'we discussed it with the prosecutor, if you make one more remark then we can kick you out'. Well, then I made

another remark, I said to my client 'with this question you can better use your right to be silent' – 'that was it, you have to leave now'. So I said 'ok get the prosecutor on the phone because you have no right to kick me out, I want to hear it from the prosecutor himself'. I explained the situation to the prosecutor and then I could remain.

(INTNeth15)

4.3 Outside of the interrogation

4.3.1 Challenging procedural breaches and the use of procedural remedies

In the respective professional discourse, Dutch lawyers are described as *procesbewakers*, 'guardians of the process', exercising control over the correct application of procedures by the authorities (Prakken and Spronken, 2009: 6). At the investigative stage, this includes, for instance, the lawyer verifying whether: the suspect's procedural rights were respected; there was legal basis for the suspect's arrest and detention; the investigative actions conformed with procedural rules and the suspect's rights; and whether the suspect was adequately treated in detention.

Breaches of the suspect's rights related to arrest or detention can be challenged during the suspect's appearance before the examining magistrate (HR 8 May 2001, ECLI:NL:HR:2001:AB1566, *NJ* 2001/587). At that moment, lawyers may attempt to argue that the detention was unlawful, which, if successful, would result in immediate release (article 59a CCP). In addition, certain pre-trial procedural violations, such as excessive use of force during arrest, or breaches in the conduct of investigative actions, may be challenged during the trial. Possible remedies include the reduction of sentence (most commonly used), the exclusion of evidence and stay of prosecution (afforded very rarely) (article 359a CCP).

Besides, lawyers may raise the issue directly with the police, or complain to the (duty) prosecutor. Raising the alleged breach directly may result in immediate relief for the client, and if it is not granted, it may help substantiate the complaint raised later in the proceedings. Yet, from the observations, it transpired that Dutch lawyers rarely challenged any procedural issues at the investigative stage, even where there were indications for doing so. In one case, for instance, a lawyer visited a suspect, who was still in detention, although he had already fully confessed (and thus his detention was probably no longer 'in the interest of investigation') (FNNeth12.09.2002). The suspect had asked his lawyer why he had not yet been released, to which the lawyer responded that 'probably, police want to interrogate him further', but that 'he [the lawyer] cannot do anything about this, but hopes that he will be released the next day' (FNNeth08.09.2002). In other observed cases, lawyers did not argue that their clients' detention was unjustifiably long, although the lawyers themselves believed that this was the case (FNNeth11.02.2002; 14.02.2002). Thus, in one example, two minors suspected of shoplifting – both had confessed at the first interrogation, and had no prior criminal record – were kept in detention over the weekend because, as the police explained to the lawyer, 'their statements did not match'. The lawyer, however, believed that they were kept in detention over the weekend 'for purely pedagogical reasons', but he did not challenge this decision at that moment.

The encountered Dutch lawyers also rarely raised motions or defences based on the breach of procedures at the investigative stage before an examining magistrate or trial judge (as transpired from the interviews). Most lawyers were only able to remember one or two occasions, when they raised an argument about an alleged procedural breach at the investigative stage in court. As one lawyer put it, 'not much happens at police stations ... This is perhaps a good sign' (INTNeth6). Typically, the examples given by lawyers concerned such breaches, for which a remedy would be afforded based on the existing case law. These were, for instance, denial of access to a lawyer, arrest or search conducted without sufficient evidentiary basis, or unlawful pressure at interrogation (HR 30 June 2009, ECLI:NL:HR:2009:BH3079, *NJ* 2009/349; HR 9 November 2010, ECLI:NL:HR:2010:BN7727, *NJ* 2010/615; HR 13 September 2011, ECLI:NL:HR:2011:BQ8907, *NJ* 2011/556; Rechtbank Gelderland 28 January 2014, *NbSr* 2014/134). One interviewed lawyer, in contrast, said that she would always try to note the violations occurring at the investigative stage and mentioned them in her submissions to court. This was also the only interviewed lawyer who gave an example of a successful argument she raised in front of the examining magistrate. She argued that her client was not given any food during 24 hours, after which, in her words, 'the magistrate got so angry about this that the client was released' (INTNeth18).

4.3.2 *Participation in the fact-finding process at the investigative stage*

The encountered Dutch lawyers rarely participated in the fact-finding process at the investigative stage. During the fieldwork observations, only once was a lawyer present in an investigative action conducted by the police. It concerned a video identification of a suspect by a witness (FNNeth26.07.2011). The lawyer was present in an adjacent room, and observed the process through a video link. He did not make any interventions. The lawyer told the researcher that he had never attended line-ups previously. He was surprised to be invited, and decided to participate, because it was an 'interesting experience'.

Duty lawyers also typically did not engage in their 'own' investigations while their clients were in police detention. Clearly, this period is too short for the lawyer to set up a full-swing parallel investigation. On the other hand, it might be necessary to conduct certain inquiries at the earliest possible opportunity. For example, an alibi witness suggested by the client might need to be approached to prevent unnecessary detention, or to determine whether the witness would confirm the client's alibi (Prakken and Spronken, 2009: 325–326).

Contact of lawyers with third parties at the investigative stage was usually limited to informing suspects' family members about their needs in detention. In these interactions, lawyers usually avoided discussing the 'case' at hand, even if the person in question wished to do so: for instance, where the suspect was arrested for domestic violence, and the family member was the alleged victim. The encountered lawyers were also reluctant to contact other (potential) witnesses. One lawyer explained that he did not do so for ethical reasons. In the words of this lawyer:

> Sometimes a suspect will say they have witnesses, who can testify in their interest. I find it objectionable to then call these people and tell them to run to the police station immediately to give a statement. I wonder if that's clean. So I always tell my client to mention these names to the police during the first interrogation, make sure these names are written down in the interrogation record, that they sign it, and that they insist that police hear them.
>
> (INTNeth17)

Another lawyer suggested that the authorities were unlikely to treat a witness who had been in contact with a lawyer as reliable:

> If I talk to a detective on the phone I will also tell them 'this guy has said that he has a witnesses, go interrogate them too'. So I will tell the police but I usually won't go calling the witnesses like 'go to the police station to give a statement'. Because this will definitely come up during questioning. 'Why are you here?' 'Well the lawyer called and told me to come.' I wonder if that adds to their reliability in the end.
>
> (INTNeth20)

However, for some lawyers the risk that the witnesses would not be treated as credible was not a sufficient reason not to contact them. As one lawyer has described it:

> Yes, naturally I am very cautious with this, because the public prosecutor can turn that around and say 'you approached those people, so you influenced them' but if the client for instance says, 'my wife was at the scene and can confirm this' then I won't say 'hey police, go interrogate the wife'. I will ask the client if I can call his wife, and then I will call her 'I am calling on behalf of ... Do you recall what happened on this day?' and then I first wait and hear what the wife will tell me herself, and if this fits with the client's story then I won't hesitate to ask her if she would tell that to the police also, and then I can give her name to the police. But if the stories do not fit together then I will tell the client 'it is not totally clear, your wife thinks she was somewhere else, we cannot take that risk right now, we could wait until a later stage'. And I will not use that information. Usually I check the stories and the information myself before I tell the police about it.
>
> (INTNeth10)

5 Conclusions

This chapter presented a snapshot of the Dutch practices of legal assistance at the investigative stage of the criminal proceedings, as experienced during the fieldwork. The role played by Dutch lawyers at the investigative stage was the role of an 'information provider' and, to a limited extent, the 'trusted person' of the suspect. However, the role of the 'trusted person' – meaning the provider of social and moral support to the client – in practice was more limited than described in the official professional discourse of Dutch lawyers. The 'informational' role of Dutch lawyers at the investigative stage was limited to providing general information about the rights and police detention procedures.

Generally, the observed Dutch lawyers did not play an 'active' or 'participatory' role at the investigative stage. Such a role was compromised by the lack of information about the impugned events and the evidence. Lawyers were almost never given access to case-related information, and they also rarely asked for such information. The observed duty lawyers were passive during interrogations, and did not participate in the fact-finding process at the investigative stage in any meaningful way. They rarely raised procedural breaches or reacted to alleged procedural violations at this stage. Lawyers' involvement into decision-making with regard to out-of-court disposals at the investigative stage was overall rather limited.

Thus, the observed Dutch practices hardly corresponded to the 'model' role reflected in the respective European regulations described in Chapter 2. The Dutch fieldwork was conducted shortly after the right to legal assistance before and during police interrogations was introduced (and before the right to interrogation assistance was given to all criminal suspects). Five years had elapsed by the time of writing, and some practices described in this chapter may have evolved. Lawyers and police may have grown accustomed to each other, and their mutual attitudes might have become less antagonistic (Vanderhallen et al., 2014: 155–156). A drastic change in the observed practices or attitudes, however, is not to be expected: which is also confirmed by more recent empirical studies (Vanderhallen et al., 2014, 2016; Thomas et al., 2016; van Kampen et al., 2018). These practices are likely to be stable, because, as argued in this research, they were formed under, inter alia, the enduring influence of the factors examined in Chapters 5–7.

Notes

1 See the website of the Central Bureau of Statistics, available from: http://statline.cbs.nl/Statweb/publication/?DM=SLNL&PA=82315NED&D1=0-1,12,18,22,25-27&D2=0&D3=0-1,6,9,24,26&D4=1-2&D5=15&HDR=G4,G1,G3&STB=T,G2&VW=T (last accessed on 16 July 2019).
2 Het Statuut voor de Raadsman in Strafzaken, Vastgesteld in de vergadering van de Nederlandse Vereniging van Strafrechtadvocaten op 13 November 2003.
3 With some narrow exceptions. This practice, however, may discontinue with the adoption of the new CCP, which would require that the information about all witnesses to be questioned at the hearing should be provided to the court in advance of the trial.

4 It was also carried out prior to the implementation of *Directive 2012/13/EU* (November 2014) and *Directive 2013/48/EU* (November 2016) into Dutch law. Where relevant, the provisions of the implementing legislation were incorporated, and their possible influence on the empirical findings was discussed.
5 The current regulations (in force since 1 March 2017) provide for the possibility of both the lawyer and the 'trusted person' to be present. OM-beleid bijstand door vertrouwenspersoon bij verhoor minderjarige en procedure bij afstand verhoorbijstand door minderjarige, *Stcrt* 2017, 2009.
6 Which also covers the situations where someone bought goods, which he should have reasonably known to be stolen (e.g. because an unreasonably low price was asked). Art. 417bis CC.
7 INTNeth1, 24; 6; 911; 15, 19, 20, 22, 24.
8 Lawyers told suspects that they could benefit from free legal assistance only in one in ten consultations. In none of the 15 observed consultations where the suspect did not speak Dutch did the lawyer explain the right to interpretation (other than that the interrogation should be interpreted, mentioned in 8 consultations).
9 In 24 out of 70 consultations that took place before the first interrogation, the right to silence was not mentioned.
10 Protocol (Best Practice) Raadsman Politieverhoor (2013), vastgesteld door NOvA.
11 Leidraad Advocaat bij Politieverhoor (2016), vastgesteld door NOvA.
12 These interrogations were observed by me personally. They were conducted in the period from June 2011 until August 2013. The cases involved allegations of varying degrees of seriousness, from squatting to attempted murder. The research for the *Inside Police Custody Project*, which partly served as the basis for this study, involved observations of 95 interrogations in the Netherlands, and its findings concerning the use of pressure at interrogations were very similar. See Blackstock et al., 2013: 383–384.
13 Other persuasion tactics, observed several times, were: appealing to the suspect's feelings (guilt, shame, sympathy, regret); insistent or repetitive questioning; expressing disbelief in the truthfulness of suspects' responses; and undermining the lawyer's advice.

4 England and Wales

Lawyer as advisor and provider of 'active defence'

1 Introduction

The English criminal procedure has adversarial roots. The locus of the proceedings, at least in theory, lies in the adversarial trial. In practice, however, the determinative nature of the trial has been undermined, as described later. English prosecutors have a less important role than their continental counterparts. They select cases for prosecution and defend charges in court, but they have no administrative powers over the police. Culturally, English police are accustomed to conducting investigations independently, although criticisms were made of their ability to adequately prepare cases for prosecution (Sanders and Young, 2007: 371, 382–385). As a result, prosecutors were given powers to guide legal aspects of police investigations and take decisions to 'charge', or open criminal proceedings following the investigative stage (although these powers were subsequently reduced, as they led to delays) (Joyce, 2017: 146). Currently, English prosecutors take charging decisions and advise police only with regard to more serious or complex offences. They also play a modest role in administering out-of-court disposals, which are mostly issued by the police.[1]

The investigative stage in England and Wales is governed by PACE, which regulates arrest, detention and questioning, and certain aspects of police investigations. Once arrested, suspects can be detained for questioning without charge for a maximum of 24 hours, which may be prolonged to 36 hours, and, in exceptional cases, to 96 hours (PACE, Sections 30, 37, 41–44).[2] Following detention, the suspect should either be charged (and released on bail, or detained longer), released with 'no further action' or offered an out-of-court disposal (Cape, 2017: 375). Another possibility, which is increasingly used, is release without a charge to enable police to continue inquiries (ibid.: 394–399).

The main difference between the English and Dutch – or other continental criminal processes – lies in their approach to the trial. While in the Netherlands, trials serve to confirm the results of pre-trial investigations presented in the dossier, in English trials evidence is presented anew by the parties to the judges or jury, unfamiliar with the contents of the defence or prosecution file. Whilst on paper this difference appears fundamental, in practice it is more modest, due to the diminishing role of the trial in England and Wales. First, only a small

64 *England and Wales*

proportion of criminal cases undergo a full-fledged trial, as about 90% of charged offences result in guilty pleas (Cape et al., 2007: 74). Besides, many criminal cases are terminated at the investigative stage without reaching the court. In 2016, 285.000 persons were issued an out-of-court disposal as compared to 1.46 million persons prosecuted in court (Ministry of Justice, 2016). The admission of hearsay evidence, including what was said by the defendant during police interview (PACE, Sections 76 and 78) and certain witness statements (Criminal Justice Act 2003, Section 116), is another cause of the diminished importance of the trial. The last, but not the least relevant factor is the so-called 'inference from silence' provision, according to which 'proper' inferences can be drawn, inter alia, when defendants rely on facts during the trial, which they did not mention during the police interview (CJPOA, Section 34). This means, in effect, that suspects must formulate their defence already at the investigative stage (Leng, 2001). This has led commentators to conclude that as a consequence of this law, the 'trial' commences already at the police station (Jackson, 2001; Cape, 2017: 3).

This chapter describes the empirical findings in relation to legal assistance at the investigative stage in England and Wales. It begins by describing the role of a lawyer in the English criminal process, and the history of police station legal assistance in this jurisdiction. It then proceeds to describing the fieldwork findings, organised around the two 'pillars' of the lawyer's role at the investigative stage: the role vis-à-vis the client and the role vis-à-vis the authorities. The chapter concludes by juxtaposing these findings with the normative view of the lawyer's role described in Chapter 2.

2 Setting the scene

2.1 The role of defence lawyers

England and Wales have a divided legal profession into 'barristers' and 'solicitors'; barristers traditionally represent cases in higher courts, and solicitors represent cases in magistrate courts and at police stations. Police station work is also carried out by so-called 'accredited representatives', who have some legal training (often, former police officers), and who comply with the respective accreditation requirements. There is no division into lawyers undertaking prosecution and lawyers providing defence services, and especially barristers often engage in both types of work. Whilst barristers are mostly self-employed, solicitors usually work for a firm, and those who do criminal defence work are usually very specialised, and do not work for the prosecution.[3]

At the investigative stage, lawyers may provide advice and assistance to their clients at any time, including before and during the police interview (PACE, Section 58(1)). Lawyers may also be present during their client's identification procedure (PACE Code D, 3.17). Besides this, the defence has no formal rights to participate in police-led investigations (Cape, 2010: 144). Defence lawyers may undertake their own investigations, but in practice such investigations are often limited. Like Dutch lawyers, English lawyers have no powers to compel individuals to provide information (although if the case reaches trial, they can ask the court to summon witnesses or request evidence).[4] The defence has no formal right to request official inquiries at the pre-trial stage (ibid.: 144). For these and other structural reasons, fact-finding by defence lawyers often 'consists of little more than the interviewing of witnesses who are willing to co-operate' (Cape and Hodgson, 2007: 76).

Thus, English lawyers, like Dutch lawyers, depend on the information from the police and prosecution to prepare for the trial (if it takes place). It has long been recognised that the prosecutor must disclose certain information to the defence (*R. v. Bryant and Dickson* (1946) 31 Cr App R 146). Recently, disclosure obligations of both parties were tightened to accelerate case progression (Hannibal and Mountford, 2016: 134). The amount and timing of required prosecutorial disclosure depend on which court deals with the case, and on the (anticipated) defendant's plea. If the defendant pleads guilty in a magistrates' court, prosecutorial disclosure obligations are very limited (*R. v. DPP*, ex p. Lee [1992] 2 Cr App R 304; Criminal Procedure Rules, Part 8, Section 8.3), and they are most extensive in cases before Crown Courts (although research points to various practical problems with obtaining prosecutorial disclosure (Plotnikoff and Wolfson, 2001; Quirk, 2006; Darbyshire, 2014). Since recently, the defence also have certain pre-trial disclosure obligations, introduced to improve trial efficiency, such as disclosing the facts and arguments that they will rely on at trial (CIPA 1996, Sections 5, 6A), and the details of defence witnesses (CIPA 1996, Section 6C).

In contrast to the pre-trial proceedings, where, as demonstrated earlier, the participatory rights of the defence are quite limited, at the trial stage, English lawyers play an adversarial role: at least, according to what is described in the law. This role encompasses, in principle, a wide range of procedural rights, including the right to call, examine and cross-examine witnesses, to introduce evidence in any form, to request adjournments to prepare a defence, and to communicate in private with one's client, protected by the legal professional privilege (Cape, 2010). These rights, however, apply only to a small minority of all criminal proceedings, namely those which involve a trial.

The SRA Code of Conduct requires solicitors to provide services to clients 'in a manner which protects their interests ... , subject to the proper administration of justice' (Ch. 1, O (1.2)). Ch. 5, O (5.2) provides that clients should be 'informed of the circumstances in which [the lawyer's] duties to the court outweigh [their] obligations to [their] client'. An explanatory note to chapter 5 states that where the duty to the client conflicts with the duty to the court, the lawyer 'may need to consider whether the public interest is best served by the proper administration of justice and should take precedence over the interests of [the] client.' Solicitors must not deceive or knowingly or recklessly mislead the court, or be complicit in allowing the court to be misled (Ch. 5, O (5.1) and O (5.2)). This implies a positive duty of the lawyer to always tell and endorse the truth, and to inform the court about any errors of facts (*Arthur J.S. Hall and Co. v. Simons* [2002] 1 AC 615; *R. v. Gleeson* [2004] 1 Cr. App. R. 29). As a result,

English solicitors may not be 'complicit' where a client (guilty or innocent), knowingly to the lawyer, deceives or wishes to deceive the police or the court about any fact (Cape, 2017: 168–169). In such cases, the lawyer must discontinue to act for the client (SRA Code of Conduct 2011, Ch. 5 IB (5.5)). Effectively, this regulation limits the options available to the defence, where the client, knowingly to the lawyer, wishes to lie: the lawyer must either withdraw, or insist that the client remains silent (Cape, 2006).

2.2 The history of the right to legal assistance for suspects in police custody

The advent of legal assistance at police stations in England and Wales is often associated with the adoption of PACE. Yet, the Judges Rules first drawn up in 1912, which intended to provide guidance to police in conducting custodial interrogations, had already envisaged the right of access to a lawyer for suspects detained and interrogated by police (Johnston, 1966). Before PACE, however, only about one in ten of all detained suspects were being assisted by a lawyer (Zander, 1972; Baldwin and McConville, 1979; Softley, 1980).

In 1978, the Royal Commission on Criminal Procedure was established, following a high-profile case of miscarriage of justice, the *Confait affair*, where three young boys were falsely convicted of murder based on confessions obtained from protracted and hostile interrogations in the absence of a lawyer (Fisher, 1977). The Commission published its report in 1981, which served as the foundation for PACE. Section 58 of PACE provides that each suspect arrested and detained in police custody has the right to consult with a solicitor privately at any time. PACE also provided for a mechanism for the provision of legal assistance at police stations through a national duty solicitor scheme.

In the first years following PACE, the rates of access to a lawyer for suspects detained by police increased, although initially only to about 20–25% (Brown, 1989; Sanders et al., 1989; Dixon et al., 1990). The low initial rates were explained by the suspects' lack of appreciation of importance of legal advice, and various ploys used by police to dissuade suspects from engaging with lawyers (Sanders et al., 1989; Sanders and Bridges, 1990; Brown et al., 1992; McConville, 1992). Since the early 1990s, the rates of access have been growing, although until now, only about half of all detained suspects ask for legal assistance (Bucke and Brown, 1997; Pearse and Gudjohnsson, 1997; Kemp and Balmer, 2008; Skinns, 2009; Kemp et al., 2012).

2.3 Arrangements and practices at the time of the fieldwork

The procedures for providing legal assistance to suspects in custody were similar in the two fieldwork sites, and have not changed by the time of writing. Detained suspects would be informed about the right to a lawyer by a custody officer. If suspects wished to consult a lawyer, they were asked whether they had a preferred lawyer or firm; if they did not, or if the particular lawyer or firm had no contract with the Legal Aid Agency, a duty solicitor would usually be appointed.

Appointments of lawyers were managed by the Duty Solicitor Call Centre, which would contact the respective lawyer or firm, providing general information about the suspect and the alleged offence(s). Having accepted the call, the lawyer would then phone the custody officer to inquire when the police was planning on commencing the interview, and would briefly speak with the suspect. Invariably, lawyers would attend the police station shortly before the planned interview time, typically several hours after the initial call.

When at the police station, lawyers 'buzzed into' the custody suite, where they were met by the custody officer. They were then given the 'custody record' for inspection, containing the clients' personal details, health status, and the time record of all actions undertaken while they were in custody. Subsequently, the officer(s) in charge of the interview provided 'disclosure'. Disclosure usually took place in a separate room, enabling lawyers to take notes. Lawyers were given the details of the allegation (such as how the suspected offence(s)) was allegedly committed, the suspect's role, how the police came to know about it, the alleged damage etc.), as well as, often, information about the existing evidence. Following disclosure, lawyers were then taken to one of the 'consultation booths' for a pre-interview consultation with the suspect. There was no time limitation on this consultation.

An interrogation, or 'interview', usually took place immediately afterwards. All observed interviews were audio-recorded. During the interview, both lawyers and clients could request a private consultation. After the interview, lawyers could, if they wished, speak with clients in private. At the end of their police station visit, lawyers could make representations to the custody officer concerning bail or release of their client, the prolongation of police custody if envisaged, or access to a doctor. Lawyers were usually informed about how the proceedings could develop further, for instance, whether an out-of-court disposal, or a decision to charge was envisaged. Where these decisions were taken by the police, lawyers could negotiate them: the custody officer had the authority to discontinue the proceedings and could determine the charges in certain minor offences (PACE, section 37(7)). In other cases, where the respective decisions were made by prosecutors, negotiation was not possible, because prosecutors were not located at police stations. At the time of the fieldwork, prosecutors determined the charges in all but minor offences, and issued or authorised cautions in more serious offences.

3 Lawyers and their clients: the lawyer as 'legal expert'

The lawyer–suspect encounters observed in England and Wales were more 'meaningful' than those observed in the Netherlands. On average they lasted around 30 minutes, and consultations of more than one hour were not uncommon. Most encounters involved in-depth discussions regarding the circumstances around the alleged offence(s), and most suspects were willing to give detailed disclosure to lawyers, and relied on their advice about how to handle an interrogation. Only half of the observed English consultations (25 out of 58) involved 'duty' lawyers, while in the Netherlands only cases involving 'duty' lawyers were observed.

68 *England and Wales*

This, however, cannot explain the difference in the country findings: in England and Wales, those consultations where lawyers acted under the 'duty lawyer' arrangements did not significantly differ from those involving 'preferred' lawyers.

At the same time, the observed English lawyers were rather directive and leading when providing advice. This was contrary to the prevailing professional discourse of 'acting upon client's instructions'. The following sections further analyse the contrast between the lawyers' professional discourse and the observed practice in respect of the lawyer–client relationship (and its supposedly 'amoral' nature), and advising clients, particularly regarding the upcoming interrogation. Finally, English lawyers perceived their role vis-à-vis their clients at the investigative stage as strictly 'legal', and they did not consider providing emotional or moral support as part of this role. This approach was also reflected during the observations, as described in the following sections.

3.1 *The discourse on the lawyer–client relationship: lawyers 'simply advise'*

In the English lawyers' professional discourse, a (criminal defence) lawyer is described as a detached and 'objective' professional, who 'simply follows' clients' instructions. This discourse consists of two inter-related elements: the 'amoral' nature of the lawyer–client relationship, and the client-directed character of the assistance provided by lawyers.

The professional ethics of lawyers in the common-law tradition envisages an 'amoral' lawyer's stance, where the latter is not concerned with the morality of the client or his cause (see Chapter 5). Lawyers must be emotionally detached from their clients in order to provide 'objective' advice (Boon, 2015: 112). The SRA Code of Conduct implicitly endorses this view. The lawyer's relationship with the client is described as a contractual one, which carries certain legal obligations and requirements concerning conduct. Lawyers are required to provide 'a proper standard of service' to their clients (Ch. 1: Client Care). They 'carry out their clients' instructions' with the help of their professional expertise. Unlike the professional codes for Dutch lawyers, the SRA Code of Conduct does not mention any moral aspects in relation to the lawyer–client relationship, such as lawyer–client trust, or the lawyer's obligation of personal loyalty to the client.

Likewise, most encountered English lawyers described the lawyer–client relationship as strictly 'professional' and devoid of any moral or personal involvement on the lawyer's behalf. As one lawyer described it,

> I only have to deal with the suspect and so I have no emotional attachment. And I just look at the law in a mechanical way, because it's what you do as a lawyer, isn't it? It's like a doctor, do you know what I mean? It doesn't matter what the patient is like you're operating on, if there's something technically wrong you are employed and paid to help them out with. That's what you do. So it's just a very mechanical and impersonal thing for me.
>
> (INTEng6)

England and Wales 69

The interviewed English lawyers stressed that they wished to provide 'objective' and 'independent' legal advice, which presumably made moral commitment to clients and their causes irrelevant. In the words of one lawyer,

> ... 99.9 per cent of the people I represent I probably would, as a member of the public, loathe and wouldn't be going to play golf with or wouldn't be out with, but I'm here to represent them ... I mean, we don't like our clients. We're not friends with them. We're just doing a proper job.
>
> (INTEng7)

Consequently, in England and Wales, unlike in the Netherlands, there was no explicit emphasis on the trust relationship as a necessary precondition for effective legal assistance at the investigative stage. The need to obtain *truthful* information from clients, likewise, was not mentioned. Thus, lawyers were careful to *avoid* using the words 'true' or 'false' when speaking about their clients' accounts, instead referring to their 'credibility' or 'coherence'. The respective professional discourse focused on the notions of 'formal truth', and of multiple versions of truth, characteristic of the adversarial procedural tradition (see Chapter 5).

Related to the previous one, in the professional discourse of the English lawyers, the decision on how to handle an interrogation was at the discretion of the client, whilst the lawyer 'simply advises'. As one lawyer noted,

> It depends on their wishes, first of all. And their instructions .... [T]hey'll give me their story and then they'll tell me what their account is. And then I'll give them advice on the law ... If they say to me 'what's the best result, what should I do?' I'll give them the options ... And unless they've got mental health problems or they're a child and don't understand, then I'm going by what their wishes are ... You can't force them anyway, you know, you just take their instructions.
>
> (IntEng4)

3.2 *The lawyer–client relationship in observations*

The presumption of the lawyer's 'amoral' and non-judgmental stance towards the client in the lawyer's professional discourse did not reflect the actual reality, as transpired from observations. The client's honesty, or truthfulness, did matter to the encountered lawyers and affected their advice, even if it was described as the 'credibility of' or 'consistency in' (the client's account). Lawyers also did not hesitate to challenge the accounts of their clients, even where this could result in admissions (which would limit the options of procedural strategy at the interrogation, as described in Section 2.1). At the same time, presumably, the ability to gather detailed information from clients helped English lawyers to formulate more concrete and realistic advice, in contrast to the Dutch lawyers.

Likewise, the assumption that lawyers 'simply advise' and clients decide on the procedural strategy was not confirmed in the observations. The observed English lawyers were rather directive and 'controlling' in their approach to consultations. This may be illustrated by how lawyers dealt with accounts which did not appear truthful, or 'credible'; their approach to explaining the right to silence 'caution'; and to presenting the options of procedural behaviour at interrogation.

3.2.1 The client's 'truthfulness' and dealing with 'non-credible' accounts

In contrast to the Dutch findings, most suspects encountered in England and Wales were willing to provide detailed accounts to their lawyers. Most observed English lawyers also spent a considerable part of the consultation taking clients' disclosure (or their 'instructions'). This was preceded by lawyers telling clients about the police disclosure. Lawyers used the information obtained from the police to encourage suspects to discuss the allegations by 'commenting' on this information. Detailing the police disclosure also felt like a means of securing client's trust (although the concept of 'trust' did not surface in the respective professional discourse, as previously discussed). Showing clients that they knew the details of police allegations enabled lawyers to come across as more 'knowledgeable' or 'competent'; and reliance on the other person's competence, as mentioned in Chapter 3, constitutes one element of interpersonal trust.

As discussed in the previous section, client's 'truthfulness' with lawyers was considered irrelevant in the respective professional discourses. This does not mean, however, that English lawyers did not habitually judge the veracity of their clients' accounts. The encountered lawyers regularly commented on whether or not they believed their client was telling them the truth. One lawyer, for example, described his approach to advising at police stations in the following way:

> You ask for the client to be produced. You explain the basics, why they've been arrested, why they've been detained. They'll then give their account of what happened … About half will admit to the crime, one-third will give some fantastical story. I listen to what they say and then advise, depending on what they tell me. It'll depend on the honesty of the client, how much he's disclosed etc. I'll usually say 'I'm not here to tell you what to say in interview, only to advise.
>
> (FNEng09.01.2012)

Such judgments were also often expressed in the interviews. In the words of one lawyer,

> Usually you know damn well they're lying, but that's been their instructions. They haven't told you that they've done it, they just say, they give you it – it's a load of bollocks. You tell them it's bollocks, but then they just say, 'Well, no, that's the way it is.' So you've got to let them say it if that's what they want to do. It's their interview. We're there to advise them, not to tell them. They want telling, but we're there to advise, not to tell.
>
> (INTEng16)

Likewise, the encountered English lawyers did not hesitate to forcefully challenge their clients' accounts, if they did not seem credible (INTEng20). In observations, lawyers often asked questions that could elicit self-incriminating information. For example, in one case, involving an allegation of fraud committed against a person in the suspect's care, the lawyer did not hesitate to probe those parts of the client's account, which sounded implausible (FNEng30.04.2013). When the suspect said he occasionally used his own money to pay for the 'victim', the lawyer questioned him in detail about his motivation for doing so. Similarly, when the suspect mentioned that he had not recorded certain expenditures in the accounting book seized by the police, the lawyer remarked, 'It might look like you have been taking this money ...'

Where suspects were reluctant to disclose certain information to their lawyers, the latter did not hesitate to 'push' further. In one such case, for example, a female suspect had initially denied her involvement in a theft committed at her workplace. The lawyer insisted on clarifying her account, as a result of which she confessed to the lawyer, and was consequently obliged to make admissions to the police (as the lawyer told her that 'now that she has told him', it was the only possible way of handling the interrogation, implying that if she gave a statement of denial, he would have to withdraw) (FNEng17.01.2012). In any event, most observed suspects (36 out of 58) made admissions or confessed to their lawyers. (One lawyer commented on such client's behaviour as 'being too honest for his own good' [FNEng24.01.2012].)

The credibility of clients and their accounts, as perceived by lawyers, affected their advice. Several lawyers said that they would rarely sufficiently trust a client who denies guilt or responsibility to let them respond to questions during the interview. This may be demonstrated by the following excerpt:

INTERVIEWER (I): And when would you advise them to respond to questions, when they're denying the allegation?
LAWYER (L): When you're confident that they can give a coherent and reasonable account themselves, ... they won't end up making admissions to something else, perhaps worse or something different. When they're strong enough to be able and intelligent enough to be able to respond to police questioning.
I: Are there many clients who you trust enough that you let them answer questions?
L: No, not really. It's a minority.

(INTEng4)

Where the encountered lawyers doubted that their clients would provide a credible account in an interview, they usually recommended a 'prepared statement'. A 'prepared statement' is a verbal, or, most commonly, a written, summary of the facts to be disclosed during the interrogation, which was drafted by lawyers on the suspect's behalf. When a prepared statement was handed in, the suspect was advised to respond 'no comment' to all questions posed during the interrogation.

Prepared statements were favoured by some encountered lawyers, because they allowed limiting the scope of client's disclosure to the police (FNEng24.01.2012; 09.04.2013).

3.2.2 Explaining the right to silence 'caution'

The right to silence and the accompanying 'caution' (PACE, Code of Practice C, para. 10.5) was the only procedural right that the observed English lawyers standardly explained to clients during police station encounters. Following the adoption of CJPOA, the police 'caution', containing information about the right to silence, has been revised as follows:

> You do not have to say anything. But it may harm your defence if you do not mention when questioned something that you later rely on in Court. Anything you do say can be used in evidence.

According to PACE, police officers must explain the 'caution' to suspects during the interrogation in their own words (Code of Practice C. Note of Guidance 10D). In the observed sites, this was done with the help of the 'crib sheet', which prompted officers to break down the caution into three parts (Blackstock et al., 2013: 376). These parts were, first, that the suspect is not obliged to respond to questions; second, that if they fail to mention a certain fact during the interrogation that they will rely upon in court, the court may draw a 'proper inference' from such a failure; and third, that the interrogation tapes may be used in evidence (FNEng11.01.2012). Most observed lawyers followed the same structure when explaining the 'caution' to their clients, although they were not obliged to do so.

The second part of the 'caution' was the most difficult for police officers and lawyers to explain, and for suspects to understand. Many observed English lawyers spent some time explaining it to their clients – although this was more often done where the case involved an 'inexperienced' client. Thus, lawyers went through this particular caution in 14 out of 16 cases involving first-time suspects, and only in 18 out of 36 cases involving 'regular offenders' (in the remaining six cases, this information was not known). However, these explanations were not aimed at ensuring that suspects truly understood the implications of remaining silent, but rather at making sure that they could correctly repeat the 'caution'. This is reflected in the following interview excerpt:

> LAWYER (L): They [police] run through it [caution] very, very quickly and then they ask their three questions and the client is very, very keen to get the three questions correct because the client doesn't want to look like an idiot, but he has no real understanding of the caution. So the lawyers quite often feed the client the answers.
> INTERVIEWER: Just to make the client feel at ease and more confident?
> L: Yes, that's right.
>
> (INTEng17)

Yet, the ability to correctly respond to police questions about the caution does not guarantee that suspects understand the implications of remaining silent in their particular situation (Pivaty, 2018). If anything, the 'caution' may lead to an *incorrect* understanding: it may discourage suspects from remaining silent, even if it would be in their best interest (INTEng3). As it transpired from observations, suspects often did not grasp the subtle difference between 'adverse inferences *may* be drawn' and 'adverse inferences *will* be drawn'. Besides, the caution warns against remaining silent, but it does not inform suspects about those circumstances, where adverse inferences from silence *cannot* be drawn, or are *unlikely* to be drawn, as demonstrated in case law (Cape, 2017: 188–191). Therefore, in the English context, the lawyer's task of informing suspects about the right to silence must be fulfilled by explaining the broader implications of the relevant (case) law. Yet, this law is so complex that it would often be impossible to explain during the limited time of the consultation. As one interviewed lawyer noted,

> The caution summarises the [implications of using the right to silence] quite neatly for someone who has studied it for several years ... But the level of education of some of the clients is really very, very low indeed, so you know, even the word 'inference' is beyond quite a lot of them.
>
> (INTEng6)

This effectively deprived suspects of their decision-making power and placed additional responsibilities on lawyers regarding the delivery of legally 'correct' advice.

3.2.3 Presenting strategy options

The two crucial decisions that suspects must make at the investigative stage are, first, whether to remain silent or to give a full (or partial) account, and, second, if deciding to give an account, whether to confess (and to what offence(s)), or to deny the allegations. The options that the encountered lawyers suggested to clients reflected these two central decisions. Some lawyers said that they would usually give the following choices: to remain silent, to confess or to respond to questions. In the words of one lawyer,

> I explain to clients what choices they have, because they're being asked to make choices ... Options, I would call them. And what are the potential consequences of these options. So you might have three – in an interview, you can admit the offence, deny the offence, or say nothing. If you admit the offence, this, that and that might happen. If you deny, this, that and that might happen. If you say nothing, this, that and that might happen. I take them through all these options within reason to help them decide which of those options they're going to make.
>
> (INTEng12)

Others said that the three options they would mention are: to remain silent (no comment), to give a prepared statement, or to give a full account or respond to all questions. As one lawyer described it,

> I always outline three options to my clients. The basics of no comment, prepared statement or full disclosure interview. I sort of give pros and cons of each. Make sure they're aware of adverse inference. Explain the benefits of each bit, and then relate it back to evidence.
>
> (INTEng16)

However, most observed consultations did not proceed in the manner described in the interviews. During most observed consultations, the lawyer presented the options, explained the consequences of each option and let the suspect choose. Most observed lawyers outlined the options in the beginning, before discussing the 'facts' with the client ('taking the client's instructions'). One advisor, for instance, began his consultations by mentioning the confidential nature of advice and the ethical constraints on his role ('If you say something to me that would mean that you did it, and you would say something else [during the interview] ..., I will have to withdraw'). He then informed clients about the police disclosure, and outlined the options in the following way:

> There are three ways of dealing with the interview: yes, I am sorry I did it; if you want to answer questions and you didn't do it, you should give an account now; and if you do not want to answer questions, you should say nothing.
>
> (FNEng06.04.2013)

Presenting the options at that moment served the goal of controlling the client's disclosure to the lawyer (and especially avoiding inadvertent self-incrimination), as much as informing his decision on how to deal with an interview. The advice, which was given following the client's disclosure, was usually geared towards one particular option. For instance, if the suspect denied guilt, very rarely did lawyers explain the resulting options and their consequences – such as remaining silent, responding to questions fully or partially, or giving a 'prepared statement'. Implicitly, this choice was for the lawyer to make (FNEng19.04.2013). The observed English lawyers were usually rather directive in their advice. In interviews, some lawyers recognised that, although they presented the decision concerning the procedural strategy as the suspect's choice or as a 'mutual' decision. In practice it is often the lawyer's choice. In the words of one interviewed lawyer,

> So as a rule, I will say, 'In a minute, I'm going to talk you through what the police are saying. I appreciate there's two sides to everything and if you want to you can give me your account. I'll advise you to the strength of the evidence and then we'll work out what we're going to do in interview.' Always say 'we', so they don't feel it's – it's their decision at the end of the day, but the reality is that most of the times it's us (lawyers) who have to take it for them.
>
> (INTEng15)

At times, where lawyers were *too confident* in their advice, their effectiveness was compromised, especially when an out-of-court settlement was envisaged. Generally, it appeared that English lawyers preferred reaching an out-of-court settlement (so-called 'caution') at the investigative stage, because they believed that this was more advantageous for the client than proceeding to trial. Thus, the observed lawyers often directed clients towards accepting a caution. The condition for obtaining a caution, however, was that the suspect gives an account and admits to committing the impugned offence. There was therefore a risk that lawyers could inadvertently lead clients to making admissions.

For example, in one case involving a theft allegation, the lawyer pressed the suspect to confess during the interrogation, because he was told by the police that she was 'cautionable' (FNEng17.01.2012). The suspect did not wish to confess to the lawyer at first, but she did so in the course of the consultation. The lawyer then advised her in strong terms to respond to questions frankly: 'For the best outcome, you need to be upfront with them ...', noting that now that she had confessed to him, she could no longer deny guilt during the interrogation. The suspect did not fully accept this advice, because at the end of the consultation she told her lawyer that she was 'baffled' about what to say at the interrogation. This became more evident during the interrogation, when the suspect was not providing 'straight' answers to the officer's questions. Even though she finally confessed, prompted by her lawyer, it emerged that she might be charged due to her 'uncooperative' behaviour during the interrogation. In another case, involving an allegation of possession of child pornography, the lawyer was told by the police that the suspect might be offered a 'caution', if he had admitted 'sexual intent' (FNEng29.04.2013). In the lawyer–client consultation, the suspect had initially denied 'sexual intent', but he later admitted that 'the girls on the pictures were beautiful'. This was sufficient for the lawyer to press him into admitting 'sexual intent' during the interrogation, with the view to securing a caution. However, it was unlikely that a caution would have been offered in this case, because this decision had to be made by a prosecutor, and it was contrary to the existing guidelines.[5]

3.3 *Supporting suspects in detention: limited obligations in the law and in practice*

3.3.1 *PACE and lawyers' professional discourse: the lawyer's role as mostly 'legal'*

Most encountered English lawyers described their role at the investigative stage as limited to 'legal' matters: providing legal advice and ensuring that police adhere to the respective procedures. In the words of one lawyer,

> My role is basically to protect my client's personal and legal rights and to make sure that the police are adhering to due process.
>
> (INTEng15)

76 *England and Wales*

This definition closely resembled the definition given in PACE Code of Practice C (Note for Guidance 6B). Only very few lawyers mentioned the task of ensuring the well-being of their client, or providing moral support and reassurance to them (INTEng1,9,16). As one lawyer noted, in response to a question about their role at the investigative stage,

> I think it's twofold. One is that it gives legal support, legal advice ... There is also a slight element of emotional support, because it just gives someone a friendly face. Or I hope. So you're actually not part of the system and so that clients know that it's not necessarily all against them.
>
> (INTEng16)

The convergence of the 'welfare' and 'legal' aspects of the lawyer's role at the investigative stage is to some extent reflected in PACE. It requires, for instance, that the lawyer is given an opportunity to inspect their client's custody record (PACE Code of Practice C, section 2.4), which includes the information concerning the suspect's welfare in detention (PACE Code of Practice C, section 15.3). Yet, Pearse and Gudjohnsson argue that PACE does not sufficiently acknowledge the lawyer's role of providing emotional support. They write,

> ... can it be the case that a solicitor's only role is to protect and advance the legal rights of his/her client? Is it always possible, for example, to divorce a suspect's legal rights from his/her actual individual or emotional needs at the station?
>
> (1996: 235)

They then go on to criticise the Law Society guideline for solicitors on advising clients at police stations, which 'does include a rather isolated reference to "Protecting throughout the well-being of the suspect and making appropriate records", following the list of 11 purely "legal" tasks' (ibid., with reference to: Law Society, Advising a Suspect in the Police Station: Guidelines for Solicitors [London: Law Society, 1994], 3).

3.3.2 *The role of providing emotional support in practice*

In line with the 'official' professional discourse (described in the preceding section), the encountered English lawyers did not address their clients' most immediate needs during their police station encounters. The observed consultations focused on the client's legal position and the upcoming interview. This might be because the police custody period was relatively short: usually no longer than 24 hours. However, even during a relatively short detention period, certain important obligations, such as attending work or school, or ensuring childcare, may remain unattended. Likewise, issues like the right of contact with the outer world (PACE Code of Practice C, sections 5.1–5.8) or the provision of meals and drinks while in custody, were never raised by lawyers during the consultation. On two occasions, where suspects complained that they were not given any food (in one case – after six hours of detention), the observed lawyers did not follow up on the matter with the police (FNEng19.04.2013; 30.04.2013). Likewise, when suspects told their lawyer that they could not make a phone call while in custody, the former either did not react at all, or told the suspect that 'he can make a complaint about it later' (FNEng11.01.2012; 30.04.2013).

In contrast, the encountered English lawyers generally acknowledged that ensuring access to medical assistance was part of their role at the investigative stage (if it had not been ensured by the police). However, in the observed consultations, lawyers usually did not discuss their client's physical or mental health issues, unless they were already known to have a health condition, or if their condition was relevant to a legal matter, for example, the possibility to obtain bail (FNEng01.02.2012; 07.03.2012). The evaluation of the suspect's mental and physical health is closely linked with the assessment of fitness for interview (see Chapter 2). Where the suspect's health condition remains undetected, this might lead to an erroneous conclusion that they are 'fit for interview'. Yet, the encountered lawyers did not undertake an independent assessment of their client's fitness to be interrogated, but relied on the assessments done by the police (FNEng12.01.2012). Sometimes this was detrimental to the suspect's interests. Thus, in one observed case, a woman, who had unknown mental health issues, and was in the lawyer's view very vulnerable, was interrogated because 'the police said she was fit for interview' (FNEng09.04.2013). The lawyer did not question this decision. When asked how this assessment was performed, the lawyer responded that he did not know, and he was only informed about its outcome. The lawyer advised the client to remain silent, because the evidence against her was weak (no CCTV images of her, but only of other co-suspects). However, she rejected this advice. In the lawyer's view, due to her mental health impairment, she failed to grasp the difference between *legal guilt* and *moral guilt*: she was suspected of co-perpetration of burglary, but she believed herself to be innocent, because she was 'only the driver'. As a result, she made a self-incriminating statement, and was given a 'conditional caution', although the lawyer thought that if she had not given this statement, the case would have been discontinued.

4 Lawyers and the authorities: the limits of the 'active defence' role

In England and Wales, the relationship between police and lawyers was less distant and formal than that observed in the Netherlands. Most observed encounters were affable and friendly; lengthy chats about family, travels, common acquaintances or 'professional gossip' were not uncommon. Many lawyers and officers knew each other well, and enjoyed close, if not familiar relationships. Most, although not all, encountered English lawyers believed that a 'friendly, chatty' approach helped them to obtain better disclosure and cooperation on other matters, such as minimising waiting time. (In contrast, one lawyer has said in the interview that 'it was not part of his role to build relationships with the police': INTEng19.)

According to the interviewed lawyers, the individual attitudes of the police towards them depended on whether they knew the lawyer. In the words of one lawyer:

> I generally find that if the officer knows you and has seen you before and knows what you're like, they're more open. If you've not met them before, they're quite guarded and they think we're the enemy when we're not. We're there just to help ... Obviously, there are some solicitors they wouldn't trust and there are others they do. They are not so guarded with certain firms than they are with others.
>
> (INTEng17)

That is not to say that English police officers treated lawyers as professional 'allies': on the contrary, as a profession *in general*, lawyers were broadly viewed in adversarial terms (Blackstock et al., 2013: 345). Thus, in interviews with the police reported in Blackstock et al., lawyers were generally presented as adversaries: some officers considered lawyers as necessary to ensure that 'things are done properly', and others saw them as being in opposition, or as 'argumentative', 'obstructive', or even suspected them of 'concocting stories' for their clients (ibid.: 344–346). Yet, many aspects of the adversarial lawyer–police relationship have become so routinised that excessive zeal or personal involvement on either side was uncommon, and was likely to be censured. Thus, many encountered English lawyers were critical of those officers who were too 'confrontational' with lawyers. In the words of one lawyer:

> Some policemen are very professional, they accept the role that you have. Some are unprofessional and take things very personally.
>
> (INTEng5)

These 'unprofessional' officers, might, for instance, play 'tricks' with the lawyer, such as refusing to answer questions in disclosure, or apply excessive zeal in relatively 'trivial' cases. Interestingly, lawyers also criticised *other lawyers* for being too 'personal' or 'adversarial'. In the words of one lawyer:

> I know there are some lawyers that go in and think it's a definite 'us and them' scenario ... I think some of them are the old school. There are very few and far between ... Two spring to my mind in my local area and they have taken issue with the police at the wrong time for the wrong reasons. The reason, I think, is because I've seen them do it and I think they believe it impresses certain clients ... There are times when you do have to be robust, but it has to be done professionally ... So always keep it professional and these people sometimes don't and they take it personally. It's a job. It's never personal.
>
> (INTEng2)

The events at the investigative stage were still viewed, or narrated, by both sides as an adversarial 'game', but a game played with moderation. It had transparent rules, the boundaries of acceptable behaviour were well-established, and the opponents' moves were predictable to each party. Thus, lawyers knew and accepted that police officers did not always disclose all information to them about the evidence before their client's interrogation, but did not accept when nothing or almost nothing was disclosed. Police officers accepted that in certain circumstances the lawyer could advise the client to remain silent, but not that lawyers could advise silence as a rule. In the words of one lawyer:

> It is a game, because they're trying to guess what you're going to do and you're trying to guess what they're going to do. Of course. But you have to apply the rules as well. You can't do it dishonestly because it would backfire.
> (INTEng6)

Likewise, most English lawyers said that their approach to the police was 'non-confrontational' and 'cooperative'. In the words of one lawyer:

> I think you can get a lot further by having a decent working relationship than you can by being adversarial, them against us, that sort of stuff ... And if you are being more reasonable ... excuse the language ... if you are not being an asshole ... the police are more willing to help you out.
> (INTEng11)

However, the lawyers' reluctance to enter into confrontation with the police was at least partly caused by their (perceived) lack of power in their mutual relationships. As one lawyer noted:

> There's no point in going into a police station and claiming police breached PACE in front of everybody, because you are on their turf. It's their time. You're not in a courtroom, which is your time, they have complete control of everything. And what you are trying is just trying to tweak things to prop your client and try and sort out what the best outcome will be for your client, but without interfering with everything or anything.
> (INTEng2)

Mutual acceptance and personal familiarity, as described in the following sections, enabled English lawyers to obtain pre-interview disclosure and enter into negotiations with the police more easily, as compared to Dutch lawyers. Indeed, in procedural contexts, where the main actors are familiar with each other, issues are usually solved by negotiation (as familiarity with each other reduces uncertainty), as opposed to contest or confrontation (Eisenstein and Jacob, 1977). At the same time, the high degree of familiarity between lawyers and police could also have negative consequences. This is illustrated in the following sections.

80 *England and Wales*

4.1 Obtaining police disclosure: a negotiated practice

In England and Wales, disclosure of case-related information by police to lawyers[6] prior to the lawyer–client consultation was a 'standard' practice, although it was not regulated by law at the time of the fieldwork.[7] This practice emerged as the result of the developments in the law on 'adverse inferences' from silence (see Chapter 6). It is, however, largely within the police's discretion whether and which information to disclose, and disclosure practices were shown to vary considerably (McConville et al., 1994; Quinn and Jackson, 2007; Blackstock et al., 2013; Kemp, 2013; Sukumar et al., 2016).

Disclosure was offered to lawyers by officers in charge in all observed cases. Most often, it was provided verbally, although in three observed cases it was given in writing (FNEng23.01.2012; 24.01.2012; 10.04.2013). Lawyers were informed in detail about the time, place and exact nature of the suspected offence(s) and of the alleged suspect's involvement, as well as the type and, often, the content of the evidence. Often, lawyers were also informed about the anticipated outcome of police detention (bail, charge or caution), and whether or not it depended on the chosen strategy in the interview. Furthermore, although previous studies found that evidence was usually not shown to lawyers during disclosure, this was not the case in this research. For instance, CCTV records and photos were routinely shown to the lawyers, sometimes before they requested it. This was regularly done even where these records did not support the police's 'case'. Sometimes lawyers were allowed to show them to suspects during pre-interview consultations.

Lawyers said that in the observed sites, police officers were straightforward in their disclosure, which was also confirmed during observations. No cases were observed or reported where police officers deliberately exaggerated or misrepresented the existing evidence (cf. Sukumar et al., 2016). On the contrary, sometimes officers openly stated that the case was 'rubbish', or that the evidence that they had was weak. In a few observed cases, for instance, the officers told lawyers that CCTV evidence, which was not yet available, was not likely to 'show anything'. This openness was explained by the generally cordial relationships between lawyers and police officers at the observed sites. This underscored the importance of prior personal relationships with the police in obtaining disclosure.

At the same time, full disclosure was not given in all cases. For example, lawyers said that the police tended to omit exculpatory evidence in disclosure. In the words of one lawyer:

> With some identification cases, they may say that your client has been identified by two witnesses who say that they saw a person fitting his description committing a particular offence. But they won't tell you that there were 15 other people who saw a person that doesn't fit your client's description at all ...
>
> (INTEng13)

Another type of information that was regularly not given in disclosure was about the forensic evidence and its location, as well as phone or surveillance records. Thus, most encountered English lawyers had to negotiate more disclosure, particularly in more 'serious' cases. Lawyers suggested that advising silence could be used as a tactic to obtain more information about the evidence, as in the following quote:

> Sometimes the police – if the police hold back for disclosure in relation to forensics or fingerprints, they do that to test the evidence against the client. My attitude is, well, 'Can you tell me if it's forensics or fingerprints?' It's not me who's got to give the account of why it's there, it's the client. And they say, 'Well, we'll test the evidence on the client.' And I say, 'Well, if you're going to go and ask him, all he's going to do is say no comment.' Until we know whether if it's forensics, if it's DNA or fingerprints …
>
> (INTEng4)

Disclosure was also used by the police in negotiations concerning the police 'caution', which is further discussed in Section 4.4.

4.2 The role at the interrogation: lawyers avoid being 'confrontational'

The observed English lawyers were significantly more active in interrogations than their Dutch counterparts: they intervened in about half of them (25 out of 52). In the remaining interrogations, there was often no need for lawyers to intervene, either because suspects remained silent or handed in a 'prepared statement', or because they followed the agreed-upon procedural strategy, and no persuasion was used by the police. In those interrogations, where the lawyers did intervene, they were usually rather active, namely they intervened more than once, and sometimes ten times or more (Blackstock et al., 2013).

Usually, lawyers intervened to provide advice to the client – for instance, by requesting a confidential consultation, or telling the client whether to respond to certain questions. They also intervened to provide emotional support to suspects, encourage them to adhere to the chosen procedural strategy, and ensure that they understand the questioning (and that the officers understand their responses). Sometimes, where the client's account did not emerge clearly, lawyers posed questions to their clients directly, thus taking up, if only temporarily, the role of an interrogating officer. In observations, the officers concerned never objected to this kind of lawyers' behaviour, although some interviewed lawyers said that they were told off on several occasions by an interrogating officer when trying to pose questions to his clients ('This is my interview!') (INTEng9,17).[8]

As far as the role vis-à-vis the police was concerned, however, many encountered English lawyers said they would exercise caution when challenging the officer(s) directly (see also Blackstock et al., 2013: 395–397). Lawyers explained this by saying that 'it was not their task to tell the police how to do their job' (INTEng5), but that their role vis-à-vis the police was only to protect their client against any unfair or oppressive behaviour. Many lawyers said that they *would not* intervene where an 'inappropriate' question or remark was given to their client if, in the lawyer's view, this was unlikely to prejudice the client. As one lawyer described it:

> At the interview I find that I take a lot more backward step[s] ... Sometimes there are questions that are not necessarily relevant, which if they're not too bad or if they're not setting the client up for a fall too much, you may allow it go.
>
> (INTEng16)

Another lawyer noted that he would not intervene to challenge the questioning if the client is responding with 'no comment', as it 'will make no difference for his case if the lawyer intervenes.' (INTEng13) As a result, the interviewed English lawyers said that interventions to directly challenge the police's behaviour were rare. This can be illustrated by the following excerpt:

INTERVIEWER: In terms of protecting clients from police, you said that it doesn't come up that often. Can you give a sort of an indication of – is it like, in every third interview that you have to intervene?
LAWYER: Oh, no, no, no. Not anything like as often as that, I don't think. I don't know what the percentage would be, though. I'd say maybe one in ten, maybe.

(INTEng17)

Where the observed lawyers did intervene to counter inappropriate questioning, they usually addressed the client, not the officer. One lawyer, for instance, described in an interview how he would intervene in such situations:

LAWYER (L): ... You say, don't answer that.
INTERVIEWER (I): So that would be your usual strategy? You would tell the client not to answer a certain question?
L: Yes, I would do that in an interview. I tell them, I will not tell the police officer why, he should know his job. I'm not going to tell you why, because it interrupts the interview.
I: OK, so you wouldn't confront the officer because that would mean interrupting – ?
L: I would do that only if the officer pursues. I've had officers that turn around and said, 'well they answered yes'. And then I will state it for the tape why I do so.

(INTEng11)

Yet, the danger of such 'indirect' intervening in response to inappropriate police behaviour is that it may not prevent the suspect from giving potentially damaging answers (Edwards and Stokoe, 2011).

Lawyers said that they usually did not need to intervene to correct police behaviour, because in their view (in this particular region), 'police were reasonable' when conducting interrogations. Indeed, persuasion or psychological pressure tactics to obtain a confession were rarely applied in the police interviews observed in England and Wales. However, instances of 'inappropriate' questioning were regularly observed and reported by lawyers – such as asking questions not related to the offence (questions concerning other offences); questions not based on the (disclosed) evidence, or so-called 'fishing' questions; asking several questions in one; questions requiring a suspect to give a legal assessment of their (alleged) behaviour; questions aimed at proving suspect's 'bad character'; questions of opinion; repetitive or (unintentionally) misleading questions. Furthermore, on two occasions (out of 52 observed interviews), interrogating officers undermined the advice given by the lawyer, and once inquired what was discussed during the confidential lawyer–client consultation. (On these occasions, however, lawyers immediately intervened to stop inappropriate behaviour.)

Indeed, intervening in an interrogation is a delicate balancing act: when a lawyer intervenes too often, this might be detrimental to the client's interest (Hodgson and Bridges, 1995: 110), for instance because it might destabilise the client. However, the main reason mentioned by the encountered English advisors for their reluctance to directly challenge the officer(s) in an interview was that they did not wish to appear confrontational towards, or to cause annoyance to, the police. In the words of one lawyer:

> [Police] don't like it obviously when you intervene not so much for giving legal advice ... Because it prolongs the interview when you intervene like that.
> (INTEng7)

Another lawyer noted:

> I would [not] endlessly pick at questions in the interview. If my client isn't sort of – sometimes they're sort of ... sometimes they can be a bit awkward, these questions. Antagonistic, really. But if the client is not rising to it, then – and it's just water off a duck's back, you might as well just let it go. But if obviously the client starts to react, you've got to stop it. But there are lawyers that just endlessly stop it and stop it and stop it, and in the end, police officers feel that they're – well, the relationship with them starts to deteriorate.
> (INTEng18)

One lawyer furthermore explained his reluctance to intervene due to the concern of being perceived as obstructive, and eventually excluded from the interrogation. In the words of this lawyer:

> Some people are very actively involved. They will ask questions, intervene, probe the evidence. I do it to a lesser degree, because I'm really conscious – I don't want to sort of become part of the evidence process, because I'm there

[only] to protect their legal rights, not give evidence for them ... I don't think it's a necessarily good idea, actually, because you may end up getting yourself excluded from the case on the basis that you sort of become, as I said, part of the interview process.

(INTEng15)

However, this was an unfounded fear, because as transpired from the interviews and observations, lawyers (in this particular location) were rarely excluded from interrogations. The general perception was that, to be excluded, the lawyer must commit a major transgression: one interviewee, for instance, talked about a notorious local lawyer who, in his words, was excluded from the interview 'for attacking the client', and was subsequently 'banned from police stations' because of 'agressing female police officers' (INTEng19).

Some encountered lawyers, however, did not subscribe to the views described earlier. One interviewed lawyer, who was known among colleagues for being 'adversarial', described his role in an interview in the following manner:

I see my role as being there to observe, to be proactive, to getting engaged, to clarify questions. Sometimes at the end of the interview, I'll ask the officer to clarify certain points. Has the victim made a statement? Try to think of all the points that will help the defence, so that they're all there, one two three ... Not every interview, but some I will actively intervene. A majority of them, I would think. 80–90 per cent of them I will intervene.

(INTEng18)

Another lawyer, who habitually took a more active stance during interrogations than other observed lawyers, noted that 'some legal advisers are too afraid to – and they haven't got the experience to – challenge the police' (INTEng19).

4.3 Challenging procedural irregularities

Most interviewed lawyers believed that breaches of PACE did not occur often, at least not with respect to legally represented suspects, which was also confirmed during observations. However, this mostly concerned the breaches of 'brightline' rules – such as, for instance, not respecting the maximum detention period, or deliberately obstructing the lawyer's access to the client, but not the rules granting discretionary powers to the police (this distinction is addressed later).

Procedural breaches at the investigative stage were rarely challenged in court. Lawyers believed that courts were reluctant to accept arguments of the defence about procedural breaches. As one lawyer noted:

I've yet to come across the case where even when the caution wasn't explained properly, the courts have decided that it's important and the reason is, it's not like in America where they say if you don't give them the Miranda rights, everything gets thrown out. Here, the judiciary and the higher court say 'Well, OK, maybe he didn't explain to you properly that you're under arrest when he handcuffed you and dragged you into the car, but you realised soon afterwards so it doesn't matter. OK, yeah, he didn't do it correctly but it doesn't really matter because, you know, you knew well enough ...'

(INTEng5)

Given the difficulties of obtaining court remedies for procedural irregularities, it is logical to suggest that relief should be sought immediately, namely already at the investigative stage. Furthermore, as the interviewed lawyers were well aware (as several mentioned in interviews), if the suspect was legally represented when an alleged breach of PACE was committed and the lawyer has not reacted to it, courts were unlikely to afford a remedy stemming from such a breach (*R. v. Dunn* (1990) 91 Cr App R 237; [1990] Crim LR 572).

Yet, the encountered English lawyers distinguished between those violations which, in their view, constituted 'fundamental' breaches or were likely to prejudice their client's position at the stage of police custody (such as interviewing a suspect without a lawyer and an interpreter), and those irregularities which allegedly would make no difference for the client's legal 'case'.[9] In the words of one interviewed lawyer:

If the violation is really fundamental, like the police only have the certain amount of time to detain somebody, then I'll go and talk to the custody sergeant and say 'Sergeant, you got 15 minutes to either charge him, get his detention agreed for another 12 hours, or he is going home with me.' If the breach has something to with, I don't know, he's not comfortable in the cell ... Or the appropriate adult was not notified ... It all depends on the significance. Some of them are minor breaches with no consequences, some of them are fundamental breaches.

(INTEng4)

'Non-fundamental breaches' were usually 'noted down', but not challenged immediately. The police's failure to adequately explain the 'caution' during the interview also belonged to the category of 'minor' breaches. As one lawyer put it:

I will have gone through [the caution] with the client to a degree, you know, really 99 per cent of the time that I'm happy that they understand it. And so really, how the police officer explains it, I don't really mind because I'll have ... it's their evidence.

(INTEng15)

If the interrogating officer does not properly explain, or omits parts of the caution (or forgets to caution the suspect altogether), most interviewed English legal advisors said that they would not voice this immediately, but would note it down in their police station attendance notes. Lawyers explained this by saying that it was not their role to 'tell officers how to do their work' (FNEng25.02.2012), and that the failure to caution the suspect properly might be invoked to exclude the suspect's account from evidence (INTEng1, 4). One advisor (an accredited representative), for instance, said that he 'tends to let it go' when the police inadequately explain the caution, because he is 'never going to be the person who conducts the case', and that 'there will be a second opinion (i.e. from another lawyer) ... if the case ends up in court' (INTEng12). Yet, when asked whether raising such an argument would 'work' before the court, these same lawyers said that it was very unlikely. In the words of one lawyer:

> I always say to my clients, I always say to them: 'if he gets the caution wrong, if there is something about it that is not properly explained or I don't think he's done it adequately, I'm not going to stop and correct it because it might help you when we get to court.' It never does, but it might. So yeah, it's absolutely academic. Doesn't really make any difference. I'm sure there are cases when it does, but those cases will tend to be the ones where there's no solicitor there.
>
> (INTEng4)

The encountered English lawyers also did not address those procedural matters which fell within the police's discretion. These were, for instance, issues like placing a 'volunteer' in police custody (FNEng25.04.2013),[10] assessing the need for an appropriate adult to be present (INTEng4; PACE Code C section 3.15; Code H section 3.17), or the decision about fitness for detention and interview (EngInt2, 12). Although the use of police powers in these areas was considered problematic by lawyers, they rarely contested police decisions on these matters. One lawyer, for instance, described a case where he represented a client, accused of murder, who came across as 'strange' during the lawyer–client consultation, and who had obvious problems in understanding him. During the interview conducted without the presence of an 'appropriate adult', it became apparent that the suspect 'thought somebody else was in the room'. The interview was stopped and a psychiatrist was invited to assess the suspect's mental health. Surprisingly, however, the lawyer had not questioned the police's decision that his client was 'fit for interview' before the interrogation began, and he had acquiesced for it to be conducted without an appropriate adult (INTEng2). In response to the question about why the lawyer did not challenge the decision to interview, the lawyer responded that the police were unlikely to consider him unfit because of the seriousness of the allegation: 'it's quite amazing how fit someone will be deemed when the allegation is murder'. Another lawyer described a very similar case, where a client, a minor with mental health issues, was clearly unable to understand the caution and therefore the interview could not proceed. It was clear to the lawyer that the client had difficulties understanding the caution already during the consultation, but he had not challenged the decision to conduct the interview, because 'the officer wished to go ahead with the interview, in spite of the fact that the suspect was clearly unfit' (INTEng12; FNEng28.06.2012).

The desire to maintain a 'good' relationship with police officers was definitely one reason why the encountered lawyers were reluctant to challenge certain actions and decisions of the police. In the words of one lawyer:

> I don't mind giving police a little bit of leeway, partly because there is the potential to go back and meet the same officer again, so actually to have a really good relationship with the policemen can benefit more clients down the line.
>
> (INTEng16)

4.4 Negotiating out-of-court disposals and bail

A significant number of criminal cases in England and Wales do not proceed further than the investigative stage. These cases are either discontinued, for instance, due to a lack of evidence (with the so-called 'no further action' decision), or are resolved by applying for an out-of-court disposal. The terminology used, and the conditions for application with respect to the different types of out-of-court disposals, has changed regularly (Cape, 2017: 375–391; 426–429). The police, however, have always had significant powers to use out-of-court disposals, most commonly in the form of a 'police' (old term) or 'simple' (current term) caution, in respect of less serious offences. The preconditions for offering a simple caution are, inter alia, that there must be sufficient evidence of the person's guilt to give a realistic prospect of a conviction; the suspect must admit the offence; and they must expressly consent to the caution (ibid.: 379–380, 427). A caution does not count as a formal conviction. However, it forms part of a criminal record, and therefore it may be cited in the subsequent criminal proceedings or used as evidence of previous misconduct, and prevent the person from obtaining certain jobs (ibid.: 382).

The cautioning practices of the English police were criticised for being inconsistent, involving incorrect legal qualification of the alleged offences (for example, as more serious than supported by evidence) and misrepresenting the evidence, so that evidentially weak cases were disposed of with a 'caution' instead of being discontinued or investigated further (Sanders et al., 2010: 404–408). Thus, in theory, legal advice at the investigative stage constitutes an important guarantee against the misuse of cautioning powers. In practice, however, the observed lawyers invariably cooperated with the police in the issuance of cautions.

Some encountered English lawyers viewed obtaining a 'caution' as a negotiation process facilitated by their good personal relationships with police officers. As one lawyer described it:

> The way it works is, you got a good rapport with the police, and you have to usually be confident enough to get away with it, so ... you sit down with them and they give you disclosure and at the end of it you say: 'Where is it going? Does he have any previous?' and they say 'Not really ...' and

I say: 'Look, I tell you what. I'll talk to my client, get his instructions. You go and talk to your sergeant, find out if they'll give a caution.

(INTEng4)

Many observed lawyers inquired already during the police disclosure whether their client was 'cautionable', or whether a caution was envisaged. The police's response to this varied from non-committal (for instance, that a 'caution' was theoretically possible, or that it would depend on the custody officer's decision) to indicating that the suspect might, or was likely to, be cautioned if they gave an account and admitted guilt. Where the caution was suggested, the observed lawyers always raised it with the client during the lawyer–client consultation. As one lawyer described it:

Well, sometimes the police will say: 'Well, this matter', and you say 'Look, if he admits, is it possible it can be cautioned?', They'll go 'I have to speak to the inspector and I'll say yes if he says it.' You take your client's instructions, and then you say 'Look in the end of the day, you're going to get a sort of telling off for what you've done if you admit. If not, it's possibly going to court. Those are your choices. The evidence's a bit strong against you. So, what do you say?

(INTEng9)

Usually, the possibility of caution was mentioned by the lawyer after the client's disclosure, after the former could gauge the latter's intentions about whether or not to admit guilt (see Cape, 2017: 383). However, sometimes, the observed lawyers informed the suspect about the possibility of a 'caution' already *before* taking the client's disclosure. Furthermore, in three of the observed consultations, lawyers actively persuaded the suspect to admit guilt – in two cases against the suspect's initial wishes – because they believed that this would help the latter to obtain a caution (FNEng17.01.2012; 23.01.2012). In two of these three cases, lawyers did not inform their clients about the possible negative consequences of a caution.

In at least one observed case, the police's suggestion that the client was 'cautionable' appeared to be a tactic to incentivise the client to confess, using the lawyer as an intermediary. (The existence of such a practice was also confirmed by some lawyers in the interviews.) In this case, an officer hinted to the lawyer that the client would be 'cautionable' if she gave 'a frank and open account', but, as it turned out later, the police had already considered sending the file to the prosecutor for a decision.[11]

Obtaining the client's release, or so-called bail, was another area for potential negotiation with police, although most interviewed lawyers said that it was difficult for them to influence police decisions on bail. In the words of one interviewed lawyer, 'if the custody sergeants made up their mind, you're not going to get it' (INTEng2). At the same time, police were observed to use bail as a leverage point to obtain admissions or certain information (such as names of co-perpetrators) from suspects, using lawyers as intermediaries. Such tactics were also described by one lawyer in an interview:

> I think sometimes some officers – in relation to bail, specifically – [they like it] if they get an admission ... rather than when it makes them work longer. For instance, ID parade, files everywhere, Crown Prosecution Service lawyer getting involved ... If they get an admission, they can bail even with a bail risk.[12] And they sometimes lay their cards on the table. Because the clients with experience, they want to know ... what's the situation with bail. Then you can maybe sort of nudge the officer ...
>
> (INTEng7)

Thus, engaging into bail or 'caution' negotiations, facilitated by 'repeat' relationships between police officers and lawyers, was presented by the latter as advantageous for both clients and police. As one lawyer put it:

> If clients admit guilt because I tell them to, I'm doing the police a favour as well, aren't I? Most people can see it as a professional, important relationship. They [the police] might have my client, really good evidence – forget later on, at the police station stage, the evidence could easily be overwhelming. I might get my client to admit that. If I wasn't there, he might not. And so it causes the police more work. So it works both ways ...
>
> (INTEng6)

4.5 Participation in the fact-finding process at the investigative stage

In England and Wales, the lawyer's participation in the fact-finding process at the investigative stage is potentially important, because, although the respective guidance requires that police should 'pursue all reasonable lines of inquiry, whether these point towards or against the suspect' (CIPA 1996, article 3 (5), Code of Practice, section 23.1 (1)), research shows that in reality, police investigations in England and Wales tend to be oriented towards constructing the case against the suspect (McConville et al., 1991). Yet, the encountered English lawyers rarely participated in the fact-finding process at the investigative stage.

In addition to suspect interrogations, English lawyers may also be present during identification procedures (PACE Code of Practice D, section 3.17; PACE Code of Practice D, Annex A; PACE Code of Practice D, Annex B; PACE Code of Practice D, Annex C), confrontations (Code of Practice D Annex D section 1), taking intimate samples (PACE s62(1)(a), Code of Practice D section 6.3), and during all investigative actions conducted while the suspect is in custody, such as the taking of fingerprints, photos or personal searches (PACE, section 58 (1)). However, during the English fieldwork, lawyers were only observed to attend an investigative action at the police station three times. The first two attendances concerned a video identification parade (so-called VIPER). In the first case, the lawyer attended the VIPER because it was held shortly after the interview

(FNEng11.01.2012). The second case was a serious allegation of involvement in an armed robbery, concerning a firm's recurrent client, who had remained silent during the interrogation. Because the other evidence was circumstantial, the findings from the ID parade were likely to be decisive, and therefore the lawyer decided to attend (FNEng25.04.2013). On a third occasion, the lawyer attended the taking of fingerprints and a photograph from the suspect invited to the police station for interview as a voluntary attendee. However, the suspect was taken in custody upon arrival to the police station (FNEng27.04.203). The lawyer chose to attend because he was already present at the police station. Thus, the lawyer's participation in investigative actions undertaken by the police at the investigative stage was more an exception than a rule, which was also confirmed during the interviews. In the words of one lawyer:

> We don't always go to VIPER. I like to go – we certainly don't always go to the capture and selection, simply because it is now recorded automatically ... If it's a case where there is some suspicion in my mind ... I tend to try and go to the viewing.
>
> (INTEng8)[13]

Likewise, English lawyers generally did not undertake their 'own' fact-finding at the investigative stage, such as contacting witnesses or gathering other case-related information. One lawyer noted that if a lawyer contacts a witness before the police do, this might be seen as inappropriate influence on the witness:

> Contacting witnesses [is] generally not [done] during the police station part because they could become police witnesses and you could be seen as ... causing problems with the police investigation. That's more for once the police station part is dealt with, you can then sort of think, 'Right, they haven't spoken to that – we'll go speak to these witnesses.'
>
> (INTEng9)

The encountered lawyers did not contact witnesses before the client was charged, although it may have been justified, for example, by the need to ascertain whether they supported the alibi put forward by the suspect. Likewise, English lawyers generally did not contact the suspect's family. For instance, one English lawyer said that he spoke with the family only 'occasionally, depending on whether the suspect has authorised [him]', because 'if they haven't given [him] permission, then [he] couldn't' (INTEng13). If the allegation involved domestic violence where family members were also the alleged victims, English lawyers were particularly careful to avoid contact with them out of a concern of being suspected of undue influence. As one lawyer noted:

> We are not allowed to talk to victims of domestic violence. It often happens that they call us to say that they do not want to go to court. We then send them to other solicitors, who would take their statement.
>
> (FNEng09.04.2013)

5 Conclusions

In England and Wales, lawyers have been assisting suspects detained by the police and attending interrogations for more than 30 years. This chapter has demonstrated important changes in the practice of police station legal assistance as compared to the early post-PACE studies (McConville et al., 1994). The quality of legal assistance at the investigative stage has significantly improved, as also demonstrated by recent research. The police have also grown to accept lawyers as legitimate players in the police detention and interview process (Blackstock et al., 2013).

The practice of legal assistance at the investigative stage in England and Wales was closer to the European normative ideal described in Chapter 2 as compared to the Dutch practice (narrated in the previous chapter). The lawyer's role at the investigative stage was conceived in the advisory and 'active defence' terms. Lawyers in England and Wales were able to secure detailed information from the police and their clients, and, as a result, provide concrete and meaningful advice to clients concerning the procedural strategy during the interrogation. They were also rather active during interrogations, intervening not only to advise their clients, but also to assist them in providing their accounts. Lawyers were also able to negotiate with the police concerning certain decisions and outcomes at the investigative stage, such as out-of-court disposals ('caution') and bail.

On the other hand, in certain aspects, the practice of legal assistance at the investigative stage in England and Wales did not reflect the 'model' implied in the European normative framework. For instance, English lawyers did not consider it part of their role to provide social or emotional support to clients at the investigative stage. Their approach to advising clients was rather directive and lawyer-centred,[14] which was not in line with the idea that the suspect decides on the procedural strategy, implied in the respective European norms. The encountered English lawyers were reluctant to directly challenge police behaviour in interrogations, which arguably did not fully reflect the concept of 'effective participation' described in Chapter 2. Legal advisors in England and Wales also rarely challenged procedural violations or irregularities occurring at the investigative stage, inter alia in order to maintain 'good' working relationships with the police. They cooperated with police efforts to nudge admissions from suspects in exchange for out-of-court settlements or bail. The English lawyers also usually did not participate in the fact-finding process at the investigative stage.

The following chapters place these findings and the findings from the Netherlands presented in Chapter 3 in the broader context of the prevailing procedural traditions, criminal justice policies such as managerialism, and lawyers' occupational cultures.

Notes

1 Criminal Justice Act 2013, sections 23–27; Legal Aid, Punishment of Offenders Act 2012, section 133; the Director's Guidance on Adult Conditional Cautions, Guidance to Police Officers and Crown Prosecutors Issued by the Director of Public Prosecutions

under Section 37A of the Police and Criminal Evidence Act 1984, section 6; the Director's Guidance on Youth Conditional Cautions, Guidance to Police Officers and Crown Prosecutors Issued by the Director of Public Prosecutions under S37A of the Police and Criminal Evidence Act 1984, section 5.

2 In terrorist offences, other time limits apply.
3 A distinct criminal defence profession emerged in late 1970s, and has become increasingly specialised in the 1980s–1990s (Cape, 2014).
4 In practice, they do so rarely, because calling an uncooperative witness to testify for the defence might not yield results favourable for the defendant (Cape, 2010: 146).
5 See Crown Prosecution Service, Legal Guidance, Indecent Photographs of Children, available from: <https://www.cps.gov.uk/legal-guidance/indecent-and-prohibited-images-children> (last accessed on 16 July 2019).
6 Police guidance states that unrepresented suspects should not be given disclosure, because it is feared that they would comment on the information provided before being informed of their rights. College of Policing, Authorised Professional Practice: Investigations, Investigative Interviewing, available from: <www.app.college.police.uk/app-content/investigations/investigative-interviewing/> (last accessed on 16 July 2019).
7 In June 2014, PACE was amended to include the provision that, if a suspect is legally represented, the lawyer must be provided sufficient information to enable the suspect to understand the nature of the offence and why they are suspected of it, in order to enable them to exercise an effective defence. PACE Code C para. 11.1A and Note for Guidance 11ZA. The new provisions allow broad discretion to the police as to which information to disclose (Cape, 2015: 57–58). A recent study, which included observations in the period after 2014, argued that they have not led to a change in disclosure practices (Sukumar et al., 2016).
8 Note that the note of guidance to PACE Code of Practice C states expressly that '[t]he solicitor may intervene [in an interrogation] in order to seek clarification'.
9 This is also related to the lack of formal procedures to remedy the alleged violations already at the investigative stage (Cape, 2017: 488–489).
10 A volunteer is a person who attends the police station voluntarily for the purpose of assisting an investigation. PACE, section 29. Their arrest is justified only where new information came to light indicating that voluntary attendance is no longer a practical alternative to arrest. Code G NfG 2G.
11 The decision concerning 'caution' belongs to custody officers, and not to officers in charge, although in practice the latter may have influence over this decision. INTEng15.
12 PACE sections 37 (pre-charge) and 38A (post-charge).
13 'Capture and selection' is the process where the suspect's image is captured and the compilation of the images is prepared, which the suspect and his lawyer may preview; 'viewing' is the presentation of the compilation of the images to the witness.
14 In the lawyer-centred model of legal counselling, the client defines the desired outcome of the proceeding(s), and the lawyer defines the objectives of legal representation and chooses the means for arriving at these objectives. The client's role is largely limited to providing the lawyer with the relevant facts. The lawyer decides which legal avenues should be explored and how the client should behave. The lawyer takes full responsibility for the chosen legal strategy (Cochran Jr. et al., 2014).

5 The influence of legal procedural traditions
Observations from the field

1 Introduction

The previous chapters have exposed the gap between the normative view of the role of a defence lawyer at the investigative stage (as implied in European laws) and the practical reality of legal assistance at this stage. This and the following chapters, in turn, aim at identifying some of the factors which are likely to shape or influence the respective practices, and which partly explain the origins of this gap. The influence of national legal cultures and legal (procedural) traditions emerges as the most obvious factor, which might explain the gap between the European normative view on the role of the lawyer at the investigative stage and the respective practice. Resistance from the procedural tradition was cited as the reason why certain national legal systems were reluctant to implement the broad right to custodial assistance (Brants, 2016). Thus, this chapter hypothesises that the practices of legal assistance at the investigative stage described in Chapters 3 and 4, which did not correspond to the normative view presented in Chapter 2, developed mainly on the basis of the prevailing procedural traditions, or (national) laws and regulations (understood broadly, i.e. inclusive of case law and rules of professional ethics), reflecting these ideas.

This chapter adopts certain presumptions concerning (the nature of) the prevailing legal procedural traditions in England and Wales and the Netherlands based on the existing literature. The Dutch system of criminal procedure is assumed to be derived from the inquisitorial tradition (see Chapter 3) and the English system, despite the latest 'managerialist' changes, and to be embedded in the adversarial tradition (see Chapter 4). It is not the goal of this chapter to contribute to the debate about the meaning or usefulness of the inquisitorial–adversarial dichotomy. It also does not aim at advancing the theory of procedural traditions, including their relationship with the empirical practice (recognising, however, that such advancement is necessary). This would necessitate a much broader inquiry, involving numerous jurisdictions, and thorough theorising about the nature of the above-mentioned relationship mediated inter alia through laws, institutions, attitudes, perceptions and behaviours.

The analysis presented in this chapter shows, however, that the differences between the lawyer's role implied in the European normative framework and the practice of legal assistance at the investigative stage cannot be fully explained with reference to the ideas embedded in the procedural traditions, or national laws reflecting these traditions. In other words, it cannot be claimed that where the observed practice did not comply with the 'model' normative view this was always and solely because of the inhibitive influence of procedural traditions. Rather, the empirical work conducted for this study, as demonstrated further in the chapter, provided examples, where the observed practices were not (fully) in line with the ideas embedded in the legal procedural traditions of the given jurisdictions. For instance, although the adversarial tradition seemingly promotes active lawyering, legal advisors in England and Wales tended to assume a very passive role shortly after the right to police station legal assistance had just been introduced. In the Netherlands, although the procedural tradition encourages the building of a 'trusted relationship' between the lawyer and the client, the observed 'duty' lawyers, overall, did not appear successful in developing such a relationship at the investigative stage.

Contrariwise, in some other instances, the observed practice reflected the European normative view of the lawyer's role at the investigative stage to a greater extent than the national laws or procedural traditions. Thus, the English ethical rules encourage a more distant, 'business-like' relationship between lawyers and clients, and discourage lawyers from probing clients for (self-incriminating) information, which would seem to inhibit lawyer–client trust and the lawyers' ability to obtain information from suspects. However, in observations carried out in England and Wales, legal advisors were usually able to obtain detailed accounts from suspects at the investigative stage. The Dutch procedural tradition discourages disclosure of case-related information to lawyers by the authorities, treating them as 'outsiders' in the criminal proceedings (although the right to such disclosure exists in national law). Yet, the Dutch fieldwork has shown that the practice of disclosure of information to lawyers, however limited, had started to develop in the so-called ZSM proceedings for an out-of-court disposal. Furthermore, in those instances where the observed practice did align with national laws or the prevailing procedural traditions, there were other forces at play, which conditioned the said practice. For example, the Dutch lawyers' passivity in police interrogations, which was in line with the restrictive national regulations and the inquisitorial tradition, as argued further in this chapter, could not be attributed solely to the influence of these regulations.

Thus, this chapter argues that the discrepancies between the normative view of the role of defence lawyers at the investigative stage of the criminal proceedings (implied in European law) and the empirical practice of legal assistance at the investigative stage should also be attributed to factors other than the prevailing procedural traditions, and the laws and regulations stemming from such traditions. Furthermore, arguably, procedural traditions are not the determinative factor explaining the developments in the practices of legal assistance at the investigative stage. The chapter concludes with suggestions concerning why the influence of the procedural traditions on the practices in this particular area appears less determinative than expected. It also calls for better understanding of the role of legal procedural traditions in shaping the empirical practice of the criminal process.

2 Procedural traditions, legal regulations and practices

2.1 Legal cultures and legal (procedural) traditions

The meaning of the terms 'legal culture' and 'legal tradition', and their mutual relationship, is subject to debate, which falls outside of the scope of this work. This section describes the operational definitions of the terms chosen in this chapter, and exposes the rationale for this choice. 'Legal procedural tradition' is viewed in this chapter as part of 'legal tradition', which is in its turn embedded in the given legal culture (Merryman, 1985: 2). Although 'legal tradition' and 'legal culture' are often considered synonymous, here 'tradition' is viewed as more specific than 'culture', as it denotes those cultural attitudes and beliefs which are rooted in history (Twinning, 2009: 85). The idea of 'legal culture' reflects the notion that the law constitutes part of the general culture, and that it should be treated or explained as such. The most general definition of legal culture proposed by Nelken is 'one way of describing relatively stable patterns of legally oriented social *behaviour* and attitudes' (Nelken, 2004: 1; my emphasis). Arguably, however, there are good reasons to define legal culture as 'normative information', i.e. attitudes, beliefs and norms, and to exclude 'empirical practice' or behaviour and institutions from this definition. These reasons are the same that apply to the definition of 'legal (procedural) tradition', and they are explained further in this section. As Nelken observes, there is little clarity regarding the use of the concept of 'culture' in relation to the law, namely: what is considered 'evidence' of legal culture (for instance, only ideas about the law, or also the actual legal practices and institutions), for what purposes the concept is used (to describe 'law as culture' or 'culture in law', or to denote and explain differences between legal systems), and whether or not it is used as a value (for instance, as an argument for or against harmonisation of legal systems) (Nelken, 2016). There is furthermore a danger of adopting an overly static or essentialist approach to legal culture. Such an approach would assume that 'legal culture' forms within the boundaries of nation-states, and that it is so deeply rooted in the nation's consciousness that it can never change. Instead, 'legal culture' should be viewed as fluid, fragmented and not bound to geographic spaces (Glenn, 2014).

Tradition was defined as 'the awareness of an earlier inherent pattern of culture, taken as the source of and inspiration to community identification, with the demand for continuity as an encouraging or justifying power' (Varga, 1992: 6). Thus, tradition represents a segment of the past that is considered worthy of perpetuating in the future, because of its intrinsic value for the given community.

96 Influence of legal traditions

Legal tradition was famously defined by Merryman as 'a set of deeply rooted, historically conditioned attitudes about the nature of law, ... the proper organisation and operation of the legal system, and about the way law is or should be made' (1985: p. 2). This and similar definitions, however, were criticised, notably by Glenn, for being too reductionist, or viewing legal tradition as a set of fixed and bounded characteristics (Glenn, 2014). Glenn, in contrast, viewed legal traditions as a 'conglomeration' of normative information in a given society, which 'bears within itself the seed of diversity or, more radically, change'. This information, according to Glenn, is constantly selected or appropriated by the respective actors. Thus, legal traditions are not homogenous, but hybrid and inherently contradictory, and they are constantly reinvented in a dialectic and reflective process ('massaging' of the legal tradition).

Glenn viewed legal tradition as 'normative information', which should be separated from legal institutions, practices and positive law (Twinning, 2009: 83–84). A similar view of 'legal (procedural) tradition', namely as different from positive laws, practices, institutions or behaviour, is adopted in this chapter. This definition allows to distinguish normative ideas as elements of procedural traditions, and positive laws, institutions or practices as 'informed' by these ideas. Glenn's work has been criticised for the failure to conceptualise mechanisms of how the information from legal traditions becomes appropriated by the actors to inform their everyday behaviour or social practice (Duve, 2018: 31). Yet, the conceptualisation of the causal links between 'law', 'legal culture/tradition' and 'non-law' or 'behaviour' or 'practice' remains a major challenge in comparative law (Siems, 2018: 150–155).

'Procedural tradition', as a sub-element of 'legal tradition', may be defined as a set of historically conditioned normative ideas or attitudes, related to the distribution of powers and responsibilities between procedural actors and institutions, considered valuable and worthy of perpetuating by the relevant participants (cf. Langer, 2004: 1). Applied specifically to the criminal process, 'procedural tradition' thus refers to the historically conditioned ideas and attitudes concerning the objectives and values of the criminal procedural system and the roles and powers of the different actors in the criminal process (judges, prosecutors, lawyers, defendants, victims and the general public). These ideas are primarily reflected in the laws pertaining to the criminal process (understood broadly, including, for instance, case law and ethical regulations for criminal justice actors). Procedural traditions, like legal traditions, have a dynamic, fluid character. As Field wrote,

> ... we should expect the adversarial and the inquisitorial traditions to bear only a contingent relationship not only to current, but also to past, practices. As a primary site of ideological conflict, we need to see legal traditions as being invented and reinvented through the debate and dialogue that feeds social change rather than as entities with objective, stable and fixed characteristics.
>
> (2009: 370)

2.2 The 'inquisitorial' and 'adversarial' procedural traditions

2.2.1 Multiple purposes, multiple meanings

The terms "inquisitorial" and "adversarial" have dominated comparative criminal justice research for about 200 years (Langer, 2004: 7). Indeed, it was noted that "it is unusual even today for any work of comparative criminal … procedure to eschew reference to these terms" (Jackson and Summers, 2012: 6). On the most general level, the two terms denote two archetypes of procedural design: an 'adversarial' procedure is such where the two parties, defence and prosecution, argue out the case in front of a neutral and passive judge; and an 'inquisitorial' procedure is the one dominated by an official state investigator, who leads the inquiry and decides on the outcome, and where the parties play a less prominent role (Langer, 2004: 4). The meaning or usefulness of these concepts are being debated. As Langer noted, the terms adversarial/inquisitorial were used by scholars for many different purposes, sometimes within the same work, namely: as the ideal-types of (Western) criminal justice systems; as the archetypes of criminal process that have existed in Europe at a certain historical moment; as normative models aimed at informing legal reforms; or as a set of social or cultural norms related to the distribution of powers and responsibilities between the main institutions of the criminal process internalised by legal actors (Langer, 2014).

Most of the recent scholarship uses the terms adversarial/inquisitorial in the last meaning of those outlined earlier, namely in distinctly cultural or sociological terms. Thus, many contemporary accounts of national criminal procedural laws point to the cultural influences of the prevailing (inquisitorial or adversarial) procedural tradition (Ringnalda, 2010; Brants, 2013; Montana, 2016; Ryan, 2016). Some authors endorse the thesis of 'convergence' of European systems of criminal procedure, pointing at the increased communication and borrowing across systems, or at the increased 'inquisitorialism' of adversarial systems as the consequence of crime control and managerialist policies (on the 'convergence' thesis, see Jörg et al., 1995; Summers, 2007; McEwan, 2011; Weigend, 2013; Spencer, 2016). Others, in contrast, argue that the 'fundamental' features of the 'prevailing' traditions are likely to endure in national legal systems (Grande, 2000; Ringnalda, 2014; Ryan, 2016). Arguably, though, the debate about 'convergence' between adversarial and inquisitorial systems becomes superfluous if one adopts a pluralist and fluid definition of 'procedural traditions' as described in Section 2.1. Such a definition would allow for the co-existence of procedural traditions, alongside other possible influences, within the same systems of the criminal process. Furthermore, the thesis of 'enduring influence' of the prevailing procedural tradition should be accepted with the caveat that the meaning behind the ideas considered 'fundamental' to the given tradition (such as 'party parity' in the adversarial tradition, or 'truth-finding' in the inquisitorial tradition – see the next section) would inevitably be contested by other contemporary influences, and change over time (Field, 2009).

98 *Influence of legal traditions*

The notion of (prevailing) procedural tradition has been used to explain why national systems resist reforms aiming at introducing legal institutions 'alien' to the given tradition, or why such reforms yield unintended results (Grande, 2000; Langer, 2004). Some sources attributed the reluctance of some European systems of criminal procedure to embrace the right of early access to a lawyer to resistance exerted by procedural traditions or local legal cultures (Brants, 2011; Giannouloupoulos, 2013). Others noted that procedural tradition cannot be the only factor causing this reluctance (Jackson, 2016a: 188). Moreover, references to 'legal culture' can be used by governments to disguise other, more pragmatic, reasons to eschew defence rights (Cape, 2019). In contrast, when introducing a certain law helps to achieve a particular policy or political objective, concerns that it is contrary to the prevailing procedural tradition can be muted. In England and Wales, for example, the introduction of disclosure obligations for lawyers under the CIPA 1996 and the 'case management' duties for judges (inspired by 'managerialism'; see Chapter 6) was clearly inconsistent with the traditional adversarial roles of the respective actors (McEwan, 2011). Yet, these new provisions, as the relevant case law demonstrates, were endorsed by the judiciary with relative ease (Owusu-Bempah, 2013). The ability of criminal justice actors to choose to endorse or forego certain elements of procedural traditions reflects their porous and contested nature.

Despite the various reservations concerning the uses of the adversarial–inquisitorial dichotomy, it remains a relevant analytical tool to describe the influences on the contemporary systems of criminal procedural law and its operation in practice, among other possible influences, such as 'managerialism', 'punitiveness' or others (Duff, 2018).[1] The following section sets out the main normative ideas of the two traditions.

2.2.2 *The contours of the two procedural traditions*

Any attempt to draw out the elements of the 'adversarial' and 'inquisitorial' procedural traditions is susceptible to being criticised as essentialist, or insensitive to the complexity of the contemporary systems of the criminal process. This section, however, should not be viewed as describing the reality of the criminal procedural systems informed by either of the two traditions. Rather, it presents, in very broad strokes, the ideas which form part of the 'theory' of the two traditions developed in the comparative criminal justice literature. It is not claimed here that the contemporary laws or practices of the criminal process in England and Wales or the Netherlands reflect these ideas. However, it is presumed – for the purposes of the subsequent analysis – that these ideas (continue to) exert influence on the English and Dutch systems of the criminal process in some form, alongside other possible types of influences.

The notions of 'inquisitorial' and 'adversarial' traditions are believed to reflect the differing historic and philosophical conceptions of the role of the state and the law in society (Damaška, 1986). The 'inquisitorial' tradition reflects the idea of an active, interventionist and benevolent state, deemed capable of limiting its own powers from within (Brants and Ringnalda, 2011: 17). The state interest, representing the common good, is superior to any individual interest; and individual or 'private' interests are seen as inherently ulterior, and treated with suspicion. For this reason, in the inquisitorial tradition, the fact-finding mission – the 'truth-finding' – should be confided to state institutions (Brants and Franken, 2009: 22). Private individuals, including defendants and their lawyers, should have no role in the 'truth-finding', other than when being questioned by the authorities. Because state officials presumably act in the common interest, 'truth-finding' within the inquisitorial tradition is understood as a thorough, impartial and objective inquiry, aimed at the establishment of the substantive 'truth' (Brants, 2013: 1075–1076). Another related element is the reliance of the inquisitorial tradition on the written evidence included in the case file (dossier). 'Evidence' in the inquisitorial tradition does not 'exist' unless it is written down and 'officialised' by the state. The dossier sets the limits of the official state inquiry against an individual and contains detailed descriptions of the authorities' actions during the preliminary inquiry to enable control by higher-level officials (judges) (Damaška, 1986: 506–507). The parties in the inquisitorial tradition are believed to have a subordinate position to that of the judge; although the prosecutor, as the representative of the state, plays a more significant role than the defence lawyer.

Within the adversarial tradition, the ideas about the relationship between the state and the individual are believed to reflect the classical liberal theory, according to which individual interests have primacy over the interests of the state. States are viewed with suspicion and mistrust, because if states accumulate too many powers, they might encroach upon the individual freedoms of citizens.[2] Consequently, the adversarial tradition strives to 'model' the process of criminal investigation, prosecution and trial, to the extent possible, as the resolution of a private dispute between two individuals: contrasting the two versions of the relevant events, followed by negotiating about the mutually acceptable outcome (Damaška, 1973: 563). Thus, both 'parties' to the proceedings supposedly undertake their own 'fact-finding', and present the results of their investigation to a neutral arbiter. To preserve a level playing field, parties are not required to disclose the results of their investigation to the opposing party before presenting them to the judge. There is also ample room for negotiation between the parties: the application of virtually any procedural rule may be altered, and any outcome may be acceptable, if it is based on the parties' consent (Damaška, 1986: 109–116). 'Evidence' in the adversarial tradition exists 'on its own' and does not need to be written down or 'officialised' by the state (Brants, 2013: 1076). It is, however, recognised that criminal adjudication cannot be modelled entirely after the process of resolving a dispute between two private parties, because the state's resources used for prosecution are infinitely greater than those available to a private individual. Therefore, this inequality of powers is compensated by, inter alia, the idea that the prosecution must prove the defendant's guilt 'beyond a reasonable doubt'.

The role of defence lawyers is conceptualised differently within the adversarial and inquisitorial procedural traditions.[3] In the adversarial tradition, the defence

100 *Influence of legal traditions*

lawyer's role is conceived as relatively important (as an 'equal party' to the proceedings). This role is amoral in the sense that the lawyer must refrain from passing a moral judgment on the client or the case while conducting the defence.[4] Defence lawyers have an obligation to advance the interest of their client, making use of all available legal means for this purpose (exercise a 'zealous defence'). It is commonly assumed that the adversarial system is not concerned with the absolute factual or moral truth, but with a consensual or 'legal' truth that can be negotiated between the parties, or proven in court. Consequently, lawyers are not supposed to engage with the issues of morality or substantive 'truth', but instead to negotiate or put forward a version of the 'truth', which would be most favourable for their client. In the adversarial procedural tradition, it is assumed that clients decide on the desired outcome of the proceedings, and take other important decisions, such as what kind of defence should be advanced at the trial (Damaška, 1986: 141). The lawyer's task is to follow and fulfil the client's wishes, unless they require that the lawyer acts unlawfully: in the adversarial legal ethics, the lawyer is often described as an 'extension of the client's will' (Simon, 1978: 142). The lawyer is also the delegated 'spokesperson' or the 'voice' of the client, who is not obligated to act during the proceedings in person. Furthermore, because in the adversarial systems lawyers are expected to refrain from engaging with moral issues, the lawyer–client relationship in such systems is understood as a professional relationship, not influenced by emotion or personal judgment. Thus, lawyers have an obligation to act for every client, who requests their services (with narrow exceptions such as a conflict of interest), notwithstanding their personal opinion of the client or the case (Cape, 2006: 57). Since the lawyer's goal is to influence the outcome of the proceedings, and because the proceedings are organised as a contest, the lawyer is responsible for researching the facts, which may exonerate the client.[5] Due to these broad fact-finding responsibilities, and because the lawyer is the only procedural figure acting in the interests of the defendant, the adversarial tradition presumably promotes an active criminal defence culture (Damaška, 1986: 142–143).

In the inquisitorial tradition, the role of the defence lawyer is supposedly less important than in the adversarial tradition (Damaška, 1986: 171; Hodgson, 2005: 116). Theoretically, the criminal process may properly function and achieve its objectives without defence lawyers. The main goal of a lawyer in the inquisitorial tradition is to ensure that the conduct of the proceedings, by which the objective 'truth' is determined, is correct and legitimate. Another objective is to provide psychological support to defendants to ensure that they have the moral strength to resist the accusation if they are innocent, or to confess, if they are guilty. In the inquisitorial tradition, defence lawyers are portrayed as guided not only by the interests of the accused, but also by some kind of (more elevated) 'common' or public interest. Thus, ethically lawyers are expected to adhere to the highest moral standards of behaviour, and to exhibit moral autonomy or 'independence' from undue influence from other parties, including that of their clients (Leubsdorf, 2001a: 39). Lawyers retain the prerogative of an independent moral judgment on all matters related to the case at hand and their clients' behaviour. Thus, lawyers do not act as an 'extended arm' of their client, as in the adversarial tradition, but rather as a 'helping hand', meaning someone who lends his 'eloquence and learning' to the client's cause (Leubsdorf, 2001b: 341). Likewise, the lawyer–client relationship has a distinctly moral character. Lawyers may refuse to act on behalf of certain clients if they have moral reservations against it (Leubsdorf, 2001a: 16). Defence lawyers do not partake in the fact-finding process in the inquisitorial tradition, because this function is reserved for the state authorities conducting an official inquiry (although they may suggest alternative lines of inquiry to the authorities once the investigation is finished). Due to the lawyer's limited responsibilities in the fact-finding process, and because state officials have an obligation to investigate objectively and secure the rights of defendants, the inquisitorial tradition presumably promotes a relatively passive culture of criminal defence (Damaška, 1986: 142–143).

3 Procedural traditions and legal assistance at the investigative stage in practice

The following sections compare the empirical findings in England and Wales and the Netherlands with the normative ideas concerning the role of the lawyer at the investigative stage of the criminal presumed to be embedded in the inquisitorial and adversarial traditions, and in the respective national laws. This research demonstrates, in particular, that ascertaining the influence of legal procedural traditions on the empirical practice is very challenging. It is, however, clear that in both researched jurisdictions, the practice of criminal defence at the investigative stage of the criminal proceedings did not fully reflect the views supposedly embedded in the 'prevailing' procedural tradition. The following sections describe the unveiled discrepancies between the normative ideas and the observed practice with regard to the following areas: the lawyer–client relationship; the degree of lawyers' participation in suspect interrogations (active or passive role and the amount of lawyers' 'procedural power'); the lawyer's role in the fact-finding process; and obtaining disclosure of case-related information.

3.1 The lawyer–client relationship

A comparison of the findings from the Netherlands and England and Wales on the nature of the lawyer–client relationship at the investigative stage of criminal proceedings (and beyond) reveals that it is viewed differently in the two jurisdictions. In England and Wales, the relationship is described as 'amoral', meaning that the lawyer is presumed to exercise their professional expertise in a manner that is morally and emotionally detached from the client and their cause. The lawyer's role is viewed as that of 'lending' the legal technical expertise to the client. Lawyers follow their clients' 'instructions' as to the desired outcome and the procedural strategy. Thus, certain moral aspects of the lawyer–client relationship, such as (mutual) trust or being 'honest' or 'sincere' with each other, are not emphasised, as they are presumed irrelevant. A similar view of the lawyer–client relationship was expressed by the interviewed English lawyers. Consequently, most English lawyers did not explicitly mention building trust, rapport or a 'relationship' with the client as a distinct element of their role at the investigative stage.

In contrast, in the Netherlands, the lawyer–client relationship is viewed as (also) having a moral or personal element, expressed, for instance, in the lawyer's personal dedication and loyalty to the client, and therefore the lawyer's role vis-à-vis the client is also described in 'moral' next to 'professional' terms. The Statute for Lawyers in Criminal Cases defines the lawyer's role as that of a 'trusted person' and 'advisor' of the suspect (Statuut Raadsman, rule 1). The professional guides for Dutch lawyers also view the lawyer's role at the investigative stage in a more 'holistic' way, namely as including both legal and 'non-legal' aspects such as providing moral and emotional support to detained clients. Consequently, there was a lot of emphasis on the development of 'trust' and the moral aspects of the lawyer–client relationship (such as mutual loyalty and being 'honest' towards each other) in the official professional discourse of Dutch lawyers, which was also reflected in the lawyers' answers in interviews. Many Dutch lawyers explicitly stated that building trust, or rapport with clients, was a distinct – or even most important – element of their role at the investigative stage. Likewise, some mentioned the need to 'trust' their client (or to maintain mutual trust) for the lawyer–client relationship to continue. Consequently, Dutch lawyers appeared more conscious or aware of the need for building rapport with the client and the various strategies to do so in the first police station encounter, than the English lawyers.

These professional views generally corresponded to the 'theory' of the inquisitorial and adversarial traditions, which reflected the differing perceptions of 'truth' as the desired outcome of criminal proceedings. Whilst in the inquisitorial tradition, the goal of the criminal proceedings is to achieve the substantive or objective 'truth', uncovered through an impartial state-led inquiry, in the adversarial tradition, the factual outcome of the proceedings is viewed as a consensual version of the 'truth' established in a contest of two opposing parties.

Indeed, most interviewed Dutch lawyers said that they found it important to hear 'the truth' from their clients, even if it meant making admissions to the lawyer, which the client did not wish to share with the police. By contrast, in England and Wales, lawyers were careful to avoid a suggestion that they wished to know 'the truth' from their clients (implying that it was for the client to decide whether or not to tell the truth to the lawyer). Likewise, most interviewed English lawyers suggested that they did not want their clients to share self-incriminating information with them, especially where they did not intend to disclose it to the police. At the same time, English lawyers wanted their clients to provide them with accounts that were logical and coherent and which could 'stand' in the face of police questioning. This view was very similar to what was described by Dutch lawyers as a 'truthful' account. However, as described in Chapter 4, in the course of the fieldwork, the encountered English lawyers regularly made comments about whether or not they believed their clients were honest with them

Influence of legal traditions 103

(even though most said in the interviews that they were not interested to know the 'truth'). Sometimes such judgments were expressed implicitly, as illustrated in the following quote:

> It's not for us to judge whether it's right or wrong. We do a job. And I don't necessarily have a problem advising anybody. I just do the job ... And I always say, and you often see, you'll see judges or prosecutors or defence lawyers defend a case and it's quite clear just by the evidence and everything else that that person may be guilty but the jury has found him not guilty and the judge says, 'The jury has found you not guilty. You're free to go.' Everybody knows within themselves that he's guilty, but it's not for us to judge. We simply put the case together and we act.
>
> (INTEng6)

Thus, in England and Wales, the professional attitudes and beliefs described earlier, which reflected the ideas embedded in the procedural tradition, did not correspond to the 'reality' of the lawyer–client relationship at the investigative stage.

Furthermore, one might expect that Dutch lawyers would be more successful than English lawyers in obtaining trust and building rapport with their clients, because they were more conscious of its importance in the first police station encounter. Yet, the Dutch lawyer–client encounters, as described in Chapter 3, were characterised by a lack of trust of suspects towards (duty) lawyers. Another discrepancy between the perceptions and the practice was observed in the nature of the accounts obtained by the observed lawyers from their clients in England and Wales and in the Netherlands. Although, in the professional rhetoric of the Dutch lawyers, it was important for them to know 'the truth' from their clients, the suspects' 'stories' given to lawyers during police station encounters often lacked detail and contained unexplained contradictions, whilst the encountered English lawyers were relatively successful in eliciting detailed accounts from suspects.

The English lawyers' approach to advising clients was rather directive and lawyer-centred, contrary to the rhetoric that the lawyer 'simply advises'. Thus, the initial lawyer–client interview in England and Wales is referred to as 'taking client's instructions'. The term reflects the notion of client autonomy and the lawyer acting as an 'extended arm' of the client, embedded in the adversarial procedural tradition. In practice, however, as described in Chapter 4, the observed English lawyers exercised considerable control over their clients' decisions concerning the procedural strategy during the initial meetings at the investigative stage. (The observed Dutch lawyers were less directive in their advice, which can most probably be explained by the fact that they knew very little about the circumstances of the impugned events, the evidence and the client's personal situation.)

This is not to say that the ideas embedded in the prevailing procedural traditions were not reflected at all in the observed practice of the lawyer–client relationship at the investigative stage. One observed difference in the professional practice attributable to the procedural traditions concerned how the encountered lawyers advised clients about the procedural strategy to be adopted during interrogation. Namely, the English lawyers took a more 'legal technical' approach, while the Dutch lawyers adopted a more 'moral' approach. Thus, the Dutch lawyers described the options of procedural behaviour at the interrogation in 'moral' terms: 'tell the truth', 'tell a lie' or 'say nothing'. As a result, the subtle differences between responding to questions fully or partially, or remaining silent and making a short denial statement, were often overlooked. The encountered Dutch lawyers were also generally reluctant to assist clients in formulating their statement to the police (if deciding to answer questions). Some interviewed Dutch lawyers, as described in Chapter 3, considered such practice 'questionable', or borderline unethical, because it might inadvertently alter what otherwise would have been the suspect's 'spontaneous' answers during the interrogation, and thus interfere with the 'truth-finding'. The English lawyers, however, presented the options of procedural strategy during the interrogation in more 'technical' terms, namely remaining fully silent, partially silent, responding to all questions or submitting a 'prepared statement'. They also did not have reservations about helping suspects to formulate their responses to the anticipated police questions; in fact, submitting a 'prepared statement' drafted by the lawyer was the preferred way of dealing with the interrogation for some lawyers (because it could limit the client's disclosure to the police).

Likewise, the different understanding of the nature of the lawyer's role at the investigative stage in the two observed jurisdictions, namely as strictly 'legal' or as more 'holistic', led to certain differences in the practice. Yet, these differences were not as pronounced as expected. Thus, whilst the observed English lawyers tended to focus on the legal matters (and primarily on how to deal with the upcoming interrogation), in line with their role implied in the procedural tradition, the Dutch lawyers also tended to inquire about the clients' well-being and broader 'social' needs in their first police station encounters. However, the Dutch lawyers approached their 'non-legal role' in a rather restrictive way, often limiting it to a set of 'standard' questions asked during the consultation and one call to the client's family to inform them that the latter was in police detention.

3.2 Active or passive role and power in the interrogation room

This study has hypothesised that the adversarial tradition (in England and Wales) would promote a more active lawyer's role at the investigative stage, whilst the inquisitorial tradition (in the Netherlands) would support the development of a more passive and limited role. This hypothesis is based on, inter alia, the assumption that defence lawyers in the adversarial systems have greater procedural power than lawyers in the inquisitorial systems (Langer, 2004).

On the surface, the empirical findings support this hypothesis. The English lawyers were significantly more active than the Dutch lawyers in the observed interrogations. These differences were also partly reflected in the existing regulations. According to the current law in force, in the Netherlands, the lawyer's statutory role during the interrogation is subject to important restrictions, whilst in England and Wales, the respective legislative framework was rather permissive. Thus, under the current Dutch regulations, the interrogating officer is in charge of the interrogation (Besluit inrichting en orde politieverhoor, article 2). The lawyer's participation during the interrogation is limited to notifying the police officer if the suspect does not understand the question, is subjected to undue pressure, or if the physical or psychological state of the suspect is such that it interferes with an effective interrogation (article 6). All other comments and questions must be made by lawyers at the beginning or at the end of the interrogation (article 5). The lawyer cannot answer questions on behalf of the suspect, unless this has been allowed by the interrogating officer and the suspect (article 4), nor can he or she directly address the suspect, but he must address the officer (article 5). The latter precludes the possibility to advise the client during the interrogation, for instance, to remain silent. In case of breach of the rules, the lawyer can be removed from the interrogation after one warning (article 9). This legislation was also translated into the working instruction for the Dutch police, which envisages that police officers must 'lead the interrogation and guarantee order ... in the interrogation room', which includes taking appropriate action when the lawyer 'acts outside of his prerogatives' (giving a warning, and ultimately, excluding the lawyer from the interrogation with prior approval of the public prosecutor).[6] Police are also advised to 'show that they have control' by 'applying the rules [described above] consequently and consistently', and reminded that '[t]he lawyer is primarily present in the interrogation to control whether things go well'.[7] At the time of the Dutch fieldwork, however, the respective legislation existed only in the form of drafts, and the only regulation in force was the internal guideline issued by the Public Prosecutor's Office for the police, which envisaged a passive role for a lawyer in the interrogation room similar to the existing legislative provisions (Aanwijzing Rechtsbijstand Politieverhoor).

In contrast to the restrictive Dutch definitions, the current formulation of the lawyer's role in the English PACE Code of Practice Code C (Note for Guidance 6C) reads:

> The solicitor's only role in the police station is to protect and advance the legal rights of their client ... The solicitor may intervene [in an interrogation] in order to seek clarification, challenge an improper question to their client or the manner in which it is put, advise their client not to reply to a particular question, or to give further legal advice.

This definition envisages a significantly more active role of the lawyer role during the interrogation than the respective Dutch regulation. In the English observations, a wide range of reasons for lawyers' interventions were accepted by the police as 'legitimate'. 'Obstructing the interrogation' was understood narrowly as behaving in such a way that the interrogation cannot continue.[8]

106 *Influence of legal traditions*

However, arguably, these practices in England and Wales did not develop (solely) under the influence of the ideas embedded in the procedural traditions. The positive definition of the lawyer's role in the interview was added to Code of Practice C of PACE in 1995, whilst the initial text contained only a negative definition (what lawyers should refrain from doing), which was considered inadequate to reflect a proper, 'active' defence role at this stage (Edwards, 2008: 227). The respective legislative amendment was the result of complex developments towards the professionalisation of police custody processes, including police interviewing and legal advice, as described later.

The research conducted in England and Wales shortly after the introduction of PACE has shown that lawyers' and polices' working practices, and the relationships between lawyers and police, were very similar to those documented in the Netherlands in this study (McConville et al., 1994). Legal advisors were hardly given any information, and were largely excluded from the key processes at the investigative stage. Police had an upper hand in all matters related to the detention and interrogation of criminal suspects, and had full control of interrogations, characterised by pervasive use of manipulation and persuasion to confess (Irving and McKenzie, 1989; Moston and Stephenson, 1993; McConville et al., 1994). Legal advisors were treated by police officers with hostility and mistrust, and had no power or influence over the events occurring with their clients at the investigative stage. Legal advisors were also ill-qualified for this work, did not give meaningful advice, and did not properly defend clients during questioning (McConville et al., 1994). Another study found that lawyers usually did not attend the interview(s) after the initial consultation (Bucke and Brown, 1997: 25, 32). Pre-interview consultations rarely lasted longer than 15 minutes (ibid.: 26–27; McConville et al., 1994: 92–93). These practices have developed in the absence of prohibitive legislation of the kind adopted in the Netherlands, and in a cultural environment which (in theory) encourages active lawyers' participation in the criminal proceedings on equal terms with the authorities.

The transformation in the lawyers' working practices in England and Wales towards more active participation was the result of several coinciding influences, which were part of the broader movement towards the professionalisation of police interviewing of suspects in custody. The impetus for this movement was given, as described in Chapter 4, by an inquiry into the *Confait affair*, which had triggered a larger investigation into the use of police powers in the criminal proceedings in practice, including the conduct of suspect interrogations (the Philips Commission or the Royal Commission on Criminal Procedure) and the adoption of PACE. This movement has resulted, on the one hand, in the adoption of a new 'ethical' police interviewing[9] model of suspects in early 1990s entitled PEACE, which seemed to contribute to eliminating the use of persuasive and manipulative tactics in interrogations (Soukara et al., 2009). On the other hand, legal advisors had been criticised for being passive during interrogations (Dixon et al., 1990; Baldwin, 1993; McConville et al., 1994). These criticisms were echoed by the judiciary. In the proceedings of a widely publicised miscarriage of justice case, the *Cardiff Three*, the appellate court forcefully censured the lawyer's passivity during the interrogation, which the court described as 'bullying and hectoring', and 'most hostile and intimidating, safe for the use of physical violence' (*EWCA R. v. Paris, Miller and Abdullahi*, 97 Cr App LR 99). In response to these criticisms, the Law Society and the Legal Aid Board (now called the Legal Aid Agency) issued professional guidance for lawyers undertaking police station work (Ede and Shepherd, 1997), and introduced accreditation requirements for the provision of custodial legal advice under legal aid arrangements.[10] These measures reportedly led to the improvement in the quality of legal assistance provided at police stations, including lawyers assuming a more 'interventionist' role during interrogations (Pearse and Gudjohnsson, 1997; Bridges and Choongh, 1998; Bridges et al., 2007; Quinn and Jackson, 2007). On the other hand, recent developments, such as the introduction of fixed fees, might have had a negative impact on the quality of legal assistance and compromised the lawyers' ability and willingness to engage into 'active' defence at the investigative stage, including during interrogations (Kemp, 2010; Smith, 2013; Welsh, 2017; Newman and Welsh, 2019).

Other sources suggest that in England and Wales the everyday reality of criminal legal aid work has never attained the ideal of active and client-centred defence practice (Newman, 2013 and sources cited in Newman, 2012). This study, likewise, has shown that, despite a significant investment into the promotion of 'active defence', the working practices of the observed English lawyers did not reflect the adversarial 'ideal' of the lawyer as a fearless combatant opposing the machinery of the state and zealously defending their clients' interests. The legal advisors observed in this study aimed to build 'good' and non-confrontational working relationships with individual police officers, whom they encountered repeatedly when attending police stations. Whilst this approach helped lawyers to obtain better pre-interview disclosure and greater access to the decision-making processes (such as the use of an out-of-court disposal or 'caution'), it also resulted in the risk of substituting the interests of their (current) clients with the interests of their future clients, or lawyers' own convenience. Thus, the legal advisors encountered in England and Wales rarely challenged procedural violations or irregularities occurring at the investigative stage, and were reluctant to intervene to challenge police behaviour in interrogations. Sometimes, they also cooperated with the police to persuade clients to admit guilt, or to provide certain information in exchange for out-of-court settlements or bail.

In the Netherlands, the observed reality generally reflected the ideas about the role of the lawyer embedded in the inquisitorial tradition, namely that of a powerless 'outsider', particularly at the early stages of the proceedings (when the pre-trial investigation is still ongoing). The prevalence of the inquisitorial discourse on the criminal process has also allowed for the adoption of restrictive regulations concerning the lawyer's role during the interrogation referred to earlier in this section. Likewise, the Dutch lawyers have commonly explained their passivity by the fact that they were not 'authorised' to be active by the existing regulations.

One lawyer, for instance, responded as follows to the question about whether he had an opportunity to intervene during the interrogation:

> Yes, a rude person could do that ... You lawfully do not have the possibility, but you can yell, but the atmosphere won't improve. I hardly have ever intervened in an interrogation, maybe once or twice with a minor. And with an adult, never. So I have never had to intervene, but I thought about it.
>
> (INTNeth14)

Another interviewed Dutch lawyer stated:

> My role in the interrogation is to figure out the protocol, whether I am supposed to sit and remain silent.
>
> (INTNeth22)

However, it is questionable that the Dutch lawyers' passivity during interrogations could be explained only by reference to the prohibitive regulations. As mentioned earlier, the only regulation in place at the time of the fieldwork was an internal guideline of the Public Prosecutor to the police, which was not binding on lawyers – however, lawyers commonly referred to it as containing generally applicable rules. (Moreover, as explained in Chapter 3, lawyers' own professional standards encouraged them to be active during interrogations.) Lawyers seemed to refer to the existing Prosecutor's guideline or, more generally, to the reluctance of the police to 'grant' lawyers a more active role to justify their passivity during interrogations. This has allowed them to legitimise passive behaviour by reference to 'external' forces (presumably) beyond their control, such as that an active stance 'was not allowed', or that it would be taken negatively by the police, and as a result harm their clients' interests. In the other words, lawyers claimed that the conditions for a 'responsible agency' were absent, namely that they were not free to determine their behaviour during the interrogation, but were 'helplessly propelled into the new situations' (Sykes and Matza, 1957: 667). This type of reasoning was described in other professional contexts as a neutralisation technique, aimed to deny responsibility for performance that provokes a feeling of moral dissonance, for instance because the professional in question knows it to be sub par (Kvalnes, 2019: 123).

Passivity was a more convenient stance for the Dutch lawyers than an 'active' role, which may be extremely challenging, especially given the novelty of the police station environment for lawyers, and the police resistance caused by the new figure in the interrogation room (Blackstock et al., 2013; Vanderhallen et al., 2014). The finding that the Dutch lawyers' passivity at the investigative stage cannot be explained (only) by reference to the procedural tradition should be contrasted with the prevailing narrative in the Dutch literature, which underscores the obstacles towards a (more) active role of a lawyer during the pre-trial stage, originating from the inquisitorial tradition (Prakken and Spronken, 2009: 8–9; van Kampen and Franken, 2013). These sources (correctly) point to the lack of 'party equality' at the investigative stage of the Dutch process, where the police and prosecutors are vested by law with the powers to limit lawyers' participation at the pre-trial stages of the proceedings with the view to facilitating the 'truth-finding' function. Thus, as described earlier, according to the Dutch regulations, police and prosecutors may exclude lawyers from interrogation of their clients if they make 'unauthorised' interventions. It should, however, be noted that the English process, which is 'adversarial' in character, likewise, does not afford any 'party equality' at the investigative stages of the criminal proceedings. In England and Wales, just like in the Netherlands, pre-trial investigations are mainly conducted by the police, who are vested with significant resources and powers without the lawyer's presence, whilst lawyers' own resources to conduct investigations (as explained in the following section) are very limited. The English police also dispose of vast resources to force suspects into cooperation with the interview process, including the vast and virtually uncontrolled powers of detention (Dehaghani, 2016). And finally, similar to the Dutch police, the English police have considerable power in the interrogation room, including the power to decide when to interrogate, to control the interrogation process, to continue with the interrogation if the suspect resorts to the right remain silent, and to exclude the lawyer from the interrogation.

Thus, the tremendously unequal distribution of powers between the police and lawyers in the interrogation room, and more generally, at the investigative stage, is not a uniquely 'inquisitorial' phenomenon. Rather, this power imbalance appears inherent in the architecture of the investigative stage as a (primarily) one-sided inquiry performed by the state authorities (informed by the hypothesis of the suspect's guilt and therefore vulnerable to confirmation bias: Leo, 2008; Meissner and Kassin, 2002). It also logically follows from the expansion of the police powers to investigate and detain for the purposes of interrogation, which occurred in the second half of the nineteenth to the early twentieth centuries in response to the growing criminality caused, in turn, by rapid industrialisation and urbanisation. Initially, these emerging police powers had been informal, and they had not been considered part of the 'official' criminal process in either the adversarial or the inquisitorial systems. These powers were not officially regulated until the early or mid-twentieth century (McConville et al., 1994: 73–74; Hodgson, 2005: 27), when the 'adversarial' and 'inquisitorial' paradigms had already been well-crystallised. It may thus be concluded that the institutions of police interrogation and detention, and the corresponding police powers, had not developed under the influence of either the 'adversarial' or the 'inquisitorial' ideas, but under an entirely different type of societal influence.

3.3 Participation in the fact-finding

The adversarial tradition supports the idea of the lawyer being an active participant of the fact-finding process, whilst in the inquisitorial tradition, lawyers are considered 'outsiders' who have no legitimate function in the fact-finding (Section 2.2.2). Thus, it was expected that the English legal advisors would be more active than their Dutch counterparts in undertaking their own inquiries and participating in pre-trial investigations. The empirical findings have shown, however, that in both jurisdictions, lawyers did not actively participate in the fact-finding process at the investigative stage of the proceedings. Both the English and Dutch legal advisors usually did not participate in the investigative actions undertaken by the police (with the exception of suspect interrogations), even though they were entitled to participate in some of them by national law.

In both jurisdictions, lawyers also generally did not undertake independent fact-finding as early as the investigative stage of the proceedings. The main reason cited by lawyers in both jurisdictions was the concern that witnesses, who were interviewed by the defence (especially if they had not yet been interviewed by the authorities), might be considered less reliable. Interestingly, this concern was also commonly expressed in England and Wales, and not only the Netherlands, where it could be explained by the ideas embedded in the procedural tradition: namely, the inherent mistrust of the defence function as representing a 'private' interest.

In addition to this general concern, in the Netherlands, there exist specific professional regulations which preclude lawyers from conducting investigations and contacting witnesses at the investigative stage of the proceedings in certain cases. No such regulations are in place in England and Wales. Thus, in the Netherlands, special rules apply to regulate lawyers' behaviour, where a suspect is detained *incommunicado* following the decision of the public prosecutor (usually, in 'serious' cases involving co-suspects).[11] According to the established line of disciplinary law, in such situations the suspect's lawyer is not allowed to share information about the case or the results of investigation with third persons.[12] As a result, lawyers are prevented from any kind of contact with persons potentially related to the alleged offence(s), including clients' family members. Another norm of professional practice, which, however, was revoked in the new 2018 Gedragsregels (Rules of Conduct),[13] was the old Rule 16 paragraph 2 of 1992 Gedragsregels, which stated that criminal defence lawyers could not come into contact with witnesses that had been called to testify at the trial by the public prosecutor (Spronken, 2001: 578–579). This norm, however, had been criticised since several decades, and was being interpreted rather liberally by the lawyers' disciplinary bodies, namely as allowing for exceptions (Mols, 2009: 317–320).

The Dutch regulations described earlier were clearly inspired by the ideas embedded in the 'inquisitorial' procedural tradition: the inherent trust in the official 'truth-finding' and the concern of preventing any interference with this process, which trumps other interests, such as ensuring the rights of the defence. Yet, when the Dutch findings concerning the practice of lawyers' participation in the fact-finding process at the investigative stage are compared with the English findings, which were very similar (in the absence of prohibitive regulations), doubts arise about whether these regulations were the only or primary cause for the lack of lawyers' active involvement in pre-trial investigations.

The scope of application of Dutch regulations preventing lawyers from contacting third persons during the investigative stage, as explained earlier, is limited to those cases where suspects are detained *incommunicado*. However, as transpired from observations (see Chapter 3), most encountered Dutch lawyers were reluctant to approach potential witnesses or to undertake other fact-finding at the investigative stage also in those cases, where suspects were not detained *incommunicado*. In the Dutch literature, this reluctance seems to be attributed to the cultural mistrust of lawyers allegedly stemming from the inquisitorial tradition (Mols, 2009: 322–323). However, very similar attitudes of mistrust towards defence lawyers by the police were observed in England and Wales (Blackstock et al., 2013: 345–346).

Similarly to adopting a passive stance during interrogations, a cautious attitude towards undertaking independent investigation at the early procedural stages is more convenient for lawyers in both procedural traditions. Active participation in the fact-finding at the investigative stage requires additional effort, as well as considerable time and resource investment (which is usually not compensated by the legal aid funding scheme). One interviewed English lawyer, for instance, spoke about the limits on lawyers' investigations at the early procedural stages:

> For instance there was a case the other week where the police said, 'We've got CCTV of your client, and he doesn't get out of the car.' He's charged, goes to court, and we follow that up to check it after speaking to him. And he said, 'No, I definitely got out of the car.' We go look at the CCTV and he had got out of the car, so the police hadn't told us the whole truth. But that's it. I mean, there's only certain things you can do once they're charged, because then that's when the legal aid and the funding comes into place, otherwise you don't get funding to travel to these places to check with witnesses and stuff.
>
> (INTEng 17)

Undertaking independent fact-finding at the investigative stage may be considered inefficient by lawyers in both procedural traditions, if they can rather identify 'loopholes' or irregularities in the prosecution evidence once it has been disclosed to them (or, as Field and West have put it, 're-read' the prosecution file to the defendant's advantage) (Field and West, 2003). Lawyers may also be reluctant to expend additional efforts on a case, without knowing whether the results of these efforts will be used: there is often little certainty at the investigative stage about whether, for instance, the testimony of a certain witness would be needed to substantiate the defence at the trial. Moreover, it is often unclear whether or not the suspect will be prosecuted, in which case the lawyer might be able to claim financial compensation in addition to the police station fee. These considerations apply equally in systems with adversarial and inquisitorial procedural traditions.

3.4 Obtaining early disclosure of case-related information

In this study, the observed English lawyers were given detailed disclosure of case-related information by the police. In contrast, the Dutch police were reluctant to share information concerning the 'case' and the evidence with lawyers.

However, as discussed in Section 2.2.2, the provision of early access to case-related information to lawyers or suspects does not form part of either the inquisitorial or the adversarial tradition. The inquisitorial tradition, which considers the suspect as the object of the inquiry at the pre-trial stages of the criminal proceedings, would presumably dictate a degree of secrecy of pre-trial investigations. Private individuals, including defendants and their lawyers, represent a 'private' interest, which is treated with inherent mistrust. In fact, disclosing case-related information to suspects before obtaining all relevant information from them would be considered counterproductive to the 'truth-finding' (causing the risk of 'contaminating' the suspect's 'spontaneous' statement). In the adversarial tradition, defence lawyers are presumed to conduct fact-finding independently from the prosecution, and in principle do not need to be informed about the contents of the prosecution case until the case is referred to the trial.

Yet, it may be hypothesised that on the level of the practice, the perceptions and beliefs embedded in the procedural traditions might provide for a favourable, or, on the contrary, inhibitive environment for the development of early disclosure practices. Namely, one might argue that the adversarial tradition caters for a more favourable environment for the development of early disclosure practices than the inquisitorial tradition because, in Langer's terms, defence lawyers tend to have greater procedural power within the adversarial systems (Langer, 2004). Therefore, in countries following the adversarial tradition, law enforcement authorities would be more willing to share information with lawyers and involve them in the respective decision-making processes than in countries with the inquisitorial tradition, where lawyers are perceived as professional 'outsiders'. On the surface, this argument is supported by the fact that in England and Wales there exists a well-embedded practice of early pre-interrogation disclosure of case-related information to lawyers, while in the Netherlands a similar practice does not exist, with the exception of ZSM procedures where the practice of disclosure of case-related information has begun to develop (as described in Chapters 3 and 4). However, one should consider the reasons for which early disclosure practices have developed in the English context.

In England and Wales, immediately after the entry into force of PACE, pre-interrogation disclosure did not exist in the same way that it does today. Legal advisors were not given any information about the evidence, nor did they request such information (McConville et al., 1994). In fact, as described in Chapter 4, the practice of pre-interrogation disclosure developed as the consequence of the CJPOA, which introduced the provisions on 'inferences' from silence, including during police interviews. The CJPOA in its turn, as described in Chapter 4, was the manifestation of the 'crime control' criminal justice policies. Thus, the practice of early disclosure of case-related information to lawyers in England and Wales should in fact be viewed as an indirect consequence of such policies, rather than the result of the influence of the procedural tradition. The emerging case law on adverse inferences from silence (*R v. Argent* (1997) 2 All ER 27; (1997) Crim LR 685; *R v. McGarry* (1998) 3 All ER 805) suggested that such an inference was unlikely to be drawn, where the case against the suspect was so weak that it did not deserve an explanation, and conversely, that it was likely to be drawn where police gave information, which reasonably should have elicited a response (Cape, 2017: 190–191). This case law encouraged lawyers to argue that it was reasonable to advise silence where police had provided insufficient disclosure (Bucke et al., 2000: 23). Police, in turn, began to provide disclosure to lawyers, knowing that this would either encourage lawyers to advise clients to provide an account during an interview, or would strengthen the case for prosecution if the suspect remains silent. Thus, in England and Wales, greater disclosure was not driven by the adversarial procedural theory of party equality, but by a desire to prevent 'no comment' interviews and to strengthen the prosecution case.

Conversely, the absence of disclosure practices in the Netherlands is sometimes explained by the fact that Dutch lawyers are viewed as professional 'outsiders' to the fact-finding process (van Kampen and Franken, 2013). In the words of one lawyer:

> In most cases you get no or barely any information from the police. A few article numbers: 310, 45, article 26 law on weapons and ammunition ... When you ask the police 'what is it about, exactly? So that I know how to advise my client.' Police: 'We don't want to reveal any information at this stage of the investigation to third parties' ...
>
> (INTNeth10)

At the same time, as described in Chapter 3, Dutch police sometimes disclosed information about the evidence to lawyers, where such disclosure could lead to quick resolution or persuade the suspect to confess. The reasons for lack of access to case-related information at the investigative stage experienced by Dutch lawyers were more complex than (simply) the cultural 'mistrust' of lawyers. These also included difficulties of logistical nature, as well as, arguably, the fact that lawyers themselves did not ask for such information.

Furthermore, as mentioned earlier, English legal advisors, like Dutch lawyers, had not been granted access to the respective information in the early days of PACE. As described by McConville et al. (1994), legal advisors were treated by English police officers very much like 'outsiders' to the police custody and interrogation procedures. Despite the existence of the practice of early disclosure, as described in Chapter 4, English legal advisors do not position themselves and are not treated by the police as an 'equal party' to the proceedings as implied in the adversarial tradition. Rather, they are greatly dependent on the police in attaining their professional goals in the context of detention and interview, and therefore aim at preserving a 'good' (non-confrontational) working relationship with the latter.

In both examined jurisdictions, the provision of disclosure of case-related information to lawyers remains largely within the discretion of the police (Blackstock et al., 2013). The amount and degree of disclosure varies depending on the nature of the case, or the prior relationship between the officer(s) and the legal advisor (see Chapters 3 and 4). Lawyers have no formal or informal powers to obtain such information, other than the possibility to advise clients to remain silent, in the hope that the police would disclose more information to persuade the client to provide a response. This, however, is a weak negotiation mechanism, which carries many risks, such as that the client or the police would not cooperate. In other words, case-related information is a resource that can be, and is, used strategically by the police in both inquisitorial and adversarial procedural traditions.

4 Conclusions

This chapter argued that the prevailing procedural tradition ('inquisitorial' or 'adversarial') was not the only or the main factor which shaped the role of defence lawyers at the investigative stage in practice in the two examined jurisdictions. This could perhaps be explained by the fact that the ideas concerning the roles of the different procedural actors within the inquisitorial and adversarial traditions are mostly applicable to the trial, and the advanced pre-trial stages. Consequently, on the level of regulations, the differences related to procedural traditions are mostly visible with regard to the trial stage, but less so with regard to the investigative stage (Cape, 2019). Historically, the investigative stage, or the period of police custody, has not been an embedded part of the criminal process in neither of the two procedural traditions. The police powers to investigate and detain suspects, and the lawyer's roles with regard to these powers, have developed in the course of the late nineteenth to early twentieth centuries outside of the traditional 'adversarial' and 'inquisitorial' procedural forms and structures. Consequently, the idea of 'active defence' at the investigative stage does not fit with either of the two procedural traditions (Jackson, 2016a).

Another possible explanation for the central finding of this chapter lies in the fact that the beliefs and ideas embedded in the procedural traditions, overall, might not exercise as much influence on the empirical practice (i.e. the everyday behaviour of criminal justice actors), as it is habitually assumed. Thus, this chapter documented numerous examples where the beliefs and ideas embedded in the procedural tradition played a 'symbolic' or 'rhetorical' function, rather than being implemented in practice by the respective actors. On some occasions, both the Dutch and English lawyers described their professional practices by appealing to the ideas embedded in the procedural traditions, while the observed reality did not correspond to these descriptions. On other occasions, the encountered lawyers seemed to use references to the prevailing procedural traditions, or regulations reflecting the ideas embedded in these traditions, to justify professional shortcomings and to dispose of taking responsibility for inaction.

Several authors have written about the rhetorical, or 'discursive', meaning of procedural traditions (Kirchengast, 2010; Langer, 2004; Field, 2009). The 'discursive' approach links the use of language, such as 'adversarialism', 'dossier', 'truth-finding', to the socio-historical context from which such language originates. Langer, for instance, points to the differences in the interpretation and meaning of the same language, such as 'prosecutor' or 'truth', used in different procedural contexts (ibid.). Viewing procedural traditions as discourse produced under the influence of particular historical circumstances demonstrates that the criminal process cannot be equalled to its underlying normative assumptions (Kirchengast, 2010: 207). In other words, it exposes the 'rhetorical' function of procedural traditions, which is to detract attention from the 'ugly' everyday reality of the criminal process by (over)emphasising its idealised normative accounts (Hodgson and Mou, 2019: 48).

It must be noted, however, that the relationship between procedural traditions and the empirical practice of the criminal process is extremely difficult to conceptualise. Whilst this study does not aim at developing the 'theory' concerning this relationship (which in any event would need to be 'tested', including through further empirical work), some building blocks towards developing such a theory can be suggested. It should first be made clear that the concept of 'legal tradition', as defined in this chapter, and consequently 'procedural tradition', belongs to the realm of the law (or 'normative information', as Glenn has put it), and not to the realm of its practical application. Combining normative ideas and empirical practices in the same concept of procedural tradition might lead to a simplified understanding of their relationship, or the presumption that the ideas embedded in procedural traditions directly shape the empirical practice (on the danger of assuming that procedural traditions are equal to empirical reality see also Brants and Ringnalda, 2010: 13).

However, the opposite statement, namely that procedural traditions do not influence the empirical practice, would probably be false. Thus, this chapter has documented instances where the prevailing procedural traditions were reflected in the lawyers' professional practices, for example with regard to how they formulated advice concerning procedural behaviour during the interrogation (see Section 3.1). Yet, the mechanisms of the influence of procedural traditions on the empirical reality need to be further understood. Several assumptions or hypotheses have been made in this regard. Empirical studies of the criminal process commonly refer to procedural traditions as part of the broader sociopolitical context in which such a process operates (Hodgson and Mou, 2019). 'Adversarialism', or 'inquisitorialism', as described in this chapter, reflects the historic ideas about the relationship between the individual and the state as applied to the area of criminal adjudication. Therefore, it is believed to be a factor determining the political, legal and institutional framework in which criminal justice actors operate and respective practices develop (Field and West, 2003; Hodgson, 2005). In this respect, procedural traditions are believed to (co-)determine the formal roles of the criminal justice actors, and their understanding of the goals of the criminal process and their roles. However, further research is needed to determine whether and how these understandings are reflected in the actors' professional practice. For instance, Langer (2004) hypothesised that procedural traditions influence the empirical practices by forming so-called 'individual dispositions', or the internalisation of the respective values and beliefs through the criminal justice actors' socialisation processes. The findings in this chapter suggest certain scepticism concerning whether such internalisation (always) directly translates into behaviour that aligns with the respective values and beliefs. The processes through which 'espoused values' (see Chapter 7) do or do not become 'enacted values' need to be better understood.

Moreover, procedural traditions may influence the existing practices through the respective regulations. Indeed, ideas related to procedural tradition find their way into law-making, because laws are drafted by those educated in the given tradition. However, procedural regulations should not be equalled to the empirical practice. In fact, the extent to which procedural regulations determine the everyday behaviour of criminal justice actors is a matter of debate (Dixon, 1997). Thus, the theory concerning the relationship of procedural traditions with the empirical reality must delineate the (mutual) influences between the ideas embedded in the procedural traditions and laws and regulations based on these ideas, on the one hand, and the various elements of the empirical practice, such as 'institutions' or 'behaviour', on the other hand. Finally, given the fluid and contested nature of procedural traditions, as explained in this chapter, the respective theory should envisage the possibility that procedural traditions, in turn, may evolve under the influence of the respective practices.

Given that, overall, the influence of the procedural traditions on the everyday working practices of defence lawyers at the investigative stage did not seem as significant as was expected, this study has sought to identify and examine other factors which shaped the development of the respective practices. These were, namely, the criminal justice policies and the lawyers' occupational cultures. These factors are discussed in the following chapters.

Notes

1 In his recent chapter on Scottish evidence law, Duff argues that it is influenced by the traditional 'internal' legal factors, and other factors, which acquire greater significance, such as 'managerialism' or 'penal punitiveness'.
2 As in the famous quote from T. Paine, one of the founding fathers of the American Constitution: 'Government, even in its best state, is but a necessary evil; in its worst state, an intolerable one.'
3 For instance, the works of D. Luban, W. Simon and other theorists of adversarial lawyers' ethics (particularly in relation to criminal procedure) – in respect of the role of lawyers within the adversarial system, and with regard to the role of lawyers in the inquisitorial system (particularly in France) – the works of J. Leubsdorf on French lawyers' ethics, and of J. Hodgson and S. Field on the role of French criminal defence lawyers in practice.
4 In adversarial legal ethics, this is described as the principle of detachment (Smith, 2013: 114).
5 Langer argues that due to the obligation to perform its own fact-finding, the defence has comparatively more power in an adversarial system than in an inquisitorial system. See Langer, 2004: 13.
6 Introduced in the national police forces via an e-learning portal. See the information on the website of the Dutch Police Academy, 'E-learning lawyer in suspect interrogation' ('E-learning raadsman bij verhoor'), available from: <https://kennismag.politieacademie.nl/12/Paginas/e-learning-raadsman-bij-verhoor.aspx> (last accessed on 16 July 2019).

7 The instruction was published on the website of the Dutch Legal Aid Board (government agency responsible for managing police station duty lawyer services and payment of legal aid fees), with an accompanying recommendation that 'it is urgently recommended to all duty lawyers to familiarise [themselves] with these instructions'. See 'Right of suspects to legal assistance in interrogation; also for adults' ('Recht van verdachten op verhoorbijstand; ook voor meerderjarigen', available from: <www.rvr.org/nieuws/2016/februari/recht-van-verdachten-op-verhoorbijstand-ook-voor-meerderjarigen.html> (last accessed on 16 July 2019).
8 Some interviewed lawyers indicated that they still had confrontations with police officers about what is an 'appropriate' intervention; however, they noted that they were rare, and that the officers concerned were mostly those with little interviewing experience (INTEng8; 9; 25).
9 The word 'interrogation' was replaced by 'interview' to eliminate any negative connotation related to the use of force or coercion implied in the word 'interrogation'.
10 Solicitors Regulation Authority, Police Station Representatives Scheme, available from: <www.sra.org.uk/solicitors/accreditation/police-station-representatives-accreditation.page> (last accessed on 16 July 2019).
11 The prosecutor may decide to keep the suspect *incommunicado* during police detention to prevent the risk that the suspect would try to destroy the evidence. Article 62 CCP.
12 Hof van Discipline 8 August 1986, *Advocatenblad* 1986, 8716; Raad van Discipline Arnhem, 19 June 2006, *Advocatenblad* 2008, 2; Raad van Discipline Arnhem, 11 January 2010, *Advocatenblad* 2010, 16; Hof van Discipline 7 December 2010, *Advocatenblad* 2011, 7.
13 *Gedragsregels Advocatuur* (Rules of Conduct for the Bar), Nederlandse Orde van Advocaten, vastgesteld op 14 februari 2018.

6 The influence of contemporary criminal justice policies

1 Introduction

In 2001, Garland introduced the term 'culture of control' to characterise the profound changes in the cultural attitudes and responses to crime that had taken place in the preceding three decades across the USA and Western Europe (Garland, 2001). Garland defined these changes as the 'crime control complex': an inherently contradictory set of criminal justice policies, aiming to create an impression that the state is capable of controlling crime and the resulting societal risks. These policies are characterised by the 'indices of change', such as the decline of the rehabilitation ideal or the growing use of imprisonment. Garland attributed these changes to the societal developments of late modernity, which have resulted in an increased sense of insecurity and fear of crime. Whilst the social climate from which Garland's account emerged might have changed, as crime rates have been steadily decreasing (Loader, 2016), the legacy of the 'culture of control' arguably remains, and its effects on the administration of criminal justice are likely to be long-lasting.

Whilst the 'indices of change' proposed by Garland refer to penal policies in general, some are relevant to characterising the recent changes in the criminal justice process. Thus, the increased punitivism and emphasis on 'swift' responses to crime is likely to result in the administration of criminal justice increasingly embracing 'crime control' values, as opposed to 'due process' values (McConville and Wilson, 2002; Newman, 2013). The concepts of 'crime control' and 'due process' were introduced by Packer and they refer to the two competing value systems, or models, underlying the operation of the criminal process (Packer, 1968). The 'crime control' model values the effective detection and suppression of crime, and, as a result, maximising time and cost efficiency, and reducing possibilities to challenge procedural decisions (which causes delay). This model dictates that procedures must be uniform and standardised, and that suspects who are probably innocent should be identified early, whilst suspects who are probably guilty should be 'processed' as quickly as possible. Lengthy trials should be avoided, both because they are costly, and because they are considered less capable of producing reliable outcomes than administrative pre-trial procedures. The 'due process' model, in turn, prioritises the goal of avoiding the conviction of an innocent person at the expense of efficiency, by introducing 'bottlenecks' and 'obstacles' for prosecution at each procedural stage. Procedural rights of suspects are the main examples of such obstacles. The ideologies underlying the 'culture of control' resonate with the 'crime control' values because they prioritise a 'resolute', but 'cost-efficient' response to crime over ensuring individual rights and liberties (Jones, 1993; Raine and Wilson, 1993; Fionda, 2000). Managerialism, which refers to a style of governance based on numeric outputs, performance targets, cost efficiency and customer satisfaction, is another element of the 'culture of control' that has a significant impact on the criminal process (Raine and Wilson, 1993: 21). Managerialism focuses on reducing individual discretion of public officials, introducing standardised working processes and reducing 'inefficiencies' and 'bottlenecks' in systemic performance. Therefore, managerialism clearly reflects the values behind the 'crime control' model. In fact, it was argued that the managerialist approach conflicts with values such as the rule of law or justice (Jones, 1993; Freiberg, 2005).

This chapter examines the influences caused by contemporary criminal justice policies on the practical exercise of legal assistance at the investigative stage of the proceedings, as observed in the two examined jurisdictions. It begins by describing the impact of such policies on the English and Dutch systems of criminal adjudication, and on the role and position of criminal defence in general. The chapter then proceeds to a comparative analysis of the relevant themes, which emerged from the fieldwork, representing different types of consequences of recent criminal justice policies on the legal assistance at the investigative stage. Based on this analysis, it is concluded that these policies have had largely negative consequences on the practices of defence at the investigative stage, although they have also had some 'collateral' positive effects.

2 Contemporary criminal justice policies and the criminal process

England and Wales is a frontrunner in 'managerialism' in public administration, which sought to make public institutions more 'business-like' and '(cost)-efficient', introduced in the early 1980s and magnified in the late 1990s (McEwan, 2011). The move towards managerialism has coincided with the increasingly crime-control-orientated character of criminal justice policies, and the rise of populist discourse on criminal justice. Since the early 1990s, the British government has sought to be seen as 'tough on crime' (Newburn, 2007).[1] This resulted in, inter alia, the proliferation of criminal law-making: in 1997–2006, about 50 crime-oriented legislative acts were passed introducing 3.000 new criminal offences (Sanders et al., 2010: 29). The powers of police to investigate crime, including by administrative or preventative means, have been steadily increasing since the early 1990s. The relevant laws comprised early legislation, such as the CJPOA (introducing inferences from silence), or the Police Act 1997 (introducing wiretapping and search without a warrant), and an explosion of laws granting new powers to the police since the early 2000s (ibid.: 29). These laws, as noted by prominent policing scholar Robert Reiner, have 'remorselessly extended police powers' (2010: 220). Many protections originally given to suspects by PACE were abolished or reduced (ibid.: 221). Most recently, managerialist tendencies in English criminal justice were reflected in the efforts to 'optimise' the working processes in courts. Another relevant initiative was incentivising defendants to indicate their 'anticipated plea' as early as possible in exchange for a reduced sentence.[2]

Likewise, the Dutch criminal justice policies have become orientated towards the 'law and order' agenda since the mid-1980s (Downes and van Swaanigen, 2007: 32). The historic emphasis on due process and humane sentencing has been replaced by the politics of crime control (Pakes, 1996). This transformation became explicit in the 1985 government plan entitled 'The Society and Criminality', which has called for, inter alia, more streamlined, efficient and coordinated administration of the criminal process.[3] A recent Dutch reform informed by managerialism is the so-called 'ZSM policy' (ZSM stands for 'as soon, smart, selective, simple, together and society-oriented as possible') introduced in 2011. Its goal is to accelerate disposal of criminal cases with a prosecutorial penal order to be issued mostly before the end of police detention (Thomas et al., 2016: 20–24). More than half of all criminal cases – 109.000 out of 197.000 – registered by the Public Prosecutor's Office and about two-thirds of 'run-of-the-mill' offences are referred to ZSM.[4] Accelerated disposal is achieved by bringing together prosecutors and other relevant 'stakeholders', such as police or social services (lawyers not included), in one location. This enables direct exchange of information regarding so-called 'frequently occurring offences', considered evidentially 'simple' (Thomas et al., 2016: 20–21). Although the ZSM policy results in increased procedural efficiency, it was criticised for its failure to enable thorough fact-finding and to provide sufficient procedural guarantees to suspects, including sufficient time and opportunity to prepare a defence (Brouwer, 2015; Spronken, 2015; van Lent et al., 2016).

Currently, the Dutch 1926 CCP is being revised with the view of 'modernising' the criminal proceedings.[5] The review is heavily influenced by the managerialist discourse, reflected in the use of words like 'streamlining', 'penal chain (partners)', their 'performance' and 'throughput times'. The Concept Note states that increasing 'efficiency' is an important objective of the reform.[6] Efficiency should be achieved by 'decreasing administrative burdens', devising clearer procedures and placing (even) greater emphasis on pre-trial proceedings. Trials would become shorter and more 'efficient', and – as openly acknowledged – would decrease in importance. The revised CCP will encourage out-of-court settlements whenever possible. Questioning witnesses or conducting further investigations at the trial stage should become exceptional. All or most evidentiary and case management issues will be handled during the trial preparation hearings. As a result, 'the need to forestall hearings and refer cases back for further investigation will be radically reduced',[7] and the defence will be expected to 'make its investigation wishes known'[8] and to supply the list of trial witnesses in advance.

Against the background of crime control and managerialism, in both England and Wales and the Netherlands, 'austerity' has emerged as a driving force behind policy reforms across various areas, including criminal justice, following the 2008–2009 financial crisis. In the English context, the 'austerity' era commenced with the banking crisis in 2008. Significant budget cuts were performed in, among other areas, the criminal justice system (which had undergone unprecedented growth between 1997 and 2010). In England and Wales, the budgets of the Home Office and the Ministry of Justice fell by about 20% and 30%, respectively, between 2010 and 2015 (Roberts, 2015). The impact of these budget cuts was felt strongly across the criminal justice system, including the police (which reduced its workforce by 20% between 2010 and 2016), CPS, prison and probation services, as well as courts and legal aid (ibid.). Although the British government declared the end of 'austerity' in 2018, further cuts to the budget of the Ministry of Justice were announced until 2020.[9]

The Dutch government implemented austerity measures, consisting of tax increases and budget cuts, between 2011 and 2017. These cuts consisted mostly of reduced expenditures in the government sector, including the criminal justice system. In the Netherlands, cuts to the budgets of the police, courts and the Public Prosecution Service, however, were less drastic than in England and Wales. Thus, the savings on the National Police amounted to about 500M euro in total in 2011–2017, whilst its annual budget constituted of about 5.5B euro (van Zanten et al., 2017). The savings were achieved mostly by cutting overhead costs and reducing the number of administrative personnel. Legal aid, including in criminal cases, seemed to suffer the most from budgetary cuts. Thus, the projected savings on state-subsidised legal assistance in 2010–2015 totalled 100M euro (against the annual budget of 470M) (Combrink-Kuiters et al., 2011: 16–18). As a result, legal aid tariffs have been progressively decreasing (in real terms) since 2010.[10] Financial pressures were also felt across the criminal justice system for reasons other than decreasing budgets: for example, courts experienced decreasing caseloads (their budgets being formed based on the number of processed cases).[11] The Public Prosecution Service, in contrast, faced increasing workloads due to a growth in the number of out-of-court disposals. Following the end of 'austerity' politics in 2017, the budgets of law enforcement institutions were increased in response to allegations that they were unable to manage crime due to financial constraints. However, no plans were made to increase expenditures on legal aid. In fact, the Minister of Legal Protection had proposed further savings in 2018, but later withdrew the proposal.[12]

The increasing shift towards the pre-trial stages as the determinative point of the proceedings (and the decreasing significance of the trial) is, arguably, another consequence of contemporary criminal justice policies. As described earlier, within the 'crime control' model, which is endorsed by the said policies, trials are being replaced by administrative pre-trial processes, which are more predictable and less costly. Managerialism, in particular, with its emphasis on productivity, cost-efficiency and reducing delays, is conducive to the declining significance of the trial (McEwan, 2011). This is caused, on the one hand, by the increased use of out-of-court disposals, which are significantly cheaper, speedier and more controllable than (public) trials. Moreover, the importance of trials is reducing due to the growing use of pre-trial case management techniques (including for instance, the early selection of evidence to be reviewed at the trial); the increased reliance on hearsay and pre-trial statements; and, in the English context, due to the 'inference from silence' provisions, which force suspects to already determine their procedural position in the first police interview.

3 The impact on the role and position of defence lawyers

The effect of the developments described in the preceding section on the position of defence lawyers in the criminal process is likely to have been significant, if not transformative. The right to defence through legal assistance is a classic due process right designed, in Parker's terms, to create 'obstacles' for speedy convictions. Thus, reforms informed by 'crime control' values are likely to be in direct conflict with the right to defence through legal assistance. Essentially, the model informed by 'crime control' shifts the responsibility for opposing to the presumption of guilt to the defence party, whilst reducing the 'time and facilities' (including financial resources) available to the defence to prepare such an opposition. If measures are introduced to reduce time or increase 'efficiency' of the proceedings, for instance, by accelerating decision-making or skipping certain procedural steps, this is likely to result in fewer opportunities to examine or question the prosecution case. Moreover, where law enforcement authorities are granted increased powers to investigate crime subject to fewer procedural restrictions, it is more difficult for the defence to challenge the authorities' actions or obtain the exclusion of evidence (Cape and Spronken, 1998).

With the proliferation of 'summary' justice and the growing importance of the pre-trial proceedings, defence lawyers are increasingly expected to argue their 'case' in a procedural setting, which does not provide the same guarantees as the court hearing (Jackson, 2008; Jackson, 2016b: 1017). If evidence is presented and examined in a trial setting, the defence can challenge the evidence and the prosecution narrative, and make further inquiries if necessary. If, however, no thorough examination of the evidence occurs at the trial stage, the defence has little choice but to challenge or complement the prosecution 'case' at the pre-trial stages. This, however, is riddled with difficulties. As described in Chapters 3 and 4, both in the Netherlands and in England and Wales lawyers have fewer participatory rights during the pre-trial proceedings, and fewer opportunities to engage in independent fact-finding, or to obtain (timely) access to the prosecution's evidence. Imposing time limits on the various defence actions or motions further complicates the position of the defence. Thus, in the Netherlands, as mentioned in the preceding paragraph, the proposed 'modernised' CCP contains a provision according to which the defence should provide the names of witnesses in advance of the trial (a similar provision already exists in the UK). In England and Wales, as described in Chapter 4, the Criminal Procedure Rules establish time limits for the submission of various materials by the defence, such as preliminary information about the client's plea, the statement of the defence and the details of the defence's witnesses. These time limits are tight, and the sanctions for non-compliance are quite serious, including the possibility of 'inference' being drawn with regard to determining the defendant's guilt (CIPA 1996, Section 11).

In addition to confounding the procedural position of the defence, managerialist pressures result in numerous ethical dilemmas for defence lawyers (Cape, 2006; Smith, 2013). The requirement to cooperate with the effective administration of justice, reflected explicitly or implicitly in the lawyer's duty to court, is almost always in conflict with the lawyer's duty to the client to ensure the best possible defence. For instance, early disclosure obligations of the defence might conflict with the client's interests, because they may interfere with thorough defence preparation, precluding the defence from 'keeping its cards close to the chest' (once considered a perfectly legitimate adversarial tactic), or lead to the waiver of legal professional privilege. Various regulations and practices, which force the defence to determine its procedural position as early as possible to increase procedural efficiency, are especially problematic. Examples of such regulations and practices in England and Wales are: the 'inference from silence' provisions and the incentives to plead guilty early in the proceedings, and in the Netherlands: the wide application of (accelerated) out-of-court disposals. These provisions often lead to impossible dilemmas for defence lawyers, where they are called to determine whether admitting guilt early would be beneficial for their clients, on the basis of imperfect information received from the authorities (e.g. because no full disclosure has (yet) been given to the defence, or because no thorough evidence-gathering has been undertaken) and within very tight time limits (Johnston and Smith, 2017). Furthermore, managerialist legislation or practices provide additional incentives for early guilt admissions, such as guaranteed sentence reductions or reduced length of court proceedings, which lawyers need to consider when formulating their advice (and which creates heavier responsibilities vis-à-vis clients, who might lose these advantages if asserting innocence). Furthermore, in England and Wales, lawyers may be liable for negligence in case of failure to give 'appropriate' advice concerning early guilty pleas (ibid.: 211).

Finally, increased managerialism and crime control are likely to have had adverse effects on the practical exercise of criminal defence. The UK government, for instance, has been progressively cutting expenditures on criminal legal aid since the early 2000s (Smith and Cape, 2017). This has led to, inter alia, the introduction of fixed fees, including for police station work, instead of an hourly fee. As a result, lawyers have been incentivised to reduce the effort invested into their clients' cases (Tata and Stephen, 2007). Thus, one study suggested that the introduction of fixed fees led lawyers to spend less time with each client, and focus on fewer issues, when attending police stations (Kemp, 2012: 50–54). Furthermore, it was argued that recent reforms of legal aid fees created financial incentives for lawyers to advise suspects to plead guilty early (McConville and Marsh, 2014: 187). Another cost-saving measure adopted in England and Wales (but not in the Netherlands) was the marketisation of legal aid services, aimed at achieving 'economies of scale', or the delivery of legal aid services 'at the most economically advantageous price' (Ministry of Justice, 2013: 38). These initiatives resulted in a decreased number of (contracts for) legal aid providers (and thus a limited choice of a lawyer for suspects), and prioritisation of large-scale providers willing to take on more cases at a lower cost (ibid.: 48–53). The cumulative effect of the cost-cutting measures described earlier, it might be argued, is that criminal lawyers will increasingly prioritise their own financial (survival) interests over the concerns of providing better services to their clients (Tata, 2007; Newman, 2013; Smith, 2013).

Fewer lawyers might be available to provide criminal legal aid in the future. For example, there is some evidence that, following the savings implemented until 2014, Dutch lawyers were more likely to refuse legal aid cases.[13] Dutch lawyers specialising in legal aid and/or criminal law expressed concerns about their financial viability. In both jurisdictions, entering the criminal defence profession becomes both increasingly difficult (due to the lack of apprentice positions) and less attractive for young lawyers; as a result, the criminal defence profession is ageing (as demonstrated by English findings). The financial pressures are furthermore likely to adversely affect the morale of criminal defence lawyers (Smith, 2013). Sommerlad found, for instance, that 'New Public Management' legal aid policies and cost-cutting initiatives caused legal aid lawyers to become disenchanted with their role, due to the internal conflict between their commitment to social justice and the pressure to adopt more 'commercial' behaviour (Sommerlad and Sanderson, 2013; Sommerlad, 2001). This was echoed by Welsh, who argued that the changes in legal aid funding placed a strain on the English lawyers' professional self-image and ethical status (Welsh, 2017). Likewise, in the Netherlands, legal aid lawyers report a decrease in their income level, an increase in their working hours, and uncertainty about their financial future, which is likely to affect their morale and commitment to criminal legal aid.[14]

4 Managerialism, austerity and legal assistance at the investigative stage

Based on the discussion in the preceding section, it may be hypothesised that the contemporary policies of managerialism and crime control have led to decreased opportunities, space and resources available to defence lawyers to carry out their day-to-day tasks at this stage. The following sections examine the different types of consequences of contemporary criminal justice policies for the day-to-day practice of legal assistance at the investigative stage, as transpired from the fieldwork. These were: the penalisation of silence at the investigative stage; the increased lawyers' duty to cooperate with the administration of justice; the growing reluctance of courts to endorse arguments based on procedural breaches; the effects of the use of out-of-court disposals; the bureaucratisation of police custody; and the decreasing criminal legal aid fees.

4.1 The penalisation of silence at the investigative stage

The fact that remaining silent, or refusing to respond to questions, was (no longer) 'harmless' for suspects was a recurrent theme during the fieldwork. In the Netherlands, the encountered lawyers pointed to the possible negative consequences of remaining silent, such as the risk of longer police detention (see also Cleiren and Nijboer, 2011: 100). Because no legislation analogous to the English 'inferences from silence' provisions existed in the Netherlands, some Dutch lawyers considered it 'safe' to advise silence, as illustrated by the following quote:

> I think there are many advantages in remaining silent. You're not helping the police in their investigation, so when there's little evidence they have to send someone home, while if you give a statement and with that give them things to investigate, 'we should check this, follow up on that', then people will be detained longer than when they would keep their mouth shut.
> (INTNeth26)

Other lawyers, however, disagreed with this view, pointing out various disadvantages of remaining silent. One lawyer, for instance, remarked:

> What I do not do is always advise to remain silent, like many criminal lawyers do. You should also take into account that exercising the right to silence may have long[-term] negative consequences. Many lawyers do not realise it. For instance, nowadays your procedural behaviour has an influence on whether you are eligible for early release. So the consequences of remaining silence are far-reaching, and clients should be informed about this. I know this sounds like blackmailing on the side of the government, but this is the reality ...
> (INTNeth3)[15]

In cases involving juveniles, remaining silent in a police interview could preclude the application of an educational (non-criminal law) measure, the so-called HALT, or of an out-of-court disposal (article 77e CCP). In the words of one lawyer:

> With minors there are more considerations that play a role. At the moment I tell a minor to use his right to remain silent, this also means that I cut off alternative disposal possibilities. To be offered HALT means he probably has confessed. The same goes for an out-of-court disposal. So I know I cut those possibilities at the moment I advise him to use his right to remain silent.
> (INTNeth10)

Similarly, in cases involving adult suspects, at the time of the fieldwork, obtaining a confession was effectively a precondition for an out-of-court disposal via the so-called 'ZSM' route. In one of the sites, the standing practice of referring cases to ZSM was 'when a suspect made a statement, and no further investigation was considered necessary': which effectively meant that the suspect had confessed, and therefore no additional evidence was needed. Furthermore, the instruction issued by the regional Public Prosecutor's Office describing the local ZSM procedure stated that police officers had to ascertain that the suspect had confessed (FNNeth11.04.2012).

In addition, some encountered Dutch lawyers also noted that although the case law precludes the use of a suspect's silence in police interviews as evidence (HR 27 June 1972, ECLI:NL:HR:1972:AB6156, *NJ* 1972/492), in practice, judges might take into account the failure to provide an early explanation to the suspect's detriment, for instance, by doubting the truthfulness of the account given later. This may be demonstrated by the following interview excerpt:

> In theory, remaining silent shouldn't have any disadvantages, but it can be used against someone when they are in front of the judge. If a situation calls for explanation, then it does. And the police do use that as a way to try to get a client to give a statement.
>
> (INTNeth4)

Another lawyer concurred:

> If there's a self-defence story, then the disadvantage is if your client remained silent in the beginning, that a judge would ask 'why are you only saying this now?' So that can also be a disadvantage.
>
> (INTNeth13)

Indeed, in the Netherlands, recent case law of the Supreme Court allows drawing an inference from a suspect's silence, or failure to respond to certain questions, where the situation calls for an explanation, and where other incriminating evidence exists (HR 3 June 1997, ECLI:NL:HR:1997:ZD0733, *NJ* 1997/584; HR 16 September 2014, ECLI:NL:HR:2014:2764, *NJ* 2014/246). In such situations, a suspect's silence may, for example, reinforce other evidence (HR 14 September 1992, ECLI:NL:HR:1992:AC3716, *NJ* 1993/54; HR 15 June 2004, ECLI:NL:HR:2004: AO9639, *NJ* 2004/464; HR 5 June 2012, ECLI:NL:HR:2012:BW7372, *NJ* 2012/369). Thus, where a suspect was positively identified by eyewitnesses, and could not explain why they possessed a bus ticket validated around the time of the criminal offence, silence in the interview could be used to reinforce the identification results (HR 3 June 1997, ECLI:NL:HR:1997:ZD0733, *NJ* 1997/584). The failure to provide an alternative explanation of the content of taped conversations, interpreted by the police as incriminating, could be used to prove that the police's interpretation was correct (HR 18 May 1999, ECLI:NL:PHR:1999:ZD1332, NJ 2000/104). Furthermore, where suspects gave partial, incorrect (compared to other evidence) or contradictory responses to police questions, this could be interpreted by the court as 'knowingly lying statements' (HR 12 November 1974,

NJ 1975/41). Consequently, the fact that suspects have lied could be used for conviction, if there was corroborating evidence from another independent source to confirm that their intention was to evade punishment (Stevens, 2005: 64; HR 3 July 2012, ECLI:NL:HR:2012:BW9968, *NJ* 2012/466; recently confirmed in HR 20 February 2018, ECLI:NL:HR:2018:228).

Similar trends with regard to the 'penalisation' of silence were observed in England and Wales. In England and Wales, however, the legal discourse (and the relevant professional practice) on 'adverse inferences' and the right to silence, and their implications for legal advice were significantly more advanced than in the Netherlands (see also Chapter 4). Research in England and Wales demonstrated that following the enactment of the CJPOA, fewer suspects remained silent in police interviews (Phillips and Brown, 1998). It was suggested that this was mainly because lawyers advised suspects to remain silent less often (Bucke and Brown, 1997: 32–33). A recently published study of Hannah Quirk (based on interviews conducted in 1999) examined the consequences of the CJPOA provisions, particularly on the police station legal advice (Quirk, 2017). Quirk concluded that custodial legal advice, and in particular the lawyer–client relationship at the investigative stage, suffered the most from the 'inference from silence' provisions. She argued that lawyers yielded to the expectation that silence would be advised only in exceptional circumstances to preserve good working relationships with the police. Moreover, whilst legal representatives could previously use silence as a bargaining tool, for instance to obtain disclosure from the police, advising silence has become tremendously risky following the introduction of the CJPOA.

The conclusions of this study corroborate the findings described earlier. Thus, the encountered English lawyers perceived advice to remain silent not as given by 'default', but only in a limited set of circumstances. Whether by coincidence or not, within this study, lawyers advised clients to remain fully silent only in about one-sixth of the observed cases. It is highly probable that, as the result of the CJPOA and its application by courts, English lawyers began to perceive the advice to remain silent as inherently risky. Thus, one interviewed advisor said in response to how she approaches advising clients to remain silent:

> Uhm, cautiously, because I think more and more in trials the adverse inference is really picked up by jurors. And when I'm doing a trial, I don't like to see a no-comment interview. I think it's so damaging.
>
> (INTEng1)

Another interviewed solicitor spoke explicitly about the implications of the law on adverse inferences on legal advice:

> Well, I think the erosion of the protection of no comment by the adverse inferences makes my job more difficult, because 20 years ago you could just say no comment and you wouldn't have to worry about any consequences arising from that other than people's possible common sense. So the

magistrates or the Crown Court jury could have, in their own minds, thought that by this defendant making no comment they have something to hide, but they weren't being specifically told from a legal point of view that that could be used against someone. But now obviously the situation is that the magistrate or the jury would feel obliged to the repercussions, so this is obviously more significant now than it was 20 years ago.

(INTEng10)

Another interviewee, a senior solicitor, commented on the actions of another solicitor (from whom he had taken over an attempted murder case). This solicitor had advised his client, who had put forward an alibi defence, to remain silent. The interviewee perceived this as a serious professional mistake:

I had one this morning, an attempted murder. The client was transferred to us. He was advised to go no comment in the police station, but he prepared a statement giving an alibi and the solicitor said, 'No, I'm not going to hand that in now. Leave it until your trial.' Well, how stupid!

(INTEng13)

Not all interviewed English lawyers, however, agreed that the law on adverse inferences affected their approach to advising clients at police stations. Some said that in their perception, their advice was driven by the considerations of the amount and strength of evidence, and not per se the concern about the inferences from silence (INTEng13,15,5). However, it is likely that these lawyers still took the risk of adverse inferences into account. Thus, before the enactment of the CJPOA, suspects could be advised to remain silent without the risk that silence would become a formal 'issue' in court, even where there was other evidence against them. Following the CJPOA, the 'standard' approach to legal advice appears to be: if there is (some) evidence calling for explanation, an account should be given already during the first interview. In other words, the English lawyers embraced the idea that the CJPOA created a 'normative expectation' that suspects should provide an account at the earliest opportunity (Leng, 2001: 246).

The statistical probability that an 'adverse inference' from a suspect's silence drawn by the court would influence the case outcome was very low. As one lawyer described it:

In the majority of cases, it never becomes part of anything, either because the suspect is not charged or either because it's a guilty plea anyway, so it doesn't matter. It's only in the rare cases that get through to trial where you haven't said anything ... I think in the Crown Court it becomes even less of a thing. But yes, the jury will be directed on it by the judge. Of course they will. But it depends on the case. Sometimes it's really important. Sometimes it depends on the rest of the evidence. The other evidence might be really strong, in which case saying nothing in the interview is hardly important. The evidence might be terrible, but there might be great defence witnesses who really contradict everything. Again, whether you said anything in the interview is hardly going to determine the result.

(INTEng15)

Despite this, the encountered English lawyers still refrained from advising silence in most cases. This finding seems to support Quirk's argument that lawyers were in part motivated by the desire to maintain good working relationships with the police (see also Chapters 4 and 7). The danger of the client complaining about lawyer's advice, if an inference is drawn from silence during a police interview, also appeared to play a role. As the lawyer quoted earlier added:

> If my client has a genuine defence and they can prove that he was involved, at some stage I'm either going to get him to talk or I'll prepare a statement for him to get his defence in from the start. That's the way I do it. Some people say, 'Why say anything ever?' But I don't buy that. Because if it goes wrong ... if we don't let them give a defence that they want to use, they're going to blame you for that. Won't they?

The option of submitting a 'prepared statement' (described in Chapter 4) was commonly chosen by English lawyers as an alternative to advising silence, as it was believed that a 'prepared statement' could counter the risk of inferences. Yet, the interviewed lawyers held differing views about prepared statements. Although the majority considered them as a useful tool to 'control' their client's account, others believed that prepared statements were a disguised form of remaining silent. One interviewed lawyer, for instance, said that she used prepared statements with caution, because she believed that the jury might consider them inherently suspicious:

> Again I think, 'how would I feel if I was a juror?' I personally would think 'what are you hiding behind that prepared statement?' I think sometimes if somebody comes over very well in interview or answers freely, even if they can't remember, I think it's more natural than a prepared statement for a juror.

(INTEng1)

Another lawyer concurred, saying that in his view, prepared statements often do not prevent adverse inferences[16] (but that they may be used as a tool to negotiate more disclosure):

> I don't really like prepared statements ... Because they don't stop inferences being drawn ... I mean, it's not a guarantee ... I use them, but I don't necessarily like using them, but I use them if I think that we're going to have to come back and do a second interview when more information has come out, but we need to get down a denial ... I actually use them in the more

complicated cases, on the basis that we haven't had sufficient disclosure for me to advise, however my client does say that he has not done the crime for which he's been arrested.

(INTEng2)

Another challenge in the use of prepared statements was determining what information it should contain. A 'prepared statement' was unlikely to prevent adverse inferences, if it failed to mention certain facts which the defence would rely on at the trial. Therefore, a very short prepared statement containing a denial of guilt or responsibility could be insufficient to counter the risk of inferences (*R. v. Lewis* [2003] EWCA Crim 223). A more detailed statement, however, could lead to disclosure of information potentially damaging for the client, such as admissions of other, or lesser, offences, or information that might become self-incriminating in the light of the other evidence (FNEng16.04.2013).

4.2 Lawyers' duties to cooperate with the administration of justice

At the time of the fieldwork, only English, and not Dutch, lawyers had the duty to cooperate with the administration of justice (although, as mentioned earlier in the chapter, certain lawyers' duties to cooperate with the speedy case processing were going to be introduced in the Netherlands by the new CCP). In England and Wales, this duty was reflected in the professional obligation to tell and endorse the truth, and to inform the court about any errors of fact (see Chapter 4). This rule of professional conduct has no equivalent in the Netherlands.

As a result, English lawyers face an ethical conflict where a client, knowingly to them, wishes to deceive or mislead the police, and in such cases they must withdraw from the case. These rules of conduct have affected the provision of legal advice at the investigative stage in several ways. First, it appeared that (some) encountered English lawyers felt constrained to press their clients for the 'whole truth' when taking client disclosure (FNEng12.01.2012; INTEng20,15). This norm seemed to create certain ambiguity in the English lawyers' position with respect to questioning clients. On the one hand, the lawyer should be interested in obtaining an account that is as detailed (and, presumably, truthful) from their client as possible, in order to provide realistic advice (Cape, 2017: 157–160). On the other hand, lawyers might wish to limit their clients' admissions to them, because if the client would not want to make corresponding admissions to the police or in court, this might cause lawyers to withdraw (unless the client remains silent throughout the entire proceedings). As one lawyer put it:

When I take disclosure from the client, see what he's got to say about the allegation, clearly I don't look initially for admissions from them, because that puts me in a position of perhaps conflict on some occasions.

(INTEng13)

Influence of criminal justice policies 131

Navigating this conflict was challenging for the observed lawyers. In one case, for example, involving a theft allegation, the lawyer first encouraged the suspect to be open in her disclosure by saying: 'the more truth you tell me the better the chances you've got later on'. He had not, however, informed her about the above-mentioned ethical rule, possibly fearing that this would confuse the client, who had no prior experience with the criminal justice system. As a result, she made admissions to the lawyer, but seemingly wished to deny the allegations in the interrogation: which, as the lawyer explained, 'was not possible anymore', because she had already confessed to him (FNEng17.01.2012).[17]

On the other hand, explaining to the client what he should or should not tell his lawyer in view of the above-mentioned ethical rule, could be equally challenging, as demonstrated by the following quote:

> I tell my clients very gently, and it gets difficult at this stage because I'm saying to them, really, without trying to spell it out, 'If you tell me that you've done it, then you've done it. I can't believe two things at one time.' All police station advisers have got that issue. We've got ethics. We've got a professional code that we can't represent someone as innocent who's told us that they're guilty. So very gently, you've got to subtly explain that to them. That's with varying degrees of difficulty from client to client.
>
> (INTEng12)

It may be speculated that if the lawyer tells the client that they 'can't represent them if they say something to them (the lawyer), but later denies it to the police', this would discourage some suspects – and not necessarily the 'guilty' ones (as people may wish to conceal the truth from the authorities for reasons other than being guilty of the suspected offence) – to disclose certain information to their lawyers. As demonstrated by the examples earlier, the explanations of what they should and should not disclose to the lawyer may be too confusing for suspects, especially for those who have no experience with the criminal justice system. It might also create an impression that the lawyer does not wish to 'hear them out'. Interestingly, though, the interviewed English lawyers did not express a concern that the above-mentioned ethical rules compromise their effectiveness. On the contrary, the lawyers who were asked this question characterised it as a 'safeguard' for the client (as well as for the lawyer). In the words of one lawyer:

> I think it protects people a bit more and it just gives us a bit more guidance on what to do. I think it's quite helpful sometimes because you're not misleading someone that you shouldn't mislead.
>
> (INTEng9)

It is plausible to suggest that the encountered lawyers appeared to willingly endorse the rules in question, in part because they helped them to avoid the moral dilemma of defending someone who they knew for certain to be guilty, but who wished to deny the allegations (INTEng14). Additionally, these rules helped lawyers to avoid being suspected of 'fabricating lies' on the suspect's behalf. In the words of one interviewed lawyer:

> And so there, I would be then complicit, in my opinion, professionally embarrassed to sit there and let them lie. If they then start saying they haven't, again, I'd have to stop the interview and walk out. And say, you either say no comment or you admit it. Otherwise I'm walking out and that's the way it's going to be. And you make a bloody record of it, why you've done it. So you've always got a record of it.'
>
> (INTEng16)

4.3 Courts' attitudes to defence arguments

Both the Dutch and English lawyers believed that courts were increasingly reluctant to grant procedural remedies, or generally to endorse the defence arguments where these arguments concerned violations of procedural rules, including at the investigative stage. Thus, one Dutch lawyer responded to the question about whether he ever raises arguments about procedural violations at the investigative stage in court:

> Sure, sure. But there's no point nowadays, is there? I'm perhaps a bit cynical. There has been some jurisprudence by the Supreme Court which says that, in short, it doesn't really matter anymore whether procedures are violated unless the prosecutor's screwed up awfully, then it can still make a difference but generally that has become very difficult. It is almost impossible to obtain stay of prosecution, then something must have gone really wrong ... And a reduction of sentence is also difficult to accomplish. Exclusion of evidence, hardly ever.
>
> (INTNeth22)

The same lawyer went on to say that, as the result of these tendencies, he 'has become more cautious with ridiculous defences that were used more easily before', and only raised those issues, which could 'touch directly upon the reliability or admissibility of evidence'. In this lawyer's words:

> See, if someone's detention is prolonged a bit too late, that doesn't really matter anymore nowadays. It's stamped and they move on to the next. It sounds a bit cynical but ... I do get the impression that that's where it's going and that it's becoming increasingly difficult for the defence to accomplish something.
>
> (INTNeth22)

Other interviewed Dutch lawyers agreed with this lawyer's opinion, stating that, in their view, the only procedural argument (with regard to violations committed at the investigative stage) which was likely to result in a remedy was an argument concerning the denial of the right to a lawyer. As one lawyer put it:

> But concerning other rights – that, for example, the right to call a lawyer, or the right to receive visits – if you try to argue that these rights were violated, you would not achieve much in court. I do not think that the Supreme Court will accept these arguments either.
>
> (INTNeth2)

In the Netherlands, arguments about procedural violations allegedly occurring at the police detention stage must be raised at the moment of the suspect's presentation before the examining magistrate. However, the only remedy available to the magistrate is declaring the detention unlawful and ordering the suspect's release, unless the suspect is immediately placed in pre-trial detention.[18] Such a remedy is used conservatively,[19] as also demonstrated by the following quote:

> Yes, I would say that court remedies are not effective. An examining magistrate only looks at whether the arrest was legal and whether there are grounds for pre-trial detention. There have been many issues which I thought should have been raised with the examining magistrate, but the magistrate did not think in that way. Of course, you can add that this or that went wrong, but it has to be something very serious, perhaps an intentional denial of a right.
>
> (INTNeth1)

Other lawyers, likewise, said that issues such as, for instance, breaches of detention time limits, were unlikely to result in declaring the detention unlawful, unless it caused a lengthy overstay in custody. One lawyer, for example, noted that he only came across one case in his career when the detention was declared unlawful due to the breach of statutory terms, and this was where the suspect was brought to the examining magistrate after five days of custody (the statutory maximum being three days and 15 hours) (INTNeth7).[20]

As mentioned in Chapter 3, concerns were expressed in the Dutch literature about excessive workloads of examining magistrates. According to the interviewed Dutch lawyers, indeed, the magistrates' busyness prevented them from carefully considering defence arguments, and caused them to adopt a 'rubber stamp' approach, in particular, to the prosecutors' requests for the prolongation of detention. In the words of one lawyer:

> And I think this has to do with the fact that the examining magistrate does not have time to study the case file in detail. He gets to see the case file just like the lawyer, 30 minutes before the hearing, and then he gets several of them. So my view is that most examining magistrates choose for a safe decision over a risky decision – they say, let the suspect stay in detention for another 14 days, and then a panel of judges will look into the case

more carefully. I think that an examining magistrate would often react to a motion about procedural violations – yes, they have happened, but there are grounds to keep the suspect in pre-trial detention.

(INTNeth2)

Another lawyer concurred:

The judiciary ... is also under pressure. I think in [site B] we have good examining magistrates, but you do see ... especially in standard cases, probably also because of the budget cuts, mistakes are often being made.

(INTNeth5)

Similar concerns about the courts' attitudes to defence arguments concerning alleged procedural violations at the investigative stage were raised by the English lawyers. In England and Wales, unlike in the Netherlands, these kinds of violations had to be raised at the trial stage (Sanders et al., 2010: 187).[21] The conditions for affording a remedy were defined by PACE. Depending on the nature of the violation, the applicable remedy would be a stay of proceedings as abuse of process, or exclusion of evidence (PACE, sections 76 and 78). Therefore, in order to obtain a remedy following a procedural violation at the investigative stage, such a violation should normally have a bearing on the evidence obtained. Furthermore, the violation should be so serious that the obtained evidence should be considered unreliable, elicited under oppression (in case of confession), or admitting such evidence should be considered to have an adverse effect on the fairness of the proceedings. In the English lawyers' view (supported by case law), only rather serious procedural violations could withstand this test,[22] particularly because they were considered jointly with the merits. In the words of one English lawyer:

[T]here has to be a really, really serious fundamental breach of the police power to get a case thrown out. What they do is to see if that breach has an effect on the proceedings, which would render it unfair to the suspect. And so ... going to trial will just take ages, just cough it and we're probably done with it by now ... If the evidence is strong and your client subsequently coughs it, what will the court do? If it did happen, it's bad tactics by the police but there's nothing to suggest that what your client did in that interview is unreliable. That's what it has to be. Unreliable. Not obtained in a bit of a dodgy way. Unreliable.

(INTEng6)[23]

Another lawyer responded as follows to the question about whether courts were likely to pick up on issues like not properly 'cautioning' the clients (meaning the right to silence caution):

Magistrates wouldn't necessarily pick up on it ... We would raise it as an issue, some judges are vocal and will express an opinion ... The more vocal ones would say are you really suggesting that is an issue and why they think this is not relevant, is it really going to affect the case or not? Is a jury going to grasp the intricacies of this or not? As well, probably not. In practice by the time a case goes to court it doesn't really affect a great deal at the end of the day. A judge will tell you: well, your client knows what happened on the day. There is so much more going on in the court case to do with forensic fact etc., rather than anything to do with what occurred in the interview in terms of how they provided a caution.

(INTEng22)

4.4 Out-of-court disposals and the role of defence lawyers

Early out-of-court disposals have now become an entrenched feature of both the Dutch and the English criminal process: in the Netherlands more than half of all criminal cases are referred for such disposal (Section 2); and in England and Wales about 20% of cases are terminated in this way (Chapter 4). In the Netherlands, initially no consideration was given to accommodating legal assistance within the ZSM procedures. Lawyers were unable to comment on the accusation, evidence and the sanction, or to even discuss these with the client (Spronken, 2012; Franken, 2013; van den Brûle, 2014). Their involvement usually ended with speaking to suspects once shortly after arrest, before they had been referred to the ZSM procedure (van der Meij, 2014). In response to criticism, attempts were made to improve lawyers' participation within ZSM proceedings.

Thus, in late 2014/early 2015, the so-called 'legal assistance pilot project' operated in four ZSM locations.[24] In this pilot, all adult suspects, except those accused of very minor offences, were offered a consultation with a lawyer before the first interrogation. They were then offered a second consultation, if their case was referred to disposal via the ZSM procedure at the police station. Lawyers could also consult the dossier before the second consultation (van der Meij and Hartjes, 2015: 39). In addition, they had some, although limited, possibilities to influence decisions taken within the ZSM proceedings (Thomas et al., 2016: 104). The target ZSM 'throughput times' were increased to accommodate the need for the provision of legal assistance (ibid.: 106–108).

Additionally, in two other regions, lawyers were permanently located at police stations.[25] Lawyers from one of these regions were interviewed for this study. These lawyers were more involved with the ZSM procedure than lawyers in other locations (INTNeth6, 16, 24). They were systematically informed about the planned outcome and could discuss it with clients. They were also given details regarding the accusation and evidence, usually by the prosecutor. Although this was only a verbal summary (prosecutors, likewise, relied on verbal police accounts), it differed from the common practice of giving no information at all. Lawyers could also engage in decision-making regarding case outcomes, although indirectly. This was done mostly by providing contextual information to the prosecutor about the client's social situation (see also Thomas et al., 2016: 105). As one lawyer described it:

> In ZSM ... there is a lot of negotiating. But that is not how the prosecutor sees it, he says 'there is no negotiating because we have guidelines'. But negotiating you should see that you as a lawyer have some information that the police do not have. So that means you can say 'my client has many debts so he cannot pay a fine, but community service might be an alternative' ... Then he will accept that. Or the other way around: 'he is too busy to do community service, but he has enough money to pay a fine'. So you actually just give an alternative.
>
> (INTNeth16)

Overall, however, Dutch lawyers' participation in the ZSM procedures was problematic, despite the improved access in certain regions. One difficulty was that the ZSM decision-making processes were fluid and informal, which created obstacles for lawyers, such as the need to contact several departments to obtain information, but also the risk of being informed with delay. In the words of one lawyer:

> Sometimes it is difficult for us to know if it is a ZSM case. I have the telephone numbers of [the] ZSM department and I have the number form the 'weekdienst' for the 'normal' client [another department within the Public Prosecutor's Office]. And if I then send the request to get the case files, then I will call right away with the ZSM department or with the 'weekdienst'. The ZSM department says 'We don't know about this case, try the "weekdienst"', and the 'weekdienst' says 'We don't know about this case, try the ZSM department.' 'We just did but they have sent us to you.' 'Oh okay let us have a look.' And then we are called back by the ZSM department and they say 'Do you still need the case files now, because actually the case will be referred to court?'
>
> (INTNeth17)

The lack of access to case-related information within the ZSM procedures, however, was seen at the greatest obstacle by lawyers. In the words of one lawyer:

> I think the biggest problem is obtaining access to the case files ... I also don't want to hear 'ask someone else', or ask the police, or that your request is being processed. No, I want the case files now. The client will be interrogated now, I want the case files ... But police and prosecutors always say 'but this is too much time and labour' ... The record of arrest, you have it on paper right, so you can give that right away, can't you. Nope, it takes two days, very annoying.
>
> (INTNeth15)

Given the fast-paced nature of the ZSM proceedings, ensuring meaningful lawyers' participation in the decision-making process during ZSM would appear problematic. This could be caused by a combination of factors, including the time pressures on the police and prosecutors; the fact that lawyers are not physically present in most ZSM locations; and the lack of practice of recording relevant information in writing. The pressure on the prosecutors to take a decision speedily may cause them to rely on the opinions and conclusions presented by the police, and be reluctant to seek further information (as requested by the defence) (van Lent et al., 2016). This finding was echoed in the Dutch interviews. In the words of one lawyer:

> Decisions are being made within ZSM while you as a lawyer think 'but ... those witnesses have to be heard, and that has to be investigated, and there are video recordings!' But I get the impression that nobody cares about that. Just get it over with fast ... The defence has no say in it. And that won't change, because a lawyer will just slow things down, make it unnecessarily complicated.
>
> (INTNeth2)

The challenges of participating in the ZSM proceedings should also be seen in the context of fixed fee arrangements for police station assistance. At the time of the fieldwork, for instance, cases referred to ZSM were treated as all other cases and lawyers were paid the same fee (75 EUR for the first consultation, and another 75 EUR for the second visit, if detention was prolonged). If this payment system remains unreformed, lawyers would not be willing to invest more effort into cases dealt with by an out-of-court disposal (INTNeth3, 13). It is difficult to imagine, for instance, that (all) lawyers would be prepared to follow up with the relevant officers, study the case file, suggest new lines of inquiry and negotiate the case outcome with the prosecutor – all for the same fee – as these tasks are additional to what lawyers habitually do during their police station visits.

In England and Wales, in contrast to the Netherlands, the encountered lawyers did not seem to experience major problems with obtaining access to information, or with participating in out-of-court settlement decisions. However, as described in Chapter 4, a tendency was observed among English lawyers to be 'complicit' with the police in persuading suspects to accept a caution (and therefore admitting an impugned crime). As described by one lawyer:

> Quite often the police say, 'Look, he's not got any previous convictions. It's his first offence. I've spoken to my inspector. He said, "Look if he makes a full frank admission, we'll caution him."' You then go into the interview, you advise your client, 'Look it's the first offence. You accept responsibility. They say if you make a full and frank admission, you'll be cautioned. Let's do that.'
>
> (IntEng8)

138 *Influence of criminal justice policies*

Yet, in doing so, as the cases described in Chapter 4 demonstrate, lawyers did not always have all the relevant information to assess the strength of the evidence, and did not always fully inform suspects about the consequences of accepting the caution. The relevant Ministry of Justice Guidance (applicable to the police) states that an offer of caution may not be used to secure admission of a crime, and that a caution may only be offered after the suspect has been fully informed about the evidence.[26] This means that using the lawyer as a 'vehicle' for securing the acceptance of the caution, and therefore, an admission by the suspect, amounts to illegal police practice. Police should also not implicitly or explicitly offer a caution, or suggest that a caution is being considered (directly to the suspect or via the lawyer) before the suspect has been interviewed, because this might pressurise the latter into admitting (Cape, 2017: 379).

4.5 *The bureaucratisation of the investigative stage*

Several English lawyers observed that the bureaucratisation, or 'formalisation', of police custody procedures made it more difficult for them to influence the decision-making at the investigative stage than, for instance, some 10 or 15 years ago. These were not the reforms brought about by PACE (which were viewed as positive), but changes of a more managerialist nature, such as the hierarchisation of decision-making and diminishing discretion (especially at mid-level, e.g. the level of custody officers), 'streamlining' procedures, proliferation of instructions and guidelines, and securitisation of custody areas, among others (Rowe, 2007; Heslop, 2011). (Another change discussed later in this section, and viewed by the encountered English lawyers as 'bureaucratic', is the transfer of certain decision-making powers from the police to the CPS.)

One lawyer described the implications of 'formalisation' in the following way:

> You're not there so much now when the decisions are being made in the backrooms ... Decisions to charge, decisions to bail, decisions even to interview ... You feel now that you will make your representations and decisions are made behind closed doors ... Now there is less of that communication line I think between solicitors and the police. It is a lot more segregated.
>
> (INTEng1)

When asked about the possible reasons for these changes, the lawyer responded:

> I think probably it has more to do with the structure of the police really. I think it's just become a lot more formal and systems are in place now, so solicitors come into the waiting room and you don't really get to see what's happening ... When there was a lot less separation I think you could really speak to a sergeant and sit down with them and say, you know, I really feel strongly about this case, sergeant, because ... So yeah, you feel that there's a lot of bureaucratic barriers in between.

Another lawyer attributed these changes to the reduced discretion of individual police officers (primarily, custody officers):

> I mean there's also an element of the custody sergeants generally tending to be a bit more by the book now. So they tend not to listen to submissions and representations as much as they did 10, 15 years ago. You know, 10, 15 years ago you ... could say to them 'look, he's got a sister in [town X]. He will go there tonight. He will not come back to this area except to see his solicitors. No contact, you know.' And quite often they would say, 'yeah, fair enough.' ... You used to be able to do it and now, not so well ... The guidelines are more rigid.
>
> (INTEng4)

Interestingly, one Dutch lawyer made a similar observation with regard to changes that, in his view, took place in the Netherlands:

> On the other hand, negotiating for suspect's release, this has become more difficult recently. Before I could just tell an assistant prosecutor [AP] – look, the suspicion is very weak, if this is all that you have against my client. Now if I say this, most APs respond: 'We will see ...' So yes, the room for negotiation has become more limited now. This is not because of Salduz, but already several years, 10 years at least ...
>
> (INTNeth30)

Similar to the English lawyer quoted earlier, he went on to explain these developments by the growing formalisation of the procedures and the increased hierarchy in the decision-making:

> Everything now is more formalised. Police just go through the prescribed steps ... And if I say that it is a weak case, they say that it is for the duty prosecutor to decide whether it is a weak or strong case. And sometimes there is a case, which is about nothing, a café fight, and the suspect has a family at home, and he needs to go to work – and I call the duty prosecutor to tell all this, and he responds that he can do nothing about it. The court will decide.

A similar trend towards reshuffling the decision-making powers at the investigative stage in favour of higher authorities, particularly the CPS, was extensively discussed in the English interviews. In England and Wales, in recent years, the CPS was given more powers with regard to police investigations, and in particular charging decisions and out-of-court disposals (see Chapter 4). Some of these powers were, in effect, taken away from the police, and specifically custody officers. The impetus for this was the concern that custody officers were not sufficiently independent from the police, and therefore tended to overcharge, and failed to vet out evidentially weak cases (Sanders et al., 2010: 379). It was hoped that charging decisions in particular would become more objective if taken by an 'independent' institution (the CPS) on the basis of written files (ibid.: 380). The CPS itself, however, was criticised for its informational dependency on the police, and the lack of capacity to cope with the new responsibilities (Belloni and Hodgson, 2000: 120).[27]

All interviewed English lawyers said that the redistribution of charging powers towards the CPS had a negative impact on their work. The most obvious concern was that the CPS lawyers (based in a different location) were less accessible to lawyers than to custody officers. In the words of one lawyer:

> Because now a lot of the decisions are taken away from the sergeant to the CPS, that representation stage seems to have gone away from us a little bit, because we don't get an opportunity of speaking to the CPS. Subsequently the sergeant says, 'Well, it's no good telling me. I'm not he one making the decision anymore.' So that is one avenue we have, I think, lost in the last five years.
>
> (INTEng16)

Lawyers also said that charging decisions issued by the CPS took weeks or months, in part because further investigation was often requested, but also due to capacity issues. In the words of one lawyer:

> Another big change is that fewer are charged at the police station. Now it's the CPS that decides ... That builds in a substantial delay, because sometimes it's not just 'go ahead and charge', it's 'you need to speak to this witness first' etc. So, pre-charge, it has been elongated tremendously, by weeks and months, as against the same case years ago ...
>
> (INTEng27)

While waiting for the CPS charge, suspects were usually bailed, and requested to periodically report to the police station ('answer bail'). The obligation to answer bail could be onerous for suspects, and the failure to answer bail was in itself, a serious criminal offence (INTENg5). Another lawyer mentioned that delays in the charging decision, and the lengthy police bail, 'do not keep people focused on their case' and 'cause frustration' (INTEng2). He gave an example of a case where one of his clients was awaiting a charging decision for ten months in a relatively simple case, although he had confessed in the interview.

In the lawyers' view, the fact that certain charging decisions were now taken by the CPS cost them additional time because of, inter alia, the need to follow up on these decisions. As one lawyer said in an interview:

> When you go to the CPS, it can be a matter of three, four hours, or three or four weeks, et cetera ... You normally have to make phone calls after you've left the police station and then later. It takes much more time.
>
> (INTEng20)

Another difficulty was that lawyers no longer had an opportunity to discuss the relevant decisions in person, but instead had to make written submissions to the CPS, and thus no real exchange of views was possible. In the words of one lawyer:

> When a custody sergeant is making that decision you could go and have a chat with the custody sergeant and put your points across. There is now no opportunity for that. They did bring that up in a form that can be faxed off with the police paperwork, but you try and write down exactly what you'll be saying to the custody sergeant and it is quite impossible at times because it doesn't mean just talking out the custody sergeant, but it means discussing certain elements of the case and now because it goes to the CPS, you've got no opportunity to go to the CPS lawyer who's looking at the case to say what is this and what went wrong.
>
> (INTEng21)

4.6 *Fixed fees and legal assistance at the investigative stage*

A prominent theme, which emerged particularly from the Dutch but also from the English fieldwork, was the discrepancy between the encountered lawyers' views of an (aspirational) 'ideal' model of legal representation at the investigative stage and their perceptions of the (pragmatic) 'everyday reality' of police station legal assistance. On the one hand, lawyers believed that their involvement at the early stages potentially results in important benefits for the clients and the justice system. Especially the English lawyers were very articulate about the added value of their participation, as demonstrated by the following quotes:

> I think the impact of being a lawyer at the police station is so significant. You can make a real difference to a case. And I often get feedback from barristers who say, not to me, I think to everybody, that the advice given at the police station made a real difference to this case down the road.
>
> (INTEng1)

> The difference it makes, I think, it is an integral part to maintaining the balance of our justice system. A Western democratic justice system where you are innocent until proven guilty ... So really what you're doing is maintaining a standard of evidence in the police station. So they've got to do it properly because if they don't do it properly then the prosecution won't stand up. So actually we're just as important to the police as you might be to the client. You're there to help the client, first and foremost. Let's not forget.
>
> (INTEng10)

Most interviewed Dutch lawyers, likewise, spoke about their presence at police stations as potentially beneficial for clients and the legal system overall:

> I see legal assistance at police stations as social advocacy. 95% of cases we do are legal aid cases, these are people that do not have enough money to pay

for a lawyer. If we wouldn't be there they wouldn't have a lawyer. And next to that, which is my way of working at least, I try to sincerely help people to pick up their life and improve it.

(INTNeth17)

My overall role at the police station is to ensure that my client gets the best starting point, whatever it takes. That is my goal, my drive, other than that, there is nothing. I believe that we do our job the way we do, so that the balance in the justice system could be maintained.

(INTNeth19)

However, for these same lawyers, in the everyday reality, their 'ideal' role was compromised by inadequate compensation. This theme was particularly present in the Netherlands, because unlike in England and Wales, where most interviewed lawyers were employees and received a fixed salary, in the Netherlands most lawyers were self-employed, and therefore their income depended directly on the legal aid fees. In the words of some Dutch lawyers:

I have seriously suffered from budget cuts. My office is still up and running, but I worked really hard and now I have to work even harder, and it ends at some point. You can't expect a lawyer to run a practice getting paid €75 for an interrogation. That's not possible. So for the first time in my life I'll consider the commercial side of it.

(INTNeth2)

Speaking of finances ... the reality is that the profession of a lawyer is a commercial profession. And it influences the amount of assistance that you provide. If I'm expected to sit in an interview for an hour, while I get paid €75, you shouldn't do that too often because your practice will go bankrupt. I always try – and I know it may not be the nicest thing to say – to round up my police station visits within a certain amount of time. I want to be out within half an hour.

(INTNeth5)

The Dutch lawyers were particularly candid concerning the influence of financial considerations on their decisions to attend interrogations (at the time of the fieldwork, the extension of the right to the presence of a lawyer for adult suspects was being envisaged). The following are some examples of the relevant interview quotes:

I do believe that as a suspect you should have the right to have your lawyer present during the interview, and I also think it's necessary in many cases, or that you should at least have the choice. But in practice, I wonder, if they would introduce that right today, without reimbursement, then you can have many ideological ideas, but if at the end of the month your bills don't get paid because you've been attending interviews instead of working on cases for which you are being paid, then the ideology ends fairly quickly. There has to be compensation, or it will be a right reserved for the rich. And maybe that one case where you think 'this is so important, it's exceptional, I will do it'. But that's it.

(INTNeth1)

An interrogation often takes a while, approximately 3 hours or more, and you don't get any compensation for it. You won't to do it for nothing. So your client should say he can pay for it, or you take care of it being paid. Another possibility is that there is such a huge interest for it, for example, with very serious cases, where your presence is desperately needed, because it is a vulnerable suspect, then you can choose to be there for free. But that is only for extreme cases.

(INTNeth8)

I am very honest about that, and this is not something you talk about in this profession, but lawyers are also entrepreneurs and you have to keep your business alive ... So I think that now without the decent financial compensation, and not in a homicide, but in a simple case, I would say 'let the mother be present'. And I am sure that I am not the only one.

(INTNeth18)

Actually I request to attend interrogations only with homicides, or when I can arrange payment for attending. We do not get paid by the government, if that was the case we would be present at every single interrogation. If a suspect asks me to be present in an interrogation I will say sure, but I want to be paid beforehand ... Look, for being present during an interrogation of a minor, I did it once, but I just can't deal with it, it takes ages, and then someone types with only two fingers, and when you read it: you begin with correcting the spelling and grammar mistakes, and that takes up so much time, even though it is about nothing, and you get about 100 euros for that.

(INTNeth13)

Thus, it follows from the quotes earlier, low remuneration for police station legal assistance, coupled with the fixed fee system, was commonly invoked by the Dutch lawyers to justify a lower 'standard' of assistance in certain, less 'meritorious' cases. Furthermore, some Dutch lawyers suggested that they would provide more comprehensive assistance to their clients paying for their services privately than to the clients funded through legal aid.

A similar tendency towards being selective in exercising activities which were not part of the 'standard package' of police station legal assistance, as documented in the Netherlands, was observed in England and Wales. It concerned, in particular, attending charging decisions, bail appointments or identification parades. As one lawyer described it:

> Whether I attend when the client goes to answer bail? Yes. I say yes. That's not 100 percent certain. What we find sometimes is that the client is solely going to be charged with an offence or rebailed, because the inquiries aren't complete. Well, if I establish that before the time, I invariably contact the client and say, 'Look, you're only going to be rebailed or you're going to be charged. There is no need for me to be there.'[28]

Likewise, some interviewed lawyers said, commenting on the practice of other firms or of their own firm, that following the introduction of fixed fees, lawyers began to spend less time on police station attendances. This was also due to the fact that, reportedly, many firms in the given location had to reduce their staff as the result of legal aid budget cuts.

Furthermore, reduced legal aid budgets incentivised law firms to make frequent use of so-called 'independent agents'. 'Independent agents' were freelance lawyers, sometimes united in firms, used by other firms to 'cover' their police station rotas, when members of staff were not available to attend, thus collecting new cases for the firm. 'Independent agents' were paid half or less of the fixed police station attendance fee (INTEng16). In the words of one 'independent agent', the demand for their work increased due to the staff layoffs in many firms:

> Because they [criminal law firms] are still on the duty scheme in town X or Y or wherever it is, they still got their duty slots so if they reduce their solicitors, and suddenly, say like firm A, we never used to do hardly anything for them. I've just done one for them now ... Firm B used us occasionally, but now they got rid of some of their staff. Town Z, the two solicitors in town Z, the two main ones have used us. Both of those have reduced their staff ...
>
> (INTEng13)

Independent agents were incentivised to limit their attendance time at police stations to guarantee sufficient income for themselves and to meet their business commitments to perform a certain number of attendances on behalf of their clients (INTEng16). Thus, one independent agent observed in this study in one night attended three suspects detained at the same police station (FNEng30.04.2013). Whilst he spent about 25 minutes in the first consultation (possibly due to the 'observer effect'), the two other consultations were significantly shorter, and felt rushed, especially because these clients, in contrast to the first suspect, were both 'first-timers'. In the interview, the same agent said that he managed to 'squeeze in' 80–100 police station attendances a month, and on average attended about 20 cases a week (INTEng11).

5 Conclusions

This chapter has argued that the contemporary criminal justice policies, described as those informed by the 'culture of control' and, more recently, 'austerity' had a negative impact on the exercise of the criminal defence in practice, because they led to decreased resources and opportunities for the defence to participate in the proceedings and influence the decision-making. Thus, in both jurisdictions, lawyers experience greater constraints when formulating their advice at the investigative stage, as the result of the tendency towards the 'penalisation' of silence at this stage (which in England and Wales was brought about by, inter alia, the CJPOA, and in the Netherlands by the recent case law of the Supreme Court). In both the Netherlands and England and Wales, courts appear to be more reluctant to endorse defence arguments stemming from alleged procedural violations at the investigative stage, and to afford remedies based on such violations. The increase in the number of out-of-court disposals at the investigative stage poses unique challenges to lawyers in both jurisdictions. These were the difficulties in accessing the relevant information and decision-making processes in the Netherlands, the challenges of dealing with the possible police tactics of pressing the suspect into accepting an out-of-court disposal in England and Wales, and the need to make quick decisions (e.g. concerning whether or not to advise clients to accept the proposed disposal) based on imperfect and incomplete information in both jurisdictions. The bureaucratisation of the proceedings at the investigative stage and the hierarchisation of the relevant decision-making processes (as the result of which, for instance, certain decision-making powers were taken from the police and given to prosecutors) created further obstacles for lawyers to influence the respective processes. And finally, in England and Wales, the ethical duty of lawyers to endorse the 'truth' has compromised the lawyer–client relationship at the investigative stage.

At the same time, some (isolated) findings described in this and other chapters show that the same criminal justice policies resulted in some 'residual' positive effects for the role of lawyers at the investigative stage. Thus, as argued in Chapters 4 and 5, the incidental consequence of the CJPOA 'inferences for silence' provisions was that English lawyers are now regularly provided access to case-related information prior to the first police interview. However, the development of this practice was not the direct or intended result of the respective regulations, which were informed by the 'crime control' agenda. Rather, they should perhaps be seen as the 'counter-response' of the criminal justice system, seeking to restore the balance between the 'crime control' and 'due process' values as described by Packer. Thus, English courts concluded that procedural fairness would be disturbed if adverse inferences were admissible from suspects' silence, where the evidence was so weak that there was no case to answer. This finding allowed English lawyers to continue using their clients' silence as a bargaining tool for disclosure after the CJPOA, and incentivised police to give disclosure, knowing that in that case lawyers were more likely to advise clients to provide a statement. In a similar vein, the introduction of early out-of-court disposals

146 *Influence of criminal justice policies*

(ZSM procedure) in the Netherlands, in some instances, has encouraged greater access for lawyers to the respective information and the decision-making processes at the investigative stage. Again, this development was not the direct consequence of the ZSM policy (which, in the very beginning, had not incorporated legal assistance), but rather the response to the mounting criticisms of the ZSM proceedings as being 'unfair', or instilled with 'crime control' values.

Notes

1 This new approach was embodied in what has become a slogan of New Labour (attributed to Tony Blair as shadow Home Secretary in 1993): 'Tough on crime, tough on the causes of crime'.
2 Reduction in Sentence for a Guilty Plea. Definitive Guideline (in force since 1 June 2017), available from: <www.sentencingcouncil.org.uk/publications/item/reduction-in-sentence-for-a-guilty-plea-definitive-guideline-2/> (last accessed on 16 July 2019).
3 Samenleving en Criminaliteit: een beleidsplan voor de komende jaren, Staatsuitgeverij 1985.
4 Jaarbericht 2016, Openbaar Ministerie, available at <www.om.nl/@98932/jaarbericht-2016/> (last accessed on 16 July 2019); Public Prosecutor's Office, 'Evaluation report 5 years of ZSM' ('Evaluatierapport 5 jaar ZSM'), available from: <www.om.nl/onderwerpen/werkwijze-van-het-om/@95111/evaluatierapport-5/> (last accessed on 16 July 2019).
5 Ministry of Safety and Justice, 'Waarom een nieuw Wet Strafvordering?' ('Why a New Code of Criminal Procedure?'), available from: <https://www.rijksoverheid.nl/onderwerpen/modernisering-wetboek-van-strafvordering/waarom-een-nieuw-wetboek-van-strafvordering> (last accessed on 16 July 2019).
6 Accompanying Letter and the Framework Note of the Ministry of Security and Justice of 3 February 2015 ('Aanbiedingsbrief en Contournota Modernisering Wetboek van Strafvordering') available from: <www.rijksover heid.nl/documenten/brieven/2015/09/30/aanbiedingsbrief-en-contourennota-wetboek-modernise ring-van-strafvordering> (last accessed on 16 July 2019).
7 Ibid., p. 13.
8 Ibid., p. 7.
9 Law Gazette, 'Budget: No end for austerity of justice', available from: <https://www.lawgazette.co.uk/law/budget-no-end-to-austerity-for-justice/5068121.article> (last accessed on 16 July 2019).
10 Nederlandse Orde Van Advocaten, 'Tussen Rapport Commissie 'Duurzaam Stelsel Gefinancierde Rechtsbijstand' (2015), available from: <https://www.mr-online.nl/wp-content/uploads/files/Tussenrapport_commissie_Duurzaam_stelsel.pdf> (last accessed on 16 July 2019), 15–6. Commissie van de Meer (2017), 'Andere Tijden, Commissie Evaluatie Puntentoekenning Gesubsidieerde Rechtsbijstand' available from: <www.rijksoverheid.nl/documenten/rapporten/2017/10/25/tk-eindrapport-andere-tijden> (last accessed on 16 July 2019).
11 Boston Consulting Group (2019), Doorlichting Financien Rechtsbijstand, available from: <https://www.rechtspraak.nl/SiteCollectionDocuments/doorlichting-Rechtspraak-BCG.pdf> (last accessed on 16 July 2019).
12 Algemene Dagblad, 'Bezuinigen rechtsbijstand van tafel advocaten blijven boos', <https://www.ad.nl/politiek/bezuiniging-rechtsbijstand-van-tafel-advocaten-blijven-boos~a922737f/> (last accessed on 16 July 2019).
13 Ipsos, 'De Gevolgen van de Bezuinigingen op de Gefinancierde Rechtsbijstand. Onderzoek onder Ingeschreven Advocaten bij de Raad voor Rechtsbijstand',

Influence of criminal justice policies 147

 18 December 2014, available from: <https://www.advocatenorde.nl/document/10-onderzoek-ipsos-nova-stelselvernieuwing-rechtsbijstand> (last accessed on 16 July 2019).
14 Uitkomsten enquête onder advocaten die lid zijn van de Vereniging Sociale Advocatuur Nederland (VSAN) en/of lid zijn van de Sociale Advocatuur Amsterdam (VSAA), 20 November 2014, available from: <https://www.mr-online.nl/wp-content/uploads/files/Uitkomsten_enquete_VSAN-VSAA.pdf> (last accessed on 16 July 2019).
15 Remaining silent at the investigative stage may be a relevant factor in the determination of the sentence, because in doing so, judges may take into account the 'procedural behaviour' of the suspect. HR 3 March 1964, *NJ* 1964/400, HR 12 November 1974, ECLI:NL:HR:1974:AB4591, *NJ* 1975/41.
16 According to the case law, a prepared statement prevents an inference only with regard to the facts mentioned in the statement. See Cape, 2017: 216–217 (also for relevant case-law references).
17 The advice given by the lawyer was wrong, because another possible option was to let the lawyer withdraw from representing the client.
18 The unlawfulness of police detention does not automatically result in the refusal to place suspects in further (pre-trial) detention. HR 16 February 2010, ECLI:NL: HR:2010:BK8537, *NJ* 2010/123.
19 Police detention is unlawful if it violates 'fair procedure' (e.g. the use of excessive force at arrest does not lead to unlawfulness, unless it had reached the level of 'inhuman and degrading treatment', which would compromise 'fair procedure'). Rechtbank 's-Gravenhage, 9 July 2008, ECLI:NL:RBSGR:2008:BD7002, *NJFS* 2008/192. The denial of the right of access to a lawyer may lead to declaring the detention unlawful for the same reason. Rechtbank Amsterdam, 26 June 2009, LJN BJ4881 (unpublished).
20 This statutory limit was applicable at the time of the fieldwork (the current limit is three days and 18 hours).
21 Unlawful or wrongful arrest could also trigger a civil action against the police.
22 Such as oppression in an interview; wrongful denial of access to a lawyer; failure to caution the suspect; failure to comply with the interview recording requirements; or using deception and inducements. See Cape, 2017: 499–505.
23 The lawyer conflates the tests under s. 76 PACE for the exclusion of confession evidence (confession should not be unreliable) and under s. 78 PACE for the exclusion of unfairly obtained evidence (it would be unfair to adduce the evidence).
24 Information brief of the Public Prosecutor's Office, 'Start pilot "ZSM en rechtsbijstand"' ("Starting of the pilot ZSM and legal assistance"), available from: <www.om.nl/@86989/start-pilot-zsm/> (last accessed on 16 July 2019).
25 *Trouw* (national news hub), 'Proef met advocaten op politiebureau ook in andere steden' ('Experiment with lawyers at the police station also in other cities'), 7 September 2011, available from: <https://www.trouw.nl/nieuws/proef-met-advocaten-op-politiebureau-ook-in-andere-steden~bd8ca23e/?referer=https%3A%2F%2Fwww.google.com%2F&utm_campaign=shared_earned&utm_medium=social&utm_source=copylink> (last accessed on 16 July 2019).
26 Ministry of Justice Guidance, Simple Cautions for Adult Offenders, paragraphs 23–26, 78.
27 'Is CPS on "Brink of Collapse"?', article on *BBC News* (15 September 2015), available at <www.bbc.com/news/uk-34246664> (last accessed on 16 July 2019).
28 EngInt16.

7 The influence of occupational cultures of lawyers

1 Introduction

The influence of occupational or professional cultures on the practical operation of the criminal process is often emphasised in literature on (comparative) criminal justice (Hodgson, 2005, Hodsgon and Mou 2019; Cape et al., 2010; Blackstock et al., 2013). However, the concept itself often remains undefined. Within the area of criminal justice, 'occupational' or 'professional' cultures have been studied mostly with regard to policing (see Section 2.1). In criminal justice literature, 'occupational cultures' are sometimes viewed as the informal, or everyday, 'working rules' related to a job, which differ from the formal norms or regulations (Ashworth and Redmayne, 2010: 64). In a more general (and neutral) fashion, 'professional' or 'occupational' cultures may be described as a set of attitudes, beliefs and ideas which characterise a certain professional or occupational group.[1] 'Occupational culture' (of police) was also defined as 'a reduced, selective, and task-based version of culture that is shaped by and shapes the socially relevant worlds of the occupation' (Manning, 1995: 472). Thus, 'occupational culture' is conceptualised as the commonly accepted beliefs and attitudes, in part embedded in history and tradition, which are used, often unconsciously, to give (selective) meaning to the present-day reality encountered by the respective professionals. The cultures embody what is taken for granted by the occupational members, the 'invisible yet powerful constraints' (ibid.) in the respective professionals' view of the world, which condition their day-to-day behaviour.

Occupational cultures are embedded in the broader culture. Culture, as described in Chapter 7, consists of the collective socially constructed symbols, ideals, values, attitudes, beliefs and perceptions which distinguish one particular social group from another. To bridge this general notion to the understanding of 'professional' or 'occupational cultures', Schein's definition of 'organisational culture' is particularly relevant (Schein, 2016).[2] Schein distinguishes three levels of organisational culture: (1) the most superficial level of rituals and 'artefacts' (such as dress or standing jokes), which are readily observable but are difficult to interpret without knowledge of the deeper levels; (2) a deeper level of espoused values and beliefs, which are articulated by the members of organisations in a conscious manner (but which may be incongruent with their actual behaviour if they do not align with the 'underlying assumptions' as defined further); (3) the most profound level of 'basic underlying assumptions', namely, unconscious beliefs which are taken for granted by the members of an organisation, but which ultimately determine their actions. These assumptions and beliefs constitute the 'learned responses to ensure the group's survival in its external environment and to safeguard internal integration' (ibid.: 6–7). They pertain to, for instance, beliefs about whether – and how – 'truth' should be determined (moralism versus pragmatism); orientation towards the past, present or future (traditionalism versus innovation); or assumptions about human relationships (e.g. within the group and towards 'others': individualism versus collectivism; or trust versus suspicion). The goal of a cultural inquiry, therefore, is to bring to light these underlying beliefs – 'push to the level of assumptions' – by critically reflecting on the knowledge obtained whilst studying the more superficial cultural 'levels' (ibid.).

Schein's conceptualisation of organisational culture provides a useful framework to study the occupational culture of criminal justice actors (Chan, 1997: 68), including criminal defence lawyers. Namely, it allows to depart from the view of occupational culture as monolithic and unchangeable, existing outside of the respective groups. Rather, Schein conceptualises culture as shared knowledge about 'reality' as it is experienced by the professional members, which is actively constructed by them. This knowledge is changeable and can be inherently contradictory, but conditions the actors' behaviour, although not in a predetermined, linear fashion. Thus, Schein's view of 'culture' is not only constructivist, but also empirical: namely, he regards culture as a contextual factor that influences 'organisational effectiveness' (Krause-Jensen, 2010: 59). A similar approach to 'occupational cultures' constituting 'constructed knowledge' – which, to a certain extent, shapes the 'reality', or the behaviour of the respective actors – is adopted in this chapter.

This chapter seeks to identify certain 'underlying assumptions' of the criminal defence lawyers' occupational cultures at the investigative stage of the criminal proceedings in the two examined jurisdictions: England and Wales and the Netherlands. It should not, however, be seen as an exhaustive representation of 'the defence lawyers' occupational culture'. This chapter is limited to the insights derived from the data collected during the fieldwork. Moreover, this chapter mainly documents the negative elements of defence lawyers' occupational cultures, rather than its positive aspects (similar criticism was expressed in respect to studies regarding policing culture – see Section 3.1). Naturally, the occupational cultures of criminal defence lawyers also include positive aspects. However, the analysis in this chapter focuses on those cultural elements which could act as barriers to the practical realisation of the normative view of the role of lawyers at the investigative stage embedded in the respective European regulations.

2 Occupational cultures of criminal justice actors

2.1 *Police occupational cultures*

This section summarises the rich tradition of research into the occupational cultures of police, whose theoretical underpinnings may contribute to our understanding of the occupational cultures of defence lawyers. The foundations for the study of 'policing (sub)culture' or 'police occupational culture' were laid by the ethnographic accounts of policing in the USA and Britain produced in the 1960s and 1970s (Skolnick, 1966; Westley, 1970; Cain, 1973, among others). These accounts emerged in response to the view of police as a legalistic, bureaucratic and rule-bound institution (Reiner, 2017: 236). They pointed at the wide range of discretion in the use of policing powers, and described the various features of police 'working personality', which Reiner referred to as the core characteristics of police culture (Reiner, 2010). These included: the exaggerated 'sense of mission', cynicism, suspicion, isolation and mutual solidarity ('us versus them', 'the blue wall of silence'), conservatism, racial prejudice and pragmatism. This characterisation of police culture, according to Loftus, has achieved the status of 'sociological orthodoxy' (Loftus, 2009), and if oversimplified, it can be viewed as a stereotypical description of police personality (Berg, 1999: 297).

Several recent writings have built on – and added nuance to – the early research into police 'worldviews'. Some authors pointed at the existence of multiple cultures depending on the rank, department, location or type of police force (Cain, 1973; Fielding, 1989; Chan, 1997; Waddington, 1999; Reiner, 2010). Chan criticised the 'traditional' view of policing culture for its failure to attribute active agency to police officers as those making individual cultural choices, rather than being overpowered by their monolithic and omnipotent 'culture' (Chan, 1997). Instead, she argued that police officers dispose of a 'cultural tool-kit', consisting of various 'stories', or alternative narratives giving meaning to police action and relating this action to certain occupational values. Another criticism raised by Chan was that the 'traditional' model of policing culture views such culture as 'given' and self-contained, being insensitive to the wider context and the possibilities for change. (Although this was likely a misrepresentation, because the 'early' ethnographic accounts did position policing within the wider structural context [Reiner, 2017: 237].) Instead, she proposed an interactive model of police practice drawing from Bourdieu's theories of 'field' and 'habitus', where the 'field' constitutes the context within which certain practices develop (including legal regulations, institutional structures and the wider sociopolitical context), and where the 'habitus' signifies the cultural knowledge of the respective actors (Chan, 1996). Policing practice develops in a fluid and interactive process, where actors react to the 'field', or contextual factors, by drawing upon their 'habitus' to justify individual behavioural choices.

Other authors argued that the 'traditional' accounts of police occupational cultures overemphasised their negative characteristics, whilst such cultures also have positive attributes such as dedication, camaraderie and sacrifice (Bittner, 1967; Muir, 1977; Cordner, 2017). Furthermore, Waddington (1999) noted that the early studies of policing assumed that the 'negative talk' of machoism, intolerance or cynicism (the 'canteen culture') determined officers' behaviour, whilst it was rather a response to their stressful and marginalising occupational experiences. He pointed to the risk of assuming that policing 'culture' (manifested through the use of language during informal socialisation) has a linear relationship with the 'practice' of policing, or in other words, of failing to note the difference between 'talk' and 'action' in policing work.

Thus, the contemporary accounts of police occupational cultures stress their dynamic and fluid character, and their non-determinative nature vis-à-vis the policing practice. At the same time, several authors observed that police cultures have a number of relatively stable features, inherent in the nature of the policing function and the role of police in society. Loftus (2009), for instance, conducted an ethnographic study among an English police force in the mid-2000s, and found that the core features associated with police culture, such as an inflated sense of mission, masculinity, dominance, isolation and mutual loyalty have persevered, despite various policing reforms (the introduction of new public management, diversity agenda and community policing). She explains this perseverance by the tensions inherent in the policing function. Reiner (2010), likewise, points at the existence of a 'typical' police occupational culture, rooted in the intrinsic elements of the policing function, such as maintaining order and fighting crime, universal across different societies. Arguably, however, those accounts of policing cultures which emphasise variability, and those which emphasise stability, are not mutually exclusive, but they rather relate to the different 'layers' of such cultures. Using Schein's terminology, certain deep 'underlying assumptions', reflecting the very core of the policing function, are likely to be relatively stable and universal across different nations, officer ranks or types of police forces. However, other kinds of 'underlying assumptions' are (much) less stable and less universal, and thus they reflect the dynamic and diversified character of police occupational cultures.

The following insights from the policing research are relevant for the characterisation of defence lawyers' occupational cultures. First, these cultures are certainly not monolithic and homogenous, but they vary depending on the types of lawyers' practices, specialisations, geographic regions or other variables. Furthermore, lawyers' occupational cultures should not be viewed as determinative of the lawyering practice, but rather as an influence in the process of interacting with the 'field', or the various contextual factors (existing laws, institutions, or criminal justice policies). The active role of lawyers in choosing which elements of occupational cultures to follow should arguably be recognised: like police officers, lawyers may draw from various cultural narratives or justifications when giving meaning to their behaviour in discretionary or problematic situations. Researchers of lawyers' occupational cultures should be mindful of the risk of equating lawyers' talk about their work to their actual behaviour; 'positive talk' may aim to disguise negative practices, but 'negative talk' might also signify a coping strategy, rather than a fair description of the lawyers' actual behaviour.

Finally, lawyers' occupational cultures are likely to contain several relatively stable and universal features, inherent in the core defence lawyers' function and their societal role, and the tensions associated with this role. Thus, the 'core' function of defence lawyers, which is arguably universal in the 'Western' systems of criminal justice, is to provide support and assistance to relatively marginalised members of society (criminal defendants), which requires lawyers to act in opposition to the investigative and prosecuting authorities. Similar to the policing function, this role is characterised by inherent tensions and pressures. Some of these tensions, such as the difficulty of empathising with their clients, or 'defending the guilty', have long become part of lawyers' folklore. Other pressures may include, for instance, the difficulty of opposing the 'state', vested with immense power and resources, and the resulting sense of isolation and powerlessness. Another challenge manifest particularly at the investigative stage is the fast-paced, unpredictable and demanding nature of defence lawyers' work, which may include long hours and lengthy waiting periods (Cape, 2017: 3). Finally, lawyers may feel lack of control over their own work, because their actions undertaken for the client must be endorsed by those actors who have decision-making power in the criminal proceedings (police, prosecutors and judges). The following sections combine these theoretical insights with the fieldwork data in order to deduce a number of general features of defence lawyers' occupational cultures at the investigative stages of the proceedings, as observed in the two jurisdictions.

2.2 Defence lawyers' occupational cultures: the state of knowledge

Before diving into the fieldwork data, a short summary of the existing state of knowledge of defence lawyers' occupational cultures should be given. The occupational cultures of criminal defence lawyers are under-researched, especially when compared to the research on police cultures (Ashworth and Redmayne, 2019: 70). Most existing studies of criminal defence lawyering represent common-law jurisdictions, while in continental-law countries, such research is generally lacking.

Originating from England and Wales, *Standing Accused* by McConville et al. (1994) is probably the most comprehensive study of criminal defence lawyering, although it dates back more than 30 years. McConville et al. conducted observations at 22 criminal defence firms during 198 weeks of observation. The study presents an accusatory account of defence lawyers' occupational cultures, showing that lawyers treated clients with disrespect, delegated work to unqualified staff, and made little effort to challenge the prosecution case or actively build a defence strategy. In a more recent study, Newman (2013) examined the relationship between criminal defence lawyers and their clients, and concluded that there was a gap between how lawyers presented their work in formal interviews and their behaviours and attitudes as transpired from ethnographic observation. In interviews, lawyers described their work as advancing the values of client-centredness and justice. However, these values were not reflected in their day-to-day practice. Lawyers talked about their clients in demeaning terms, assumed them to be guilty, disregarded their clients' needs, and pushed them into pleading guilty and accepting substandard service, plagued by lack of continuity and by time constraints. Although some of the lawyers' 'negative talk' observed by Newman might be similar to the police 'canteen culture' as described by Waddington (serving as a coping mechanism with the pressures inherent in the lawyers' work), the findings reported by Newman depict a very similar picture of lawyers' occupational culture to the one portrayed in McConville et al. (1994).

Other studies, such as those of Travers (1997) in the UK and McIntyre (1987) in the USA, present more sympathetic accounts of defence lawyers' occupational cultures. Travers, for instance, depicts a glorifying account of the work of a law firm staffed by 'radical' lawyers, committed to their clients' causes and doing their utmost to deliver best-quality service. Likewise, McIntyre's account of the daily work of the Cook County Public Defender Office is 'probably more sympathetic than available data suggests' (Ryan, 1989). She portrays public defenders as highly ethical professionals, striving to provide zealous defence to their clients despite the various political constraints and the negative publicity around them. Both studies, however, were limited to one particular defence practice, and they both seemed to pursue a certain goal. Travers's objective was to counter the scepticism against 'radical' (socialist) lawyers, while McIntyre's study seemingly aimed to refute the negative image of public defenders. Therefore, the risk of over-identification with the researched subjects in both studies cannot be ruled out.

Criminal defence lawyering was also examined as part of larger research studies. For instance, Hodgson studied French lawyers' professional practices as part of her research into the French criminal justice system (Hodgson, 2005). She found that French criminal defence lawyers were marginalised and were given limited space by other powerful participants (investigative judges, prosecutors and police), particularly at the pre-trial procedural stages. Field and West (2003) described the prevailing French lawyers' professional culture as 'rereading' the dossier to the client's advantage, rather than attempting to build an 'active' defence strategy. In the USA, numerous studies demonstrated that defence lawyers acquiesced into the pressures to cooperate with the prosecution, namely towards the mass production of guilty pleas (Hessick and Saujani, 2002: 206–215). In the UK, recent studies documented a similar tendency, tracing it to the managerialist reforms and reduced legal aid fees (McConville and Marsh, 2015; Newman, 2016). Another study examined, inter alia, whether the occupational cultures of defence lawyers inhibited or facilitated the practical realisation of suspects' procedural rights in four jurisdictions: England and Wales, the Netherlands, France, and Scotland (Blackstock et al., 2013). It has shown that in France and the Netherlands, lawyers were (still) marginalised at the investigative stages. In all examined jurisdictions, lawyers were generally passive at this stage and did not attempt to provide more than a minimum acceptable standard of service, with the exception of England and Wales, where a more active role had been promoted through accreditation and training. Similar findings were documented in a study of interrogation practices of young suspects in five European jurisdictions. Furthermore, Skinns (2010: 118–119) and Kemp (2010: 91–92) found that some clients arrested at police stations mistrust 'duty lawyers'. Another theme examined in recent research (discussed in Chapter 6) is the lowering standard of service provided by legal aid lawyers due to the decreasing fees and other cost-saving initiatives.

3 Lawyers' occupational cultures and procedural traditions

The relationship between occupational cultures and legal procedural traditions on the one hand, and behaviours or practices on the other hand, is difficult to theorise, and such theorisation falls outside the scope of this research. Rather, this study was concerned inter alia with whether the ideas forming part of the 'inquisitorial' or 'adversarial' procedural traditions were reflected in the observed occupational cultures of criminal defence lawyers at the investigative stage.

As mentioned in Section 2, occupational cultures are partly derived from history and tradition, and therefore procedural traditions may be viewed as one source of such cultures. Relying on Schein's theory of culture, the ideas embedded in the procedural traditions may be reflected in the occupational cultures on three levels: on the level of 'artefacts' (such as crimson gowns of French judges symbolising the 'King' or state power) or 'rituals' (such as the use of legalistic language in English courts) (Hodgson, 2006); on the level of 'espoused values or beliefs' (which are consciously articulated by occupational members); and on the level of 'underlying assumptions'. Applying Schein's logic, legal procedural traditions may be considered as truly part of lawyers' occupational cultures, if they have penetrated to the deepest level of the 'underlying assumptions'.

As described in Chapter 5, the ideas embedded in the two procedural traditions were usually reflected in the lawyers' 'official' professional discourse related to the practice at the investigative stage, as well as in the interviews with lawyers in the two jurisdictions. It was observed, however, that the actual behaviour of lawyers often did not reflect the values or ideas embedded in the lawyers' professional discourse, and their perceptions expressed in the interviews. Thus, for instance, the Dutch lawyers' discourse emphasised the importance of building trust with the client, even though in practice, lawyers made limited efforts to ensure 'trust' in the investigative stage. In the English lawyers' discourse, clients were presented as the ultimate decision-makers with regard to the procedural strategy, whilst in practice decisions were usually taken by lawyers. The incongruence between the 'espoused values and beliefs' of one's occupational culture and the actual behaviour, as mentioned in Section 2, is a likely sign that the articulated values and beliefs do not correspond with the 'underlying assumptions' of the given culture. Therefore, it may be concluded that in this study – which was, however, limited to examining the lawyers' professional practices at the investigative stage of the proceedings – the values and beliefs embedded in procedural traditions often did not seem to penetrate to the level of the lawyers' 'actual' occupational cultures. (With the exception of certain aspects of procedural traditions, which, as described in Chapter 5, were found to be reflected in the lawyers' practices at the investigative stage: namely, the lawyers' approach to formulating advice [whether in the 'moral' or 'technical' terms] or their preparedness to formulate answers on the clients' behalf.)

At the same time, as described in the following sections, certain commonalities in the defence lawyers' occupational cultures, manifested during observations at the investigative stage, were observed in the two jurisdictions. These commonalities existed notwithstanding the differences in the prevailing procedural traditions. This finding provides additional support for the hypothesis that procedural traditions were not the only – or the determinative – factor influencing the defence lawyers' occupational cultures at the investigative stage.

4 Observations from the fieldwork

This research has documented certain recurrent patterns in the 'working personality' of criminal defence lawyers in the two examined jurisdictions, which were exhibited at the investigative stage. These patterns concerned the beliefs and values which seemed to inform lawyers' behaviour vis-à-vis their clients and the investigative authorities, as well as lawyers' discretionary decision-making (for instance, with regard to which advice to give to the client, or whether or not to make certain representations). The following aspects of defence lawyers' occupational cultures, observed at the investigative stage, are described later: the lawyers' tendency to mistrust clients; risk avoidance; the emotional distancing from clients; and a non-confrontational stance vis-à-vis the investigative authorities.

4.1 Mistrust of clients and assumptions of their guilt

As described in Chapter 3, the encountered Dutch lawyers were generally cautious in believing that their clients were telling them the truth during their meetings at police stations. Likewise, Chapter 5 describes how the English lawyers habitually judged whether or not their clients were honest or truthful with them, even though these kinds of moral judgments were discouraged by the procedural tradition. Both the Dutch and English lawyers were regularly observed commenting that their clients were 'obviously lying' or telling a 'load of bollocks'. This finding is supported by other observational research, such as McConville et al. (1994), arguing that 'many advisers, like the police, instinctively believe that, without requiring further substantiation through evidence, that there is a case to answer, and that it is the client who must give the answer. *This in turn springs from an assumption that the client is factually guilty*' (126–127; my emphasis). Likewise, Newman found that the lawyers he encountered in the course of ethnographic observation at English criminal defence firms routinely presumed their clients to be factually guilty (Newman, 2013: 47–48).

The attitudes of 'professional mistrust' to clients seemed to develop mostly as the result of the professional socialisation of lawyers. As one Dutch lawyer noted:

> '[a] beginner's mistake is that we think we can trust our clients right away, and you think "I am sure he did not do it", and it turns out not to be the case'.
>
> (INTNeth18)

Likewise, another lawyer encountered during the fieldwork said, like the lawyer quoted earlier, that 'many young lawyers, who believe their clients, go on asserting things on their behalf, only to discover later that they had been false'. He then went on to say that 'with experience you learn to doubt everything that your client says, even their name could be false' (FNNeth14.02.2012).

The lawyers' tendency to mistrust their clients manifested itself also in other ways than assuming their dishonesty or guilt. For instance, the encountered lawyers were often sceptical about their clients' intelligence level, their ability to present a coherent and logical account, or to follow their lawyer's advice. In the words of one encountered English lawyer:

> Without too much disrespect to my clients, they're not always the brightest bunch. Although they're very intelligent in certain ways, in terms of the discipline to conduct an interview, they might get wangled up. They might say things they regret. They'll express it in a way – they're not particularly well-educated, most of them. They might express it in a way that actually reads or sounds pretty poor. That's not what they meant. We're the educated ones, so it should be – a common question a police officer asks, 'Did you write this or the solicitor did?' The answer always, it's their instructions, but I wrote it out.
>
> (INTEng15)

Another lawyer said that the main aspect of her role in the interview was to 'protect his clients from themselves' to ensure that they do not make self-incriminating admissions: 'you're endlessly in the interview watching for anything like that. To prevent them from saying it'. In response to the question about why she felt the need to protect clients from themselves, the lawyer responded:

> They are – I don't know whether – I would say that they have a lower IQ, rather than a higher IQ and have been disadvantaged in one way or another, which has an impact on the level of education that they have. And therefore, they don't seem to make decisions which you would claim rational. They just don't make them. Yeah, you have to protect them all the time. They could say anything.
>
> (INTEng12)

As a result, as also demonstrated by the quotes earlier, many encountered lawyers, in both jurisdictions, stated or implied that they prefer to in some ways 'control' their clients' accounts and behaviour, particularly in the course of the police interview. In this respect, the following interview quote is illustrative:

INTERVIEWER (I): And how often do you advise silence?
LAWYER (L): Maybe one in every five cases.
I: OK. And how often do you advise prepared statements?
L: Three or four times out of five.
I: So you're saying that mostly you advise – ?

Influence of occupational cultures 157

L: Mostly I prefer the prepared statement, because it allows you to control the interview process.
I: So what you're saying is that you actually don't often advise the client to respond to questions.
L: No, I very often advise them to make a prepared statement or go no comment. And maybe the odd case where I will think, 'No, this client is good. They're capable of holding their own.'

(INTEng13)

Thus, mistrust of clients appeared to determine the lawyers' decisions to advise silence. Likewise, the majority of the interviewed Dutch lawyers, as also described in Chapter 3, said that they preferred advising their clients to remain silent, unless they believed that their defence was genuine. The quotes given here illustrate the respective lawyers' attitudes:

> [Silence] is often advised, it seems to be the best choice most of the time. Because a lot of those people they lie to their lawyers. They think they are smarter than the police, judge, and lawyers. However they don't understand ... In most situations I do advise the right to remain silent or say 'I'm innocent, but I'm using my right to remain silent on advice from my lawyer ...'
>
> (INTNeth21)

> If someone tells me 'I didn't do it' then I say 'then you should say it'. But still, you have to be very careful, because rarely people are condemned even though they are innocent ... Also the personality, sometimes when I talk to a client I think 'you are a liar' they will just make something up, and then I will advise to remain silent because otherwise it won't go well. So these are all factors that play a role.
>
> (INTNeth25)

> And very rarely, if you really feel like someone is telling the truth, a statement of self-defence for example is more forceful when it's given immediately during the first interrogation. So that's the consideration. And it's partially based on feelings, 'is this true or not?' But I always find that difficult myself.
>
> (INTNeth4)

A small minority of the interviewed Dutch lawyers went as far as suggesting that they would advise their clients to remain silent even where the latter provided a defence, which contradicted what lawyers said about the risks of not allowing suspects to state their defence at an early opportunity, as described in Chapter 6.[3] In the words of one Dutch lawyer:

> If someone is determined to deny and says 'I have absolutely nothing to do with it' then my advice is invariably 'I would invoke my right to remain

silent' because a denial can be of disadvantage later on if from the evidence it appears that the opposite is true. And if your statement is 'a knowingly lying statement', then it becomes particularly difficult. So I advise to remain silent at least to circumvent that problem.

(INTNeth26)

Another lawyer noted:

So even when they tell me: 'I am innocent', then I can have my own thoughts about it but even when I am convinced, and you have to be careful with that because you never know who you are talking to, that they're telling me the truth, then I would advise to remain silent, unless.

(NethInt8)

Lawyers' mistrustful attitudes towards clients were also manifested in how they approached advising 'experienced' clients or 'regular offenders'. Thus, as described in Chapter 3, some encountered Dutch lawyers did not give any guidance or advice to 'regulars' at the investigative stage, effectively leaving them to their own devices for the upcoming interview. Similar tendencies were documented in England and Wales in the study of McConville et al. (1994: 76–81). Dutch lawyers felt that they were not 'competent' to give advice, particularly in the absence of prior disclosure, because they felt that such clients would not be truthful with them. Similarly, the encountered English lawyers felt that such clients would not tell them 'what actually happened'. In the words of one interviewed lawyer,

Somebody in my position or the other people that you interview, when we go in to a situation, we know less than the client and the police. The client was there, and he knows what happened, and the police have gathered all the evidence. So they both know more than us and so we're trying to navigate between the two. Which is a strange position.

(NethINT17)

Consequently, in both the English and Dutch observations, there was a tacit understanding that 'regulars' would decide themselves about how to approach the interrogation, and lawyers would not assist, or interfere, with this decision. In many such cases, suspects announced their decision upfront, which was usually to remain silent. The observed lawyers, in turn, rarely tried to challenge the client's decision: only in one observed case did a lawyer suggest that 'maybe giving an account would be more understandable', but the suspect disagreed (FNNeth21.02.2012). Following the observed encounter, the lawyer explained that in respect of regulars, he would always go along with their wishes to remain silent, because experienced suspects take a 'business risk' to remain silent, hoping that in the end there will be insufficient evidence against them (implying that they are usually guilty).

Influence of occupational cultures 159

A similar tendency was observed among the English lawyers. For instance, in two cases that involved regulars, lawyers did not give any advice (FNEng17.04.2013; 28.06.2012). One interviewed English lawyer responded to the question about how he approached advising clients at the investigative stage in the following way:

> [I]t depends on the client, again, because some clients, of course, are more experienced with police interviews than I am. They'll come and say, 'I'm not saying anything to them.' And if they're that forthright, I'll probably just say OK. Well that's – it might be against what my instincts were. I'll say, 'Look. I'm saying I think you should do this. If you're saying you want to go no comment, you're the boss here. Fine.' Because at the end of the day, they're going to be satisfied with what they want to do. They know the system ...
> (INTEng17)

It is, however, doubtful whether the 'hands off' approach to advising 'regular' suspects adopted by lawyers was only a result of their belief that these suspects were more 'expert' or 'intelligent' than them. Thus, as described earlier in this paragraph, lawyers regularly referred to clients, including 'regulars', as lacking in intellectual capacity. Arguably, the lawyers' 'detached' stance towards advising such suspects was also rooted in lawyers' perceptions of them as 'less worthy' or factually 'guilty'. As one interviewed lawyer stated, talking about advising 'regulars':

> ... [A]t the police station, it isn't for me *to force them to admit the offence*. If the client wants to go no comment, and if he's chosen to do that, that's up to him. I will not try to convince him. He knows the consequences.
> (INTEng14; my emphasis)

4.2 Risk avoidance: silence as the 'safest' strategy

In both jurisdictions, the majority of the encountered lawyers considered silence in interrogations as a more preferable strategy than giving an account, setting aside the possible 'sanctions' for remaining silent described in Chapter 6. Most interviewed Dutch lawyers said that they considered the advice to remain silent as 'default' advice, or 'remain silent, unless ...' Some went as far as saying that they advised clients to remain silent in the majority – or in 90% – of all cases (INTNeth1) (which was likely an overestimation, but it showed the value that Dutch lawyers attached to advising silence).[4] In the words of one lawyer:

> Silence is my starting point. Remain silent, unless ... Remaining silent is the safest starting point. Because everything you say in the starting phase while you don't know against which background you're saying things, even though you mean well at the time, and I also say that to people who sit in front of me and swear to God they're innocent, when you give a statement which can, against an unknown background, be interpreted differently from what

you meant to say, you're lagging behind. In the end, we [lawyers] have to be rational, which also means you have to act cautiously.

(INTNeth5)

Another lawyer likewise responded to the question about how often he advises silence as follows:

In almost all cases. When I do not know what the evidentiary position is, and I cannot make an estimate, and certain things still need to be investigated, for example traffic reports, telephones, statements from co-suspects, then I advise to remain silent. Cases in which I do not advise them to remain silent is for example when the client turned in himself, then there is no point to remain silent.

(INTNeth7)

One possible reason why the encountered lawyers in both jurisdictions appeared to prefer – at least, in theory – that their clients remained silent in police interrogations was their desire to control the risks, stemming from the uncertainties of the decision-making at the investigative stage. These uncertainties were often evoked by the interviewed English and Dutch lawyers when describing the difficulties they encountered when assisting clients at police stations.[5] In the words of one English lawyer:

[Why would it be] difficult to know what to do in terms of dealing with an interview in terms of your options? Well, I guess because there's a great deal of unknown quantities in the case. So when you've got some disclosure, but there's clearly a lot more investigation to be done. It's difficult to really know then if you want to commit fully to giving too much of an account, but of course you also don't want to lead them in the situation where they've said nothing at all and then the adverse inference comes in ... I mean, you'll know it when you see it. You know when you've got a bit of a conundrum. You can be a bit undecided about things.

(INTEng15)

The same lawyer went on to say that in the end, however, it is not so difficult to make a choice, because in case of doubt, the 'proper' course of action is to advise silence:

I guess your options are limited, though, aren't they, so it's not that hard ever, because either they're going to say nothing – if in doubt, say nothing. That's got to be the right advice. If you're not certain, say no comment, because at the end of the day you can rectify that.

Indeed, the phrase 'in case of doubt – advise silence' was repeatedly encountered during the fieldwork in both countries, as a sort of 'professional wisdom' transmitted between lawyers. Moreover, some encountered lawyers explained their cautious attitude towards advising clients to respond to questions by their general propensity towards risk aversion, allegedly characteristic of lawyers as a profession. (Characterising lawyers as 'risk averse' is one of the common stereotypes about lawyers.[6]) One English lawyer, for instance, said:

> I mean, I am a lawyer and I'm instinctively quite cautious and therefore a no comment interview would suit my personality, almost. If in doubt, if there's any doubt whatsoever, just give a no comment interview. That would be my fall-back position. Because obviously otherwise it can go wrong, hideously wrong.
>
> (INTEng13)

The alleged tendency towards minimising risks, which might explain why many encountered lawyers considered the advice to remain silent to be more advantageous, should also be seen in the context of the trend described in the previous paragraph, namely a certain propensity towards mistrusting clients.[7]

It appeared, however, that lawyers wished to minimise risks not only for their clients, but also, or primarily, for themselves. Thus, as mentioned in Chapter 3, the interviewed Dutch lawyers talked about the risk of professional embarrassment when advising clients to respond to questions by giving a denial account, and then finding out that there was overwhelming evidence contradicting the clients' 'story'. Indeed, endorsing their clients' accounts, which contradict the existing evidence, could raise a suspicion of the lawyer being complicit in fabricating a false account. In fact, lawyers encountered in both jurisdictions often emphasised that it was not their professional role to 'concoct lies' on their clients' behalf – which possibly demonstrates that they were concerned about being perceived as dishonest by other procedural actors. As described in Chapter 6, the English lawyers, for instance, willingly endorsed the ethical rule that states that the lawyer must withdraw if a suspect wishes to give a different 'story' in a police interview, than what was discussed in the lawyer–client consultation. This was probably in part because these rules helped lawyers to avoid being suspected of 'fabricating lies' on the suspect's behalf. In the words of one interviewed lawyer:

> And so there, I would then be complicit, in my opinion, professionally embarrassed to sit there and let them lie. If they then start saying they haven't, again, I'd have to stop the interview and walk out. And say, 'You either say no comment or you admit it. Otherwise I'm walking out and that's the way it's going to be. And you make a bloody record of it, why you've done it. So you've always got a record of it.'
>
> (INTEng16)

The concern to avoid the impression of being 'dishonest', or complicit in fabricating false accounts, should also be seen in the context of the criminal defence lawyers' role as 'repeat players' at the investigative stage, as described in the following section.

4.3 Emotional distancing from clients

As described in Chapters 3 and 4, lawyers in both jurisdictions were generally cautious about stretching their role at the investigative stage to include emotional or social support to the (detained) client. In observations, particularly in the Netherlands, some lawyers adopted a detached, formal tone, rushed through the consultation, and were only interested in the circumstances relevant to the legal 'case'. These lawyers did not engage with the personal circumstances or broader needs of their clients, or they approached their 'support' role in a rather formal way. In this respect, the following example is illustrative (FNNeth04.03.2013).

A lawyer encountered in one of the Dutch sites was visiting a young man who was suspected of causing bodily harm to his girlfriend in a domestic fight. (He had already been interrogated and told his 'story' to the police; the lawyer visited him after his detention had been prolonged.) The man was in a very agitated emotional state, and consumed with the thoughts about his relationship, rather than the criminal accusation against him. He had started telling the lawyer about his relationship with the alleged victim, but the lawyer impatiently interrupted him, stating that 'he understands that he has difficulties in his relationship, but he [the lawyer] is there to talk about his case', namely the events that took place the previous night. When the suspect told the lawyer that in his view he was not responsible, because according to him his girlfriend suffered no bodily harm, the lawyer asked: 'So why would the police say that she had bodily harm?' The lawyer then told the suspect that 'he has the right to silence, but in his case it would probably be better to speak'. This comment was not applicable, because the client had already confessed. At the end of the consultation, the lawyer asked his client whether there was someone to pick him up once he was released from custody. The latter responded that he 'had no one, only a mother in his care, who was bed-bound'. The lawyer had not inquired whether his mother had the necessary care, nor offered to give her a call. His last words to the client were that he would 'try to do everything to get him out of there as soon as possible, today or tomorrow', which was untrue. (As it turned out, the lawyer believed that the suspect would be released the same day anyway, but the custody officer told him that he would stay overnight and would be presented to the investigative judge.) Following this encounter, the lawyer told the researcher that 'there was little he could do for such a confused person: this was someone who cannot find his way in our society'.

As described in Chapters 3 and 4, the encountered lawyers also usually did not attend to their clients' well-being while in custody (with the exception of access to medical care). The fact of being on 'police territory' seemed to further discourage lawyers from acting upon such needs. In one case, for example, a suspect who was under the influence of alcohol had difficulty talking – as his throat was very dry – to the extent that the lawyer was unable to understand what he was saying (FNNeth27.02.2012). When the lawyer asked a police officer to bring a drink to the suspect, the officer responded that 'he will get a drink at regular hours'. The lawyer did not insist any further, even though he could hardly understand his client. In another observed exchange, the suspect was feeling cold, and asked the lawyer if she could have her jacket (FNNeth31.08.2012). The lawyer asked the custody officer whether he could bring the suspect's jacket, to which the former responded that 'it was not possible'. The lawyer did not respond and told the suspect that if she was cold, she should ask the officers for a blanket later.

Likewise, the encountered lawyers typically did not react to their clients' complaints about the conditions of their detention. Where suspects complained about not having been able to make a telephone call, to smoke or to have sufficient 'airing' time outside of the cell, the observed lawyers simply told them that they should 'ask the police' about it. Thus, in one case, involving a minor, the suspect told the lawyer that she had not been able to call her parents, had not eaten anything since she was arrested (the preceding evening), and that she wished to smoke. The lawyer told her that she should ask the police to let her make a call, as well as for food and a cigarette, or otherwise she should ask her parents to bring her cigarettes (FNNeth14.02.2012). In another case, in response to the suspect's complaint about an alleged illegal arrest, the lawyer typically told the latter that 'they will be able to request compensation for an illegal arrest later'. After the consultation, the lawyer told the researcher that 'such clients are all the same': now he 'raves about being mistreated', but it will later turn out that he is 'guilty as hell' (FNNeth08.08.2012).

The lawyers' lack of attention to clients' emotional or social needs at the investigative stage could be explained in several ways. As described in Chapter 6, the legal aid payment structures, such as fixed fees, and the decreasing compensation for police station assistance could incentivise lawyers to focus mostly or solely on the 'legal' issues, and avoid dealing with any broader clients' concerns. Practicing empathy, inquiring into their clients' well-being and emotional needs, and addressing their 'social' needs while in detention, requires considerable time. Many encountered lawyers whose practices were fully or mostly dependent on legal aid funding could not invest the necessary time to provide a more 'holistic' service to their clients at the investigative stage. Rather, they adopted a routinised 'meet 'em, greet 'em and plead 'em' approach (Rhode, 2004: 12) to legal assistance, depersonalising the client and minimising the time spent on each case (Newman, 2016).

Lawyers' reluctance to engage with the clients' emotional or social needs could also be explained by what is described in literature as 'emotional distancing' or 'detachment' of certain professional workers (Oakley and Cocking, 2001: 137; Kerasidou and Horn, 2016). Emotional detachment has two facets. On the one hand, it is viewed as an element of 'professionalism' in certain occupations, such as doctors or lawyers (Oakley and Cocking, 2001: 137). These professions value status, expressed as, inter alia, assuming emotional distance from the client (Lively and Powell, 2006), and/or require exercising an objective judgment (doctors), or adopting a particular moral position (e.g. criminal defence lawyers, who must be partisan towards the client's interests: Oakley and Cocking, 2001: 146–147). In the professional ideology of both doctors and lawyers, acting 'professionally' means relying exclusively on technical skills, logic and rational judgment and bypassing emotions, feelings or personal judgments vis-à-vis patients or clients (Kiser, 2015; Kerasidou and Horn, 2016). This type of professionalism is ingrained in the training and socialisation of the respective occupational members (Lief and Fox, 1963; Townsley, 2014).

Lawyers, for instance, are trained to approach clients' problems in a rational and structured way, focus solely on the 'legally relevant' facts, and pursue the 'bottom line' legal outcomes (the final 'win' or 'lose') (Shaffer, 2005: 21). Thus, as described in Chapters 3 and 4, lawyers in both jurisdictions were only 'picking up' on certain types of procedural violations occurring at the investigative stage – namely, those that were likely to lead to a legal remedy and potentially influence the case outcome. Lawyers did not know what else they could do to help the client, if not to request some sort of a legal remedy. This can be illustrated by the following Dutch lawyer's response to the question about which kinds of procedural violations he would try to challenge at the investigative stage:

> Well [I would raise] Salduz and things like that of course. That sometimes goes wrong. And sometimes a client will say he was handled a bit roughly but that's always difficult. It's just something your client is telling you and if you can't base it on anything it's difficult to really do something with it.
> (INTNeth10)

In the second meaning, 'emotional detachment' is a coping mechanism used by professionals who regularly deal with stressful or emotionally challenging situations (e.g. nurses in intensive care units) (Hayward and Tuckey, 2011). Coping mechanisms are employed when professionals are required to perform 'emotional labour', namely to display or hide certain emotions as required by the (unspoken) professional rules (ibid.; Kadowaki, 2015). Research has shown that lawyers working across legal fields engage in emotional labour to manage negative emotions, particularly towards clients and their causes (Yakren, 2008; Westaby, 2010; Kadowaki, 2015). Assisting suspects detained in custody is possibly the most stressful and emotionally challenging aspect of defence lawyers' work. Police custody is a highly emotional environment (Skinns, 2010; Wooff and Skinns, 2018). During my fieldwork I often observed clients who were stressed, frightened, angry or seeking release, or police officers who were unwelcoming of lawyers (particularly in the Netherlands) or under time pressure to get on with the interrogation. It is easy to imagine how encounters with certain clients in police detention may provoke strong emotions: anger, repulsion, frustration or sadness. Lawyers were often stressed due to the need to make important decisions within a short amount of time and limited available information. The stress was augmented by the fact that they were often required to attend police stations in the midst of other appointments, or during the hours intended for social life or rest. Nonetheless, it seemed that any display of emotions such as anger, repulsion or sadness would be highly inappropriate according to the unspoken professional rules: instead, lawyers were expected to be 'civil' and emotionally 'neutral' towards both the clients and the police.

Systematic exercise of emotional detachment may result in depersonalising clients and desensitising towards their needs, becoming unresponsive or even unaware of the extent of their suffering (Oakley and Cocking, 2001: 138). This might in part explain lawyers' insensitivity to the clients' complaints about the conditions of their detention, or to their plight for making telephone calls, getting some fresh air, food or drink described in this chapter. Another likely factor, or consequence of emotional detachment is that some lawyers perceived their work tasks at the police station as boring, repetitive and intellectually 'unengaging' (Niks et al., 2017). Most encountered lawyers in this study (in line with the McConville et al. [1994] study) considered police station work significantly less challenging than court representation. Some Dutch lawyers, for example, have candidly described attending interrogations as 'tedious' (although this was partly because they believed they had no meaningful role in interrogations). As one lawyer noted:

> The interrogation will last three or four hours, and you have to keep your mouth shut all the time ... And it is not so exciting like you see it on TV. It is a 'social interrogation' for two hours, with an officer typing each question and answer with two fingers ... In the first half hour you fall asleep! So then you think, perhaps I could spend my time in a more lucrative way.
> (INTNeth31)

These perceptions were likely false, because although assisting clients at police stations often does not require to apply or interpret the law (FNNeth14.02.2011), it involves other types of challenges, such as the effective use of communication and interpersonal skills, or processing large amounts of information (Mols et al., 2016).

Some interviewed Dutch lawyers went as far as describing the events occurring at the investigative stage as relatively 'trivial', and not 'worthy' of their time and personal investment (INTNeth15, 28, 31). Interestingly, in the Netherlands, these views, and the general tendency of lawyers to take emotional distance vis-à-vis their clients appeared contrary to the ideas embedded in the procedural tradition, which encouraged lawyers' personal dedication to clients and moral investment into their causes.

4.4 The non-confrontational stance with the authorities

As described in Chapter 4, the encountered English lawyers, being 'repeat players' at the investigative stage of the proceedings, tended to adopt a cooperative, non-confrontational stance vis-à-vis the police authorities. Similar findings were reported by McConville et al., and in other studies (Dixon, 1991; Baldwin, 1993). As Sanders et al. (2010) wrote, 'adversarialism is not a natural stance for most defence lawyers, particularly those who spend a lot of time advising suspects. To such lawyers, the police station is a workplace and maintaining good relations with work colleagues is important' (244).

Dutch lawyers, like English lawyers, also tended to adopt a non-confrontational stance towards the police. Most lawyers encountered in both jurisdictions believed that maintaining good relationships with the police made them more effective at the investigative stage. An overwhelming majority of the Dutch lawyers said that they tried to behave in a 'friendly' manner towards the police, and some said that they used confrontation only as a last resort. As one lawyer described it:

INTERVIEWER: In general, how would you describe your attitude to the police?
LAWYER: Cooperative. I will hold with the hare and hunt with the hounds. One of the first pieces of advice I was given. Because otherwise you won't get much cooperation from the other side either. So only when there's no way, when it's unacceptable, I'll be harsher. But that actually never happened.

(INTNeth5)

Another lawyer echoed this:

Generally I am for friendliness. I think you can get more out of it by being friendly, than by being a strict lawyer. The police are normally already quite reluctant towards lawyers and if I would enter like a strict lawyer they would right away remove me from the interrogation ...

(INTNeth12)

In the words of yet another lawyer:

You go in with the friendly, professional attitude and this is the way to do it. I know there are some lawyers who go in and think it's a definite 'us and them' scenario. I find that this doesn't work very well. It puts their backs up and you end up being there longer when you don't need to be ... And that's how the relationship down with the police would be, of, I would say, professional friendly nature.

(INTNeth13)

As described in Chapter 4, English lawyers tended to rationalise taking a non-confrontational stance towards the police by emphasising the need to protect the interests of their (current and future) clients. Indeed, establishing a good rapport is key to obtaining cooperation, even if the other party in the relationship has differing, or even conflicting goals.[8] Lawyers might also wish to develop 'friendly' relationships with the police to increase their negotiating power (Newman and Welsh, 2019: 88). At the same time, by rationalising their efforts at 'building rapport' with the police as being (only) in their clients' benefit, lawyers might have downplayed more self-serving concerns. Thus, for instance, lawyers depended on the police to facilitate their work at police stations. This also included a range of 'administrative' matters such as scheduling interviews and other appointments and informing lawyers about the progress of the proceedings. Lawyers repeatedly came across the same police officers – which gave them an additional incentive to invest in building 'good' relations with these officers. In the words of one English lawyer:

> I mean, it has to do with your reputation. Because you go to the same police stations again and again and again, and so some solicitors get a reputation for being awkward, difficult, and they get back awkwardness and difficultness from the police officers, whereas if you are relatively straightforward, you're there to do a job.
>
> (INTEng14)

A Dutch lawyer expressed a similar sentiment:

> I am cooperative, so with that I mean I take into account the agenda of the police. I am always friendly, because you will need these people in the future, so therefore I am always very friendly at the police station. You achieve the most with this.
>
> (INTEng7)

It was argued elsewhere that the need to maintain 'good' ongoing relations with police officers might cause lawyers to be less assertive when defending their clients' interests at police stations (Baldwin, 1993). In other words, lawyers may fail to speak up and challenge the officers' behaviour, out of concern that this might damage their future relationship with the latter. Early research conducted in the UK, depicting lawyers' passivity, their frequent alignment with the police's objectives and the lack of appropriate concern for their clients' interests and goals, provides some support to this claim (ibid.; McConville et al., 1994; Blackstock et al., 2013: 407–408). Theoretical support for this hypothesis could be found in the so-called 'repeat player versus one-shot player' theory (Galanter, 1974). This theory suggests, inter alia, that the interests of one-shot players (suspects) may get overshadowed in interactions between repeat players (police and lawyers) (Bloomberg, 1967). That is because the latter might be guided by other, longer-term, incentives, than simply obtaining a desired result for their current client. Thus, in the context of police detention, it may be suggested that the wish of lawyers, for instance, to secure (future) police cooperation on scheduling matters, or to ensure a 'pleasant' atmosphere in their future encounter(s) with the police, might at times interfere with the need to oppose the officers in the interests of the client.

168 *Influence of occupational cultures*

The lawyers' reluctance to enter into confrontation with the police also seemed to be caused by lawyers' lack of power in their mutual relationships. As one English lawyer noted:

> There's no point in going into a police station and claiming police breached PACE in front of everybody, because you are on their turf. It's their time. You're not in a courtroom, which is your time. They have complete control of everything. And what you are trying is just trying to tweak things to prop your client and try and sort out what the best outcome will be for your client, but without interfering with everything or anything.
>
> (INTEng2)

5 Conclusions

Occupational cultures of criminal defence lawyers played an important role in shaping the practical exercise of the role of lawyers at the investigative stage. Professional or occupational cultures were defined in this chapter as the 'underlying assumptions', namely, the unconscious and taken-for-granted beliefs which determine the professionals' worldview, and are formed in response to the tensions inherent in the given occupation and its societal role. Thus, the 'core' of these cultures, stemming from the very nature of the occupational role, is rather stable and universal across those contexts where such occupational roles exist. Occupational cultures (the 'habitus') shape the practice, or the respective professional actors' behaviour, alongside the 'field', or the procedural, institutional or sociopolitical context, in which these professionals operate. Thus, procedural traditions and criminal justice policies (see Chapters 5 and 6) may be considered part of such a context. Procedural traditions, however, do not appear to play a determinative role in shaping the defence lawyers' occupational cultures at the investigative stage of the proceedings for the reasons outlined in Section 3.1.

Whilst this research was not per se a study of the lawyers' occupational cultures, it has documented certain common tendencies in the encountered lawyers' behaviours and attitudes, arguably informed by their 'underlying cultural assumptions'. Thus, in both countries, lawyers tended to mistrust their clients and assume them to be guilty. Clients were often perceived as incapable of taking reasonable decisions, or acting rationally (in the given context). As a result, lawyers in both jurisdictions wished to control their clients' behaviour, which could arguably result in a lawyer-centred and paternalistic approach to the lawyer–client relationship (Rosenthal, 1974; Cochran et al., 2014).

Another tendency observed across jurisdictions was the lawyers' desire to control and manage risks, manifested in particular in their reasoning behind advising clients to remain silent. Whilst lawyers explained their risk-avoiding behaviour as a means to protect the interests of their clients, they were (also) likely to protect their own interests, such as avoiding possible professional embarrassment, or being accused of fabricating false exculpatory stories. In both jurisdictions, lawyers tended to adopt a non-confrontational stance towards the police, which could be explained by their role as 'repeat players', as well as by the asymmetries of power at the investigative stage. Finally, this chapter suggests that the lawyers' reluctance to invest in their clients' emotional and social needs noted in Chapters 3 and 4 was partly the result of lawyers' 'emotional detachment' from their clients. This detachment could originate from, first, the unspoken professional rules, imprinted through professional learning and socialisation, requiring lawyers to bypass emotions and keep an emotional distance from clients. Second, it could be the manifestation of a coping mechanism in response to the highly stressful and emotional nature of police station work.

Whilst the various elements of defence lawyers' occupational cultures described in this chapter constituted 'negative' behaviours, arguably they were also the manifestations of the tensions and challenges inherent in the defence lawyer's procedural position and societal role. These were likely to be, for instance, the need to adopt a partisan stance and to 'mute' other moral concerns (such as the plight of crime victims), the challenges of empathising with clients and of dealing with power imbalances (lawyers vis-à-vis investigative authorities), as well as the relative lack of control over the work results (namely, procedural outcomes).

By focusing exclusively on certain observed patterns, this chapter inevitably presents an oversimplified picture of the defence lawyers' occupational cultures at the investigative stage of the proceedings. Thus, the patterns described here should not be viewed as unchangeable and omnipresent features of such cultures. Indeed, not all encountered lawyers in the two examined jurisdictions exhibited these attitudes and behaviours. The lawyers' attitudes towards their role at the investigative stage were in reality quite diverse. For instance, some English as well as Dutch lawyers disagreed with the prevalent view that they should adopt a 'non-confrontational' approach towards the authorities, but emphasised the need for adopting a more critical and confident attitude. In both jurisdictions, some observed lawyers adopted an empathetic attitude towards their clients, took the time to dive into their personal stories and the context of the impugned events, were respectful of their clients' wishes and opinions, attentive to their 'non-legal' needs, and adopted an assertive stance vis-à-vis the authorities. (Although these behaviours and attitudes diverted from those that seemed 'common' or 'typical' in the given context, as described in this – and the preceding – chapters.) This finding underscores the idea that defence lawyers play an active role in shaping their occupational cultures and behaviours by accepting or rejecting certain elements of these cultures. Thus, lawyers' occupational cultures, being relatively stable, are also amenable to change.

Notes

1 Because criminal defence is an occupation, rather than a profession, this chapter uses the term 'occupational' culture when referring to criminal defence lawyers.
2 Although 'occupations' and not 'organisations', the definition is relevant, because the concept of 'organisational culture' situates the general notion of 'culture' within the domain of professional or occupational activity.
3 Three out of 32 interviewed lawyers. See INTNeth4, 21, 26.

4 In observations, Dutch lawyers advised silence in about one-fifth of all observed cases. The encountered English lawyers advised silence in 12 out of 58 observed cases.
5 For instance, virtually every interviewed Dutch lawyer evoked these uncertainties, in connection with their lack of access to the relevant information.
6 A US consultancy, Hildebrandt International, ran personality surveys with 1898 lawyers in four American law firms, and compared them with the findings of personality surveys of managers across different industries. Lawyers scored about 20% higher than managers on the scale of 'cautiousness' defined as the willingness to take risks in decision-making (Foster et al., 2010: 5).
7 It should be noted that this tendency was observed only on the level of perceptions. The methodology of this study did not allow for examining whether and how often the encountered lawyers sought to avert risks when advising clients to remain silent in practice.
8 An analogy may be made with the suspect–police relationship in an interview, where the suspect's objectives may be different or opposing to the police's objectives. However, it was demonstrated that building rapport is an effective technique for obtaining suspects' cooperation in the interview (Vanderhallen and Vervaeke, 2014: 63).

8 Concluding remarks

1 Introduction

The traditional role of a criminal defence lawyer as (primarily) a trial advocate is challenged by the contemporary developments in the European systems of criminal procedure. Due to the shifting focus of the criminal proceedings to the pretrial or investigative stages, lawyers are increasingly expected to exercise 'active defence' from the earliest moments of the proceedings. These developments have become embedded in the national and European laws on criminal procedure, and they constitute the new work reality for European criminal defence lawyers. This study sought to shed light onto the question of whether – and how – the new, extended role that defence lawyers are expected to play at the investigative stage of the proceedings is realised, or is 'realisable', in practice.

To respond to this question, it was first necessary to develop an understanding of what the 'new' role of a lawyer at the investigative stage of the proceedings entails according to the relevant normative sources. As the impetus for change towards a more 'active defence' at the pre-trial stages of criminal proceedings originated from Europe, European normative pronouncements (EU and ECtHR) were used as the sources to distil these normative views. The second step of the research was to examine the practice of legal assistance at the investigative stage in two European jurisdictions, which differed in their procedural background and the amount of experience with police station legal assistance (the Netherlands and England and Wales). The next task was to compare the observed practices with the normative 'model' of the role of lawyers at the investigative stage, and assess whether – and to what extent – they were aligned with this model. As the next step, the findings concerning the 'compliance' of the observed professional practice at the investigative stage in the two jurisdictions, with the normative view of the role of lawyers at this stage, were placed in the broader context. Could the discrepancies between the normative 'model' and the observed practice within each jurisdiction, or the differences between the jurisdictions, be attributed (only) to the influence of procedural traditions? What is the impact of the contemporary criminal justice policies, which prioritise efficiency, cost-saving and crime control, on the practice of criminal defence at the investigative stage? Which features of lawyers' occupational cultures might hinder the practical realisation of the normative role of a lawyer at the investigative stage in practice? Finally, what can be said about the possibilities to instigate change in lawyers' professional practices? In which area(s) should the effort lie: legal regulation, policy, or elsewhere?

This chapter synthesises the findings of this research with the ultimate goal to inform the development of a plausible 'theory of change' with regard to the professional practice of criminal defence at the investigative stage. Section 2 reflects on the nature of the normative 'model' of the role of lawyers at the investigative stage of the criminal proceedings described in Chapter 2. Section 3 compares the empirical findings from the Netherlands and England and Wales in light of this normative view. Section 4 describes the findings concerning the respective influence of procedural traditions, criminal justice policies and lawyers' occupational cultures on the practical realisation of the role of lawyers at this stage. Section 5 presents insights intended to guide practical change. The chapter concludes on an optimistic note, arguing that, despite the inherent complexities, an 'active' and 'participatory' role of criminal defence lawyers at the investigative stage can be achieved in practice.

2 The normative model of the role of lawyers at the investigative stage: between aspiration and rhetoric

Chapter 2 of this book argued that the contemporary normative view of the role of lawyers at the investigative stage of the criminal proceedings reflected in the respective European pronouncements is that of 'active' and 'participatory' defence. Affording this role to defence lawyers is the necessary precondition of procedural fairness at the pre-trial stages of the proceedings. Yet, the normative 'model' presented in Chapter 2 contains elements that are not systematically present or enforced in all European legal systems. For instance, in most European jurisdictions, the possibility to access case-related information prior to the first interrogation of the suspect is not afforded on the level of the right, nor of the practice (see Pivaty and Soo, 2019 for further references). Most Member States, did not consider affording the right of access to case materials prior to the first suspect interrogation necessary for adequate transposition of *Directive 2012/13/ EU* (ibid.). The normative 'model', as argued in Chapter 2, also presupposes the possibility for a lawyer to play an active role during the interrogation of the client, and to intervene for various reasons. However, some European countries, including the Netherlands, Belgium or France, have placed important restrictions on the role of lawyers during suspect interrogations (see Pivaty, 2018 for further references).

Ensuring adequate access to case-related information for the defence prior to the first interrogation, and the possibility for a lawyer to participate actively during the interrogation, is essential for the practical realisation of an 'active' and 'participatory' defence role at the investigative stage. Access to case-related information facilitates several aspects of the role of lawyers at this stage (Blackstock et al., 2013: 10–11). Lawyers are often unable to provide meaningful advice concerning the strategy to be used in the interrogation, if no information is provided about the accusation and evidence. Effective lawyers' participation in the interrogation may also be compromised by the lack of prior access to the case materials, because lawyers might be focused on trying to understand the nature of the accusation and the evidence, rather than being alert to any improper questioning tactics (ibid.: 407). Without access to the case-related materials, lawyers might be unable to challenge their clients' arrest or argue for pre-trial release (*Mooren v. Germany* [2009]). Effective defence participation in the decision for an out-of-court disposal may also be compromised if lawyers (and suspects) are not given prior access to the case file. Lawyers are unable to assess the completeness and legality of the evidence collected by the authorities, or verify the appropriateness of the charge(s) and the proposed settlement or penalty. Finally, when lawyers do not enjoy access to case-related information before meeting clients at the investigative stage, this may hinder the development of trust and the establishment of an effective lawyer–client relationship. For instance, as demonstrated by several examples observed in the Netherlands (see Chapter 3), police might suggest to suspects that their lawyers are incompetent because they 'know nothing about the details of their case'.

In turn, the requirement to afford a broad participatory role to criminal defence lawyers during suspect interrogations follows from the notion of centrality of police interrogations (Pivaty, 2018: 28–30). If pre-trial procedural stages increasingly become the 'centre of gravity' of criminal proceedings, police interrogations of suspects are usually the 'centre of gravity' of pre-trial investigations. Suspect interrogations are crucial for the evidence-gathering process and for determining the avenues for further investigation. Often, the first police interrogation(s) are the moment when the procedural position of the suspect is determined and fixed. In any legal system, retracting statements made during the interrogation, or giving a statement after having remained silent, carries a risk that the suspect's account given at a later stage would not be believed. A change in the suspect's procedural position may also be interpreted as evidence that they are lying, and therefore guilty of the impugned offence(s). Consequently, in the contemporary criminal proceedings oriented towards the pre-trial stages, suspect interrogations at the investigative stage become the focal points for active defence-building. To enable active defence in the context of suspect interrogations, lawyers should be given the possibility to exercise a broad range of functions, described in Chapter 2. Clearly, statutory limitations such as the possibility for lawyers to ask questions only in the beginning or in the end of the interrogation, which exist in the Netherlands (see Chapter 5) are incompatible with the lawyer's ability to freely exercise their normative role implied in the European regulations.

The above-mentioned examples show that if taken seriously by governments, the normative model of the role of lawyers at the investigative stage developed in Chapter 2 can serve as a source of inspiration to inform national law-making. It can also be used by national courts or CJEU to assess compliance of national regulations with EU law, as well as to determine, in concrete cases, whether suspects have benefited from effective legal assistance at the investigative stage. It can be relied on by lawyers' professional organisations to inform debates about the nature and 'content' of the appropriate professional role at the investigative stage. Finally, it can be invoked by individual lawyers to substantiate defence motions in court, particularly with regard to the compliance of national law with European norms. On the other hand, if certain elements of the normative model are not reflected in national law, there is a higher risk that in these Member States, the right of early access to a lawyer would play a rhetorical or legitimising role, instead of being a real guarantee of 'effective participation' of the suspect in the pre-trial proceedings.

3 England and Wales and the Netherlands compared

Chapters 3 and 4 described the findings of the empirical study into the role of Dutch and English criminal defence lawyers at the investigative stage of the proceedings. It was noted that the observed Dutch practice was particularly far from the 'model' normative view of such role embedded in the European regulations. The observed Dutch lawyers were generally unable to secure 'trust' in the first police station encounters and to obtain detailed (or coherent) accounts from their clients. Dutch lawyers were almost never given access to case-related information ('disclosure') by the police, and nor did they ask for it. Likewise, at the time of the fieldwork, they generally did not attend suspect interrogations, with the exception of interrogations of minors. In those observed interrogations where lawyers did attend, they generally remained passive.

The observed English practice of legal assistance at the investigative stage was closer to the normative view described in Chapter 2. English lawyers seemed to secure sufficient trust to enable clients to give detailed disclosure to their lawyers, and to follow their advice. The encountered English lawyers were usually given detailed disclosure of case-related information by the police prior to meeting with the client. Most lawyers also sought additional disclosure from the police. Furthermore, English lawyers were rather active during interrogations, intervening not only to advise their clients, but also to assist them in providing their accounts, and to react to inappropriate or abusive questioning.

Several possible explanations of these differences between the English and Dutch practices can be put forward. First, the difference might stem from the fact that the Dutch system of criminal procedure follows the inquisitorial tradition, which encourages a more 'passive' defence lawyers' role and defence culture, and the English system follows an adversarial tradition, which encourages a more 'active' role. It is, however, unlikely that the difference in the procedural traditions account for all observed differences (see Chapter 5 for more detail). Another possible explanation lies in the different amounts of experience with police station legal assistance in the two jurisdictions: England and Wales had had more than 30 years of such experience, and the Netherlands only 2–3 years at the time of the fieldwork. It may be hypothesised that in England and Wales, lawyers obtained greater access to the investigative procedures than in the Netherlands, because the authorities have become accustomed with their presence, and the initial mistrust of lawyers has been overcome (Vanderhallen et al., 2014: 167–169). However, this mutual accustomisation cannot explain why lawyers became more 'active' or 'assertive' in the interrogation room. Rather, it was likely to incentivise lawyers, as 'repeat players' in the respective procedures, to be non-confrontational with the police as described in Chapters 6 and 8. Thus, another, more plausible explanation of the difference between the English and Dutch findings lies in the fact that in England and Wales a concerted effort had been made to reform deficient professional practices of legal assistance at the investigative stage, as described in Chapter 7.

At the same time, the observed English lawyers' professional practices were often not aligned with the normative 'model' of the role of lawyers at the investigative stage. For instance, lawyers played a rather dominant, 'lawyer-centred' role in the lawyer–client relationship. They also exercised caution when intervening to directly challenge police behaviour in order to preserve good working relationships with the police. Some English lawyers have furthermore initiated or facilitated 'deals' with the police incentivising suspects to confess or cooperate with the investigation in exchange for bail or an out-of-court disposal. In this work, such practices were explained with reference to lawyers' occupational cultures, such as the tendency to mistrust clients, the desire to control risks, and lawyers acting as 'repeat players' in the proceedings at the investigative stage.

Most importantly, in both jurisdictions, lawyers approached their role at the investigative stage in a narrow fashion, focusing mostly on the pre-interrogation advice and the interrogation itself (Blackstock et al., 2013: 446). Other tasks embedded in the normative model described in Chapter 2 – such as providing moral and social support to the client, or challenging procedural irregularities – were either not acknowledged by lawyers as part of their role, or were not exercised in practice. These tendencies were explained mainly by the influences from the lawyers' occupational cultures and the contemporary criminal justice policies, which incentivised lawyers to reduce time and resources spent on individual cases at the investigative stage.

For similar reasons, lawyers in both jurisdictions did not actively participate in the fact-finding process at the investigative stage, although they were not prohibited from participating by national law. Furthermore, as the consequence of recent criminal justice reforms, lawyers in both jurisdictions had reduced possibilities to access important decision making processes at the investigative stage, such as the decisions on the out-of-court disposal in the Netherlands, or charging decisions in England and Wales. Yet, ensuring meaningful participation of lawyers in the fact-finding and decision-making processes is key to the practical realisation of the contemporary view on the role of the lawyer at the investigative stage, which underscores the ability to build an 'active defence' at the earliest possible moment in the proceedings.

4 The interplay of procedural traditions, criminal justice policies and occupational cultures

Ascertaining which factors influence the role of defence lawyers at the investigative stage in practice across several jurisdictions is a difficult task. The difficulty is augmented by the complex nature of the relationship between legal norms, institutions and other similar categories (procedural traditions, social and political structures), and the day-to-day practice – or behaviour – of criminal justice actors and their professional cultures.

This research, whilst not pretending to provide a comprehensive theory concerning the above-mentioned relationship, provided insights that could be used as 'building blocks' for developing such a theory. First, this study examined the possible influence of legal procedural traditions on the practical operation of the criminal process in one particular area: legal assistance at the investigative stage (Chapter 5). Procedural traditions were defined as a sub-element of 'legal tradition', or as a set of historically conditioned normative ideas or attitudes related to the objectives and values of the criminal procedural system, and the roles and powers of the different actors in the criminal process, considered valuable and worthy of perpetuating according to criminal justice actors. These ideas are primarily reflected in the laws and regulations on the criminal procedure (in a broad sense, including ethical and professional regulations). Although procedural traditions are not monolithic or omnipotent, most European systems of criminal procedure are originally 'shaped' by either the 'inquisitorial' or 'adversarial' tradition. It is, however, less clear whether and how (by means of which mechanisms) procedural traditions influence the day-to-day practice or behaviour of criminal justice actors. Besides exerting influence through the respective regulations, procedural traditions – as suggested in the literature (Langer, 2004) – may influence the practice because the respective actors internalise the values and beliefs embedded in these traditions (and so these ideas become part of their 'occupational culture', see Chapter 7).

The present study – which, however, focuses only on one aspect of criminal procedural practice: that of legal assistance at the investigative stage – did not reveal much evidence of the influence of procedural traditions on such practice. 'Traces' of the influence of procedural traditions were found in how lawyers in both jurisdictions formulated their advice to clients at the investigative stage. Furthermore, the ideas embedded in the prevailing traditions ('inquisitorial' or 'adversarial') were often reflected in lawyers' 'official' professional discourse, for instance concerning the lawyer–client relationship. However, observations revealed that these ideas were usually not reflected in lawyers' day-to-day professional practice. Furthermore, this study argued that certain practices, such as the prior disclosure of case-related information to lawyers in England and Wales or Dutch lawyers' 'powerlessness' in the interrogation room, which seemed congruent with the prevailing procedural tradition, actually (also) developed under other types of influences. The study has moreover shown that lawyers in both jurisdictions used references to the procedural traditions to justify deficient professional practices, pointing at the possible 'rhetorical' function of procedural traditions. These findings highlight the need for further exploration of the role of procedural traditions vis-à-vis the practical operation of the criminal process, and the professional practices of its actors.

In addition to procedural traditions, contemporary criminal justice policies of managerialism and crime control have certainly affected the practical exercise of the role of defence lawyers at the investigative stage in both examined jurisdictions (Chapter 6). Their influence on lawyers' professional practices at this stage has been mostly negative: thus, these policies reduced the resources, space, time and other opportunities available for lawyers to exercise the role as envisaged in the normative 'model' presented in Chapter 2. In the English literature, this influence is described as severely compromising the role of lawyers and quality of legal assistance, including at the investigative stage of the proceedings (Smith, 2013; Newman, 2016; Newman and Welsh, 2019). This study has shown that Dutch lawyers are currently facing very similar influences. At the same time, this research presents a more nuanced analysis of the impact of managerialist policies, showing that they have also had residual positive effects. These were, for instance, the development of pre-interview disclosure practices in England and Wales, or the nascent practice of sharing case-related information within the ZSM proceedings in the Netherlands.

Finally, this research examined whether the occupational cultures of criminal defence lawyers constitute an obstacle for the practical realisation of the normative 'model' of the role of lawyers at the investigative stage (Chapter 7). The hypothesis that these cultures may have such an influence was derived both from the literature on comparative criminal justice and from the studies of policing. Indeed, this research has shown that certain elements of lawyers' occupational cultures, common across the two researched jurisdictions – such as the tendency to mistrust clients and view them as guilty, the desire to control risks to avoid, inter alia, professional embarrassment, the non-confrontational approach towards the police, and emotional distancing from clients – were likely to prevent lawyers from acting in line with the normative view of their role at the investigative stage. This study, however, focused solely on the negative manifestations of defence lawyers' occupational cultures at the investigative stage, and it did not focus on the positive elements of such cultures. Further research into defence lawyers' occupational cultures therefore appears necessary, particularly given the dearth of such research as compared to the studies of policing culture.

5 Reforming the practice of criminal defence at the investigative stage

The insights on the 'theory of change' presented in this final section are inspired, first, by the works of Janet Chan on changing police cultures (Chan, 1996, 1997). As described in Chapter 7, Chan developed a model of interaction between the police's occupational cultures ('habitus'), the broader context within which the police operate (the 'field') and the policing practice. This model appears suitable to explain the nature of relationships between lawyers' professional practices, lawyers' occupational cultures and other factors, such as procedural traditions or criminal justice policies, as described in the preceding section. Thus, defence lawyers' occupational cultures, some elements of which were described in Chapter 7, constitute the 'habitus' within which criminal defence practices develop. The 'field' consists of various 'contextual' structures and influences which are external to the given professional practices: such as procedural traditions, criminal justice policies, the institutional context of the investigative stage and the respective legal regulations. The respective practices develop as the result of the interaction between the 'habitus' and the 'field': thus, the 'habitus' and the 'field' influence each other, and jointly shape the respective practices.

Chan argued that achieving the desired change in the professional practices requires action both on the level of the 'habitus' and the 'field'. Although practices are likely to change if only one of the parameters (either the 'field' or the 'habitus') is modified, such change is likely to be unpredictable or short-lived. If action is taken only on the level of occupational cultures, the change is unlikely to be sustained in the absence of broader structures to support the emerging professional practices. If action only involves the 'field', for instance changing legal regulation, it cannot be predicted whether it would achieve the intended goal (as it would possibly conflict with occupational cultures) (Chan, 1916: 131). These insights, developed from an empirical exploration of police reforms, are also relevant in explaining the processes of change and resistance observed in this work.

In this research, there were numerous examples of (national) legal regulations pertaining to lawyers' professional practices, which were not enforced or used in practice. These were, for instance, the provisions on early access to case-related information in the Netherlands, or in both countries: the provisions on lawyers' participation in investigative actions at the investigative stage (see Chapters 3 and 4). These provisions were not used by lawyers due to, inter alia, the clash with lawyers' occupational cultures. The English example, where changes in lawyers' professional practices at the investigative stage were achieved, as argued in Chapter 7, due to acting simultaneously on the level of regulation and on the level of 'culture', provides further support for the 'theory of change' advanced by Chan.

Further insights on the role of legal regulation (European or national) in changing lawyers' professional practices can be derived from the works of David Dixon. Dixon (1997) outlined three theories explaining the relationship between legal regulation and the professional practice of criminal justice actors in his study of police. The 'legalistic' view assumes that the mere existence of a regulation ensures conformity of the practice with that regulation. The 'culturalist' approach argues that regulations are ineffective, because the practice is shaped exclusively by occupational cultures. The 'structural' approach states that regulations provide structural frameworks within which professional practices operate, and they may be effective, when they are in harmony with the existing social structures (Dixon, 2008: 21–45). In other words, laws must be complementary and conceptually compatible with the 'informal normative environment' (Licht, 2008: 734). The findings of this research do not support either the 'legalistic' or the 'culturalist' theory, but rather align with the 'structural' view.

This research has identified at least two ways in which laws and regulations concerning the role of the lawyer at the investigative stage could have influenced the relevant practices. First, at times they served to reinforce the already-existing practices by clarifying them, or providing better enforcement procedures. The articulation of the role of lawyers during suspect interviewing in the PACE Code of Practice is one example of a regulation that, arguably, had a positive impact on the practice of legal assistance during interviews, alongside other measures, such as training police station lawyers to apply the respective regulations (Edwards, 2008). Second, laws and regulations arguably served as a catalyst for the development of the underlying social structures and attitudes, which would, in turn, promote compliance with the respective regulations. The English example of PACE being a catalyst for critical research into various aspects of police detention, suspect interviewing and legal assistance – which then inspired several policy measures aimed at improving the implementation of PACE in practice – illustrates this kind of influence.

More generally, the expressive theory of law might explain why legal regulations may be effective in achieving change in (lawyers') occupational cultures. The expressive theory argues that law affects social judgments and sends messages to people about what is good or bad behaviour (Sunstein, 1996). Law might influence professionals' behaviour and act to change attitudes and beliefs by sending a signal that adhering to a certain legal norm would help maintain esteem and gain approval within the reference group of professionals (McAdams, 2009). Thus, legal regulation could help endorse certain beliefs, which form part of occupational cultures, over other, equally powerful competing beliefs. For instance, aligning the formal roles of criminal defence lawyers with the elements mentioned in the normative 'model' would signal the preference for due process values over crime control values (see Chapter 6), which both appear to be embedded in the occupational cultures of the relevant actors.[1] (In the professional practice of criminal defence, crime control values are implicitly promoted by the contemporary criminal justice policies, for example, through requiring lawyers to cooperate with the truth-finding [Cape, 2006; Smith, 2013].) Sending such a signal might incentivise professional actors to align their behaviours to the due process – rather than the opposite – values. The fact that PACE, together with other accompanying measures, as argued by Dixon (1997), triggered change in the approaches of the English police to suspect interviewing and police custody towards greater alignment with the due process values, provides support to this argument.

In addition to laws reflecting the normative view of the role of a lawyer at the investigative stage described in Chapter 2, further regulations may be needed to off-set negative effects of the contemporary criminal justice policies on the lawyer's role described in Chapter 6. For instance, revising the scope of the professional obligation of English lawyers to tell and endorse the truth and to inform the court about any errors of fact might be helpful to ensure the realisation of such a role in practice. Likewise, detailed regulations affording a participatory role to Dutch lawyers in the ZSM procedures might contribute to the practical implementation of this role.

However, legal regulation alone is insufficient to achieve the desired change in lawyers' professional practices at the investigative stage. Change is required also on the level of 'habitus', or the occupational cultures of criminal defence lawyers. To achieve such change, first and foremost, adequate funding of legal assistance at the investigative stage is essential. One could rightfully argue that increased funding alone is unlikely to improve the quality of lawyers' services or, even less so, have a transformative effect on the underlying professional cultures (Newman, 2013). Yet, adequate financing is the necessary precondition for the successful implementation of any measures aimed at ensuring the quality of legal assistance in criminal cases. Adequate remuneration is the basis for legitimacy of any quality assurance intervention. It is difficult to imagine that lawyers would genuinely comply with the prescriptions concerning the expected 'standard' of service without being adequately remunerated for that service.[2]

In addition to appropriate funding, some kind of quality assurance measures – concerning particularly the provision of legal assistance at the investigative stage, appear necessary. For example, accreditation of lawyers in assisting suspects at the investigative stage might be considered. As described in Chapter 4, in England and Wales, for instance, all lawyers wishing to assist suspects at the police station and receiving remuneration from the legal aid fund (both non-solicitors and solicitors) must undergo an accreditation process consisting of a 'reflective portfolio' and a test aimed at assessing critical skills, such as intervening during suspect interviews. The accreditation process, together with other measures, is believed to have contributed significantly to the professionalisation of English lawyers providing police station legal assistance.

Finally, professional training is key to the development of cultures that facilitate the practical implementation of the normative 'model' of the role of lawyers at the investigative stage. As a spin-off of this research project, for instance, a highly successful training programme for defence lawyers was implemented in Belgium, Hungary, Ireland and the Netherlands, which focused specifically on legal assistance at the investigative stage.[3] This programme aimed to develop the practical skills considered critical for the effective exercise of the various lawyers' functions at the investigative stage. These were the skills required to build rapport with clients, effectively gather factual information, intervene assertively in the interview, and negotiate with the police. The training also aimed at developing 'reflective practice' (Schön, 1984) as a tool enabling lawyers to, inter alia, become cognisant of the 'underlying assumptions' of their occupational cultures, and of other factors motivating their professional actions.

Across Europe, changes in lawyers' professional practices at the investigative stage of the proceedings are needed to adapt to the contemporary developments in their professional role. These developments, triggered on the one hand by the shifting centre of gravity of the criminal proceedings to the pre-trial stages, and on the other hand by the recent European regulations on suspects' procedural rights, envisage an increasingly 'active' and 'participatory' role for criminal defence lawyers at the investigative stage of the proceedings. This research concludes that this role can be effectuated in practice, provided that action is taken simultaneously on the level of (European and national) legislation, and of lawyers' occupational cultures. In addition to legislative reforms, attention must be given to adequate funding of criminal legal aid, quality assurance of legal assistance at the investigative stage, and training lawyers in the skills needed to provide such assistance.

Notes

1 On the role of 'due process' and 'crime control' values in the construction of police powers and their use in everyday policing, see Sanders and Young, 2008.
2 In her research examining the impact of managerialist policies on English legal aid lawyers, Sommerlad found that lawyers were cynical about government quality initiatives, because of the simultaneous pressure to cut costs – and that some lawyers even considered quality control measures as an 'indirect' way of exercising control over lawyers with the view to containing the costs of legal aid. See Sommerlad, 1999.
3 SUPRALAT: Strengthening the Protection of Suspects' Procedural Rights in Pre-Trial Proceedings in the EU through practice-oriented training for lawyers (JUST 2014/JTRA/AG/EJTR/6844) (1 October 2015 to 30 September 2017). See also Mols, 2017.

Appendix
Notes on the research methodology

1 Critical realism and constructivist grounded theory

The current research combined a critical realist (CR) ontology with elements of constructivist grounded theory (GT). CR is a philosophical framework of science situated between relativism and positivism.[1] In contrast to relativism, CR acknowledges the existence of a reality independent of the observer's mind (Sayer, 1992: 5). Unlike positivism, CR recognises that human knowledge is fallible, and only captures a small part of it (ibid.). Some aspects of the reality, however, are more accessible to human knowledge than others. This knowledge may be achieved as 'theories, which may be more or less truth like' (Danermark et al., 2002: 10). These theories have an explanatory character, namely they help us identify causal mechanisms behind social phenomena, activities and events, using rational judgment. Thus, the researcher's active role in the construction of knowledge is explicitly recognised.

CR is applicable to this study, because it engages with the explanation – or understanding – of the social reality, which goes beyond 'thick description' (Fletcher, 2016: 182). In doing so, it assumes that social problems may be studied and analysed from an external viewpoint, and that results may be transferable to other (similar) contexts than the one being studied. The presumption of transferability of findings, together with an emphasis on identifying explanations assumed to be inherent in the social phenomena, and to exist independently from their interpretations given by the relevant actors, renders the CR approach useful for making recommendations for social change. Furthermore, CR defines causality as a complex interplay of processes and mechanisms, rather than statistical regularities (Delanty, 2005: 147). Therefore, it implies that causal processes can be directly observed, rather than inferred by measurement. Thus, a CR approach allows engagement with causal explanations based on a qualitative inquiry.

CR views the reality as consisting of three levels.[2] The first level is the *empirical*[3] level, where meanings of social phenomena constructed through human interpretation can be directly observed (Fletcher, 2016: 183). This level is viewed as 'transitive' in the sense of being socially produced. Thus, critical realists are first interested in ascertaining the perceptions, beliefs and ideas of the relevant social actors about the studied reality. The second level is the *actual* level, where events occur independently of the human experience (for this reason characterised as *intransitive*), which may objectively differ from the theoretical (mind-produced) concepts about these events (Danermark et al., 2002: 20). The third and deepest level is the *real* level, where 'casual mechanisms' exist. Causal mechanisms are trends or tendencies, which may produce certain events, or enable or constrain the development of certain social phenomena in a certain way, depending on the existence of particular social conditions, or contextual factors (ibid.: 55–59). For critical realists, social objects or phenomena exist within 'open systems', namely those that constantly interact with their environment, and are therefore subject to numerous simultaneous influences (and demonstrate no constant regularities, or definitive relationship between variables) (Sayer, 1992: 122; Bhaskar, 2008). Because the objects within social systems – and relationships between them – are transient, it makes little sense to study these objects and relationships as such. Rather, the goal of a CR inquiry is to elicit the influences that shape these objects or relationships, and the conditions under which they might take effect. Thus, Schein's definition of occupational cultures used in this study (see Chapter 7) closely resembles a CR approach.

This research was structured to reflect the three above-mentioned levels of 'reality'. The information on the *empirical* level – consisting of the existing theories and actors' beliefs and perceptions – was obtained mostly through studying the literature (laws, regulations, ethical codes) and qualitative interviewing. The information on the *actual* level was gathered mainly through naturalistic observation. Any discrepancies within the data on the *empirical* level were carefully noted. Finally, the information on the *real* level was deduced by: identifying patterns of regularity on the *empirical* and *actual* levels (so-called 'demi-regularities') (Fletcher, 2016: 185) (Chapters 3 and 4), and reinterpreting – or explaining – the observed patterns by referencing certain theories (Chapters 5, 6 and 7). For instance, it was observed that English lawyers tended to consider remaining silent the 'safest', or the most 'advantageous', option for suspects (*demi-regularity on the empirical level*), whilst observations have shown that this advice was rarely given (*demi-regularity on the actual level*). Thus, the second step was to try and explain this discrepancy by referencing the existing theoretical frameworks (*causal mechanisms*). Indeed, lawyers considered silence the 'safest' option in order to avoid professional risks (*occupational cultures*). Contextual factors were also present: namely, the existence of the law on 'adverse inferences' (*criminal justice policies*).[4]

Insights from constructivist GT were used to inform the collection, interpretation and analysis of the data for this study. The purpose of constructivist GT is 'to learn how people make sense of the situations and act on them' (Charmaz, 2006: 11). The goal is to achieve in-depth understanding of a particular social process (ibid.: 22–23): in this study, legal assistance at the investigative stage. This includes unveiling the various explicit and implicit meanings given to this process by the participants, and ascertaining how these meanings shape their behaviour. Thus, the focus is not only on studying the 'talk', but also the 'action'. Moreover, an account must be given of the broader (local, social or institutional) context, in which interpretations and actions occur, to understand how – and why – these processes unfold in the given social conditions (this viewpoint is very similar to CR) (Willig, 2016). Constructivist GT recognises the researcher's active and subjective role in the construction and interpretation of the data. It encourages 'methodological self-consciousness' (Charmaz, 2017: 36), or paying close attention to how the researcher's own values, personal characteristics and positioning in the field affect the construction of research findings.

In line with the constructivist GT (Charmaz, 2006: 20), the empirical study was initiated with a general question: How does legal assistance at the investigative stage unfold? The research approach was fairly open-ended, and the analysis and early writing (in the forms of memos and drafts) were carried out simultaneously with the data collection. I continuously checked my interpretations of certain situations and the possible explanations for the observed patterns with the participants, other stakeholders (e.g. other academics), or by means of data triangulation. Data analysis and coding were guided by the recommendations from the CT approach and constructionist GT combined (Charmaz, 2006; Sobh and Perry, 2006; Bygstad et al., 2016; Fletcher, 2016). Coding was carried out in two steps. The initial coding was undertaken to establish the most prominent 'demi-regularities', or the emerging trends: such as, for instance, lawyers being directive in their advice. In the text, these demi-regularities were described as 'frequently observed practice', or opinions expressed by 'many' or 'the majority of' lawyers (where more than half of interviewed lawyers referred to a certain phenomenon or practice). References to the respective fieldnotes or interviews (kept on record) were omitted to avoid bulky citations. After that, additional data were collected to try and explain these trends (by means of 'theoretical sampling'). The second step consisted of the 'abduction' or 'theoretical redescription', namely, the data was recoded using the explanatory theories (procedural tradition, criminal justice policies and occupational cultures) each broken into several subthemes, to arrive at the underlying causal mechanisms.

2 Data collection

In the Netherlands, observations were conducted in June–July 2010 and February–September 2012, and the interviews in June–August 2014. In England and Wales, observations were conducted in January–July 2012 and April–July 2013, and the interviews in July–September 2013. The work on this study coincided with the European-funded project 'Procedural rights of suspects in police detention in the EU: empirical investigation and promoting best practice' (*Inside Police Custody*).[5] The project was developed on the basis of my PhD research. I was also a research team member and one of the field researchers.[6] Some data collected in this project were used in this study, but I also gathered extensive additional data. From the *Inside Police Custody* dataset I used: observations with lawyers in the Netherlands (18 weeks, conducted by me); observations with police in the Netherlands (15 weeks, conducted by me) and observations with lawyers in England and Wales (10 weeks, conducted by others); 7 interviews with English lawyers and 5 interviews with Dutch lawyers. The additional data I gathered myself consisted of: 6 weeks of observations in the Netherlands; 12 weeks of observations in England and Wales; and interviews with 20 lawyers in England and Wales and 27 lawyers in the Netherlands.[7] In total, I spent 51 weeks conducting observations, and an additional 4 weeks conducting interviews. Decisions on the length of immersion and number of interviews were driven by the need to have a sufficient amount of data to detect recurring patterns, and sufficient quality of data to achieve theoretical depth (Saunders et al., 2018).

The Dutch fieldwork was carried out in two sites in the central and southern parts of the country. The sites corresponded to the districts drawn for the purposes of the duty rota of police stations. I shadowed lawyers from the duty rota list. The southern site comprised four police stations located in three towns. The largest police station had a throughput of 1.300 arrests per year, and was located in a middle-size town (population: about 120.000). The duty rota list comprised about 160 lawyers, of which half were criminal law specialists. The second site, likewise, comprised four police stations, the largest having a throughput of 1.800 arrests a year, which was located in a somewhat larger town. The duty rota list included about 180 lawyers, of which just under half specialised in criminal law.

In England and Wales, most fieldwork was undertaken in a larger-sized urban area (population about 500.000), complemented by observations in a smaller-sized urban location (population about 40.000), both located in the south. At the time of the fieldwork, there were four police custody suites in the larger site (in different city districts), and one in the smaller site. The largest police station in the larger site had a throughput of about 9.500 arrests a year. The police station at the smaller site had a throughput of about 4.000 suspects a year. In England and Wales, other researchers and I were based in law firms. The larger site included two middle-sized firms: one specialised in criminal and family law, comprising seven criminal solicitors (six doing police station work) and two accredited representatives; and another specialised exclusively in criminal law, and included six staff who attended police stations (two solicitors and four accredited representatives). Overall, the site comprised about 25 criminal defence practices. The area included, for the purposes of the duty rota, the larger city, and a number of adjacent smaller towns. In the smaller site, the researcher was based at two firms employing specialised criminal lawyers (two each), and sharing the same police station accredited representatives.

3 Being in the field

The fieldwork commenced with naturalistic observations. The role I adopted in the field resembled that of an 'observer as participant' (Adler and Adler, 1994: 13). I was clearly identified as researcher, and could freely interact with the participants. My role was relatively non-intrusive, as most lawyers were used to having trainees observe them at work. I was never asked to perform any other role than that of a researcher, although I sometimes volunteered to take on practical tasks, such as interpreting introductions while waiting for an interpreter.

I took written notes simultaneously where possible (sometimes I refrained from taking notes because I considered it to be too intrusive) and then transcribed them, mostly electronically. I kept a log of all field notes noting the date they were taken, and which lawyer(s) I shadowed on that day (all encountered lawyers were assigned a particular number). All field notes were anonymised. In this study, field notes are referred to as 'FN' followed by a country identifier ('Eng' or 'Neth') and the date.

Following the observations, in-depth semi-structured interviews were conducted with most observed lawyers, as well as other lawyers, in both jurisdictions. The purpose was to learn about lawyers' own perspectives and interpretations of the observed practices. Interviews are referred to as 'INT', followed by the country identifier and the interview number. Additional participants were selected mostly by means of snowball sampling. However, care was taken to include different types of interviewees (e.g. women and men; partners and employees; solicitors and accredited representatives (in England and Wales); experienced and relatively inexperienced; specialised only in criminal law, or also in other areas; 'super-specialists' (financial crime, youth crime) and 'mainstream' criminal lawyers) to cover different perspectives. The topics loosely followed the sequence of the events at the investigative stage to provide structure. All topics were raised in each interview to ensure comparability, but there was much variation in the questions within each topic.

While in the field, I was aware of my status as a double outsider, namely someone who does not belong to the given profession (law academic vs. practicing lawyers) and a foreigner in both jurisdictions studied.[8] Given my 'outsider' status and the relatively short period of immersion, I expected that professionals might provide the 'public relation' answers rather than their real opinions on the studied topics (Charmaz, 2006: 20). This, however, was mostly an unfounded concern. The encountered lawyers were quite open about engaging with practices which did not seem to align with the norms of 'good professional practice'. Dutch lawyers, for instance, freely talked about being passive during suspects' interviews, or deciding not to attend clients' interrogations. They endorsed these attitudes as more 'pragmatic' or 'realistic' than the viewpoints given in the professional guides. At times, however, the interviews did result in more polished and idealised accounts than those transpired from observations (similar to what Newman (2013) has encountered during his study). Thus, more general questions ('How do you do X? What is your role with regard to X?') often seemed to invite accounts of the 'ideal' professional practice. These responses were valuable, because they demonstrated lawyers' 'espoused values and beliefs' (see Chapter 7), which could be compared with the observational data. The interviewees often switched perspectives within the same interview, first providing a more idealised account in response to the opening questions, and a more 'pragmatic' account later in the interview, or when discussing concrete examples.

I was mindful of how my presence may have affected the 'field' and the lawyers' behaviour. For instance, some lawyers seemed to be making a greater effort than they would usually do, due to the fact that they were being observed.

These lawyers, for instance, might have taken more time for the consultation because of my presence (see e.g. an example of an independent agent given in Chapter 6). Moreover, some lawyers, particularly in the Netherlands, where the role of providing legal assistance at the investigative stage was new to them, made references to them being 'under observation', or asked for feedback. (I would then point at something positive that I noticed them doing.) However, despite the possible 'research participation effect' (McCambridge et al., 2014) in both jurisdictions, the observed professional practice of lawyers at the investigative stage in both jurisdictions was very different from the 'model', normative view as described in Chapter 2.

I was furthermore aware of the possible influence of gender, status and other power-related issues whilst being 'in the field' (Charmaz, 2006: 27–28). About 70% of the lawyers I encountered in both countries were male. As a young female researcher, I ran the risk of my research subjects wishing to assert control of the interview process or even sexualising the encounter (Pini, 2005; Vähäsantanen and Saarinen, 2012). On the other hand, a woman researcher is likely to be viewed as an empathic and attentive listener, which facilitates rapport-building and encourages respondents to speak freely about their feelings and emotions (Arendell, 1997). Being interviewed by a woman invites men to talk about their work as a means to assert their masculinity, as 'work' is often central to masculine identity (Broom et al., 2009). During the fieldwork, I was mostly able to capitalise on the advantages of the inherent gender dynamics. Occasionally, I was the object of 'chivalrous' behaviour (Arendell, 1997: 362) (more so in England and Wales than in the Netherlands), but I never felt patronised or dominated due to being a woman. I also did not experience interviewees engaging in 'minimising' (giving terse answers) or 'maximising' strategies (providing overly detailed but superficial and patronising accounts, i.e. acting as a teacher) reported in other studies (Horn, 1997; Pini, 2005; Vähäsantanen and Saarinen, 2012). One exception was an interview with a partner in a law firm. In the interview, he gave succinct 'public relations' answers, which remained superficial, despite my attempts to achieve greater depth. I experienced his demeanour as domineering, or even aggressive. (Later when I got to know this lawyer better, the nature of our rapport changed.) My status of 'university researcher' or 'university lecturer', which was perceived by the research subjects as relatively high, appeared to mitigate the potential power disbalances of age and gender (Belur, 2014).

Achieving balance between understanding the perspectives of the research participants (Charmaz, 2006: 19) and the risk of 'going native' (Adler and Adler, 1994) was a particular challenge. Often I felt that lawyers were better able to judge whether action (or inaction) was 'appropriate' in a certain situation than an 'outsider' like myself. This especially concerned matters which were within lawyers' professional discretion: for instance, whether or not to intervene in the interrogation, or whether or not to challenge a certain procedural irregularity. When encountering such situations in the field, I was often inclined to take the lawyer's perspective. This was even more the case due to the fact that lawyers usually explained their (in)action by referring to the client's best interest: for instance, had the lawyer intervened, the client would have been disadvantaged in a certain way. However, later I began to observe patterns of certain actions, or, usually, inaction, which were repeated despite the differences in context. I also began to doubt whether the argument of lawyers that clients would be 'disadvantaged' through their action, e.g. because the police would become 'uncooperative', was 'real', or whether it was rather raised out of convenience. I observed other lawyers who did intervene in similar contexts, and did not experience the 'reprimands' that were often mentioned in interviews (see Chapter 5 for relevant examples). I have also heard lawyers invoking other reasons for not intervening, rather than (just) the interest of their client, such as being uncertain about when and how to intervene. My initial perspective would then switch, and I would become more critical. Yet, in order to pay sufficient respect to the perspective of lawyers, I did my utmost to understand the contextual factors that influenced/led to their (in)action (described in Chapters 6–8).

4 Ethical issues

The empirical methodology was developed within the framework of the *Inside Police Custody* project and obtained ethical approval from Maastricht University. In my own fieldwork, I have also followed the recommendations given in the *Statement of Principles of Ethical Research Practice* of the UK Socio-Legal Studies Association (SLSA).[9] Particular attention was paid in this study to avoiding harm to criminal suspects, however minimal their level of participation. Although the SLSA recommendations advise that (at least) implicit consent from the research participants should be obtained, in my own observations I sought explicit consent from suspects (for practical reasons, in verbal form). I told them that I was a university employee doing research on lawyers, that I had the duty of confidentiality (i.e. I was not allowed to share my notes with the police), and that I was not recording any personal information. I have also obtained explicit (usually written) consent from all accompanied lawyers, which was renegotiated for every new 'case'.[10] Sometimes, either the lawyer or the suspect objected to my presence. Informed consent was also sought from other research participants, such as the police, to the extent possible. With regard to the interviews, all interviewees were informed in writing, or verbally at the beginning of the interview, about the nature and objectives of the research, about researcher anonymity and confidentiality obligations. Explicit consent was asked to audio-record interviews (two interviewees refused to be recorded).

5 Limitations of the chosen methodology

Because the fieldwork for this study was only conducted in one or two regions in each country, my findings are not generalisable on the national level.[11] However, my goal was not to draw a representative picture of the national practices of legal assistance at the investigative stage. Rather, the purpose was to describe, in as much detail as possible, the practices and attitudes encountered in the given locations, taking into account the broader institutional and legal context. According to the CR approach, the identification of the 'causal mechanisms' – and detailed description of the context in which they operate – ensures the transferability of the findings (Maxwell and Mittapalli, 2007: 9–10).

My representation of the processes studied in this research, namely of legal assistance at the investigative stage, is necessarily selective. For instance, in Chapters 3 and 4, I described what I considered the most 'typical' or 'common' practices or viewpoints of the encountered lawyers in the given sites. Certain alternative viewpoints and practices, which were 'weak' but still present in the fieldwork data, were muted in the final narrative. (This was in line with the CR approach, which requires searching for stable patterns or 'demi-regularities' in the fieldwork data.) Furthermore, in my 'explanatory' chapters, I decided to focus on the more general contextual factors (namely, procedural traditions, criminal justice policies and occupational cultures) and not, for instance, on the local factors, such as local institutional structures. This decision was driven by the need to ensure comparability and transferability of the findings across jurisdictions. It must be noted that both the CR and constructivist GT approaches consider selectivity to be inevitable in social science research. Within both approaches, researchers are recognised as authors of theoretical reconstruction (in constructivist GT achieved by means of focused coding: Charmaz, 2006: 57), selecting the theories, which in their view have the greatest 'explanatory power' of the studied 'reality' (Archer et al., 2013: 157).

Another limitation of this study is that it does not take into account the perspective of criminal suspects. Given that suspects are the right-holders and beneficiaries of the assistance provided by lawyers, their perspective on legal assistance at the investigative stage, and how it unfolds in practice, would indeed be very valuable. For this reason, I had considered conducting interviews with (former) suspects, namely in prisons, in the early stages of this study. However, due to the various practical and ethical challenges (Abbott et al., 2018), undertaking such research was considered unfeasible, given that observations and interviews with lawyers were chosen as the primary data collection methods.

Notes

1 Critical realism was originally conceived as a broad philosophical movement in human sciences and it is associated with the works of R. Bhaskar. On critical realism as a philosophy of science see Archer et al., 2013. On the application of the critical realist approach to doing research in social sciences see Sayer, 2010.
2 The summary given here is based among others on: Sayer, 1992: 11–12.
3 Note that this description relates to social and not natural phenomena (which can often be experienced directly). The word 'empirical' is used here in its most general meaning, i.e. as the knowledge about the reality, which may be obtained through investigation, experimentation, observation or experience.
4 Interestingly, only a very small fraction of cases (less than 10%) in England and Wales was likely to reach the trial stage, when the issue of adverse inference could potentially arise. From those cases, only in a very small proportion of them, the issue was likely to be raised by prosecution, and even more rarely was it likely to influence the

case outcome. Nonetheless, English lawyers appeared to routinely factor in the risk of inference from silence when giving advice at the investigative stage.
5 JUST 2010/JPEN/AG/1578. The project ran between May 2011 and September 2013.
6 The results of the project were published in Blackstock et al., 2013.
7 The 27 Dutch interviews were conducted by a junior researcher under my supervision.
8 Language, however, did not represent an important barrier, as long as 'standard' English or Dutch, and not a local dialect, was spoken. All encountered lawyers spoke 'standard' Dutch or English, including with their clients, but a small minority of suspects preferred to respond in a dialect. I was mostly unable to understand their responses, but I was at least able to understand what was said by the lawyer.
9 Adopted by the SLSA Executive Committee in January 2009, available from: <www.slsa.acuk/images/slsadownloads/ethicalstatement/slsa%20ethics%20statement%20_final_%5B1%5D.pdf> (last accessed on 16 July 2019).
10 I also provided each lawyer with a written statement regarding confidentiality, anonymity and the intended use of data.
11 It should also be noted that the quantitative data described in this study are not derived from a representative sample. Therefore, it is only used to illustrate, contextualise or scrutinise the qualitative findings.

Bibliography

Abbott, P., DiGiacomo, M., Magin, P. and Hu, W. (2018) A Scoping Review of Qualitative Research Methods Used with People in Prison, *International Journal of Qualitative Methods*, 17, 1–15.

Adler, P.A. and Adler, P. (1994) *Membership Roles in Field Research* (Thousand Oaks, London, New Delhi: SAGE Publications).

Archer, M., Bhaskar, R., Collier, A., Lawson, T. and Norrie, A. (eds.) (2013) *Critical Realism: Essential Readings* (London and New York: Routledge).

Arendell, T. (1997) Reflections on the Researcher-Researched Relationship: A Woman Interviewing Men, *Qualitative Sociology*, 20(3), 341–365.

Ashworth, A. and Redmayne, M. (2010) *The Criminal Process* (1st edn., Oxford: Oxford University Press).

Ashworth, A. and Redmayne, M. (2019) *The Criminal Process* (2nd edn., Oxford: Oxford University Press).

Baldwin, J. (1993) Legal Advice at the Police Station, *Criminal Law Review*, 371–373.

Baldwin, J. and McConville, M. (1979) Police Interrogation and the Right to See a Solicitor, *Criminal Law Review*, 145–152.

Belloni, F. and Hodgson, J. (2000) *Criminal Injustice: An Evaluation of the Criminal Justice Process in Britain* (New York, Basingstoke [etc.]: Macmillan).

Belur, J. (2014) Status, Gender and Geography: Power Negotiations in Police Research, *Qualitative Research*, 14(2), 184–200.

Berg, B.L. (1999) *Policing in a Modern Society* (Oxford: Gulf Professional Publishing).

Bhaskar, R. (2008) *A Realist Theory of Science* (London and New York: Routledge).

Bittner, E. (1967) Police Discretion in Emergency Apprehension of Mentally Ill Persons, *Social Problems*, 14(3), 278–292.

Blackstock, J., Cape, E., Hodgson, J., Ogorodova, A. and Spronken, T. (2013) *Inside Police Custody: An Empirical Account of Suspects' Rights in Four Jurisdictions* (Mortsel and Cambridge: Intersentia).

Bloomberg, A.S. (1967) The Practice of Law as Confidence Game: Organisational Cooptation of a Profession, *Law and Society Review*, 2(1), 15–40.

Boksem, J., Brouwer, D.V.A., van der Hoeven, R. and Nan, J.S. (2011) *Strafprocesrecht* (Den Haag: Boom Juridische uitgevers).

Boon, A. (2015) *Lawyers' Ethics and Professional Responsibility* (Portland, OR: Hart Publishing).

Bradley, A.W. and Ewing, K.D. (2007) *Constitutional and Administrative Law. Volume 1* (London: Pearson Education).

Brants, C. (2011) The Reluctant Dutch Response to Salduz, *Edinburgh Law Review*, 15, 298–305.

Brants, C. (2013) Wrongful Convictions and Inquisitorial Process: the Case of the Netherlands, *University of Cincinnati Law Review*, 80(4), 1069–1114.

Brants, C. (2016) 'What Limits to Harmonising Justice?', in: Colson, R. and Field, S. (eds.), *EU Criminal Justice and Challenge of Diversity* (Cambridge: Cambridge University Press), 221–241.

Brants, C. and Franken, A.A. (2009) The Protection of Fundamental Human Rights in Criminal Process, General Report, *Utrecht Law Review*, 5(2), 7–65.

Brants, C.H. and Ringnalda, A. (2011) *Issues of Convergence: Inquisitorial Prosecution in England and Wales? (Pre-Advies NVVR 2011)* (Nijmegen: Wolf Legal Publishers).

Bridges, L. and Choongh, S. (1998) *Improving Police Station Legal Advice. The Impact of the Accreditation Scheme for Police Station Legal Advisers* (London: Law Society, Research and Policy Planning Unit, Legal Aid Board).

Bridges, L., Cape, E., Fenn, P., Mitchell, A., Moorhead, R. and Sherr, A. (2007) *Evaluation of the Public Defender Service in England and Wales* (London: Legal Services Commission).

Broom, A., Hand, K. and Tovey, P. (2009) The Role of Gender, Environment and Individual Biography in Shaping Qualitative Interview Data, *International Journal of Social Research Methodology*, 12(1), 51–65.

Brouwer, D.V.A. (2015) ZSM en de Verdediging, *Delikt en Delinkwent*, 26, 265–278.

Brown, D. (1989) *Detention at Police Station under the Police and Criminal Evidence Act 1984*, Home Office Research Studies, No. 104 (London: Home Office).

Brown, D., Ellis, T. and Larcombe, K. (1992) *Changing the Code: Police Detention under the Revised PACE Code of Practice*, Home Office Research Studies, No. 129 (London: Home Office).

Bucke, T. and Brown, D. (1997) *In Police Custody: Police Powers and Suspects' Rights under the Revised Codes of Practice*, Home Office Research Study, No. 174 (London: Home Office).

Bucke, T., Street, R. and Brown, D. (2000), *The Right of Silence: The Impact of the Criminal Justice and Public Order Act 1994* (London: Home Office).

Bygstad, B., Munkvold, B.E. and Volkoff, O. (2016) Identifying Generative Mechanisms Through Affordances: A Framework for Critical Realist Data Analysis, *Journal of Information Technology*, 31, 83–96.

Cain, M. (1973) *Society and the Policeman's Role* (London: Routledge Kegan Paul).

Cape, E. (2002) Incompetent Police Station Legal Advice and the Exclusion of Evidence, *Criminal Law Review*, 471–484.

Cape, E. (2006) Rebalancing the Criminal Justice Process: Ethical Challenges for Criminal Defence Lawyers, *Legal Ethics*, 9(1), 56–79.

Cape, E. (2010) 'National Approaches to Effective Criminal Defence: England and Wales', in: Cape, E., Namoradze, Z., Smith, R. and Spronken, T. (eds.), *Effective Criminal Defence in Europe* (Antwerp, Oxford, Portland, OR: Intersentia), 107–165.

Cape, E. (2014) The Rise (and Fall?) of a Criminal Defence Profession, *Criminal Law Review*, Supplement (50th Anniversary Edition), 72–84.

Cape, E. (2015) Transposing the EU Directive on the Right to Information: A Firecracker or a Dump Squib?, *Criminal Law Review*, 1, 48–67.

Cape, E. (2017) *Defending Suspects at Police Stations* (6th edn., London: Legal Action Group).

Cape, E. (2019) 'Defence Rights, Duties, Norms and Practices in Civil Law and Common Jurisdictions', in: Brown, D.K., Iontcheva Turner, J. and Weisser, B. (eds.), *The Handbook of Criminal Process* (Oxford: Oxford University Press), 189–209.

Cape, E. and Hodgson, J. (2007) 'The Investigative Stage of the Criminal Process in England and Wales', in: Cape, E., Hodgson, J., Prakken, T. and Spronken, T. (eds.), *Suspects in Europe. Procedural Rights at the Investigative Stage of the Criminal Process in the European Union* (Antwerpen, Oxford: Intersentia), 59–79.

Cape, E. and Spronken, T. (1998) 'Proactive Policing: Limiting the Role of the Defence Lawyer', in: Field, S. and Pelser, C. (eds.), *Invading the Private: State Accountability and the New Investigative Methods in Europe* (Farnham: Ashgate Publishing), 291–322.

Cape, E., Hodgson, J., Prakken, T. and Spronken, T. (eds.) (2007) *Suspects in Europe: Procedural Rights at the Investigative Stage of the Criminal Process in the European Union* (Antwerp, Oxford: Intersentia).

Cape, E., Namoradze, Z., Smith, R. and Spronken, T. (2010) *Effective Criminal Defence in Europe* (Antwerp, Oxford, Portland, OR: Intersentia).

Chan, J. (1996) Changing Police Culture, *The British Journal of Criminology*, 36(1), 109–134.

Chan, J. (1997) *Changing Police Culture: Policing in a Multicultural Society* (Cambridge, England: Cambridge University Press).

Charmaz, K. (2006) *Constructing Grounded Theory: A Practical Guide Through Qualitative Analysis* (London, Thousand Oaks, New Delhi: SAGE Publications).

Charmaz, K. (2017) The Power of Constructivist Grounded Theory for Critical Inquiry, *Qualitative Inquiry*, 23(1), 34–45.

Cleiren, C.P.M. and Nijboer, J.F. (eds.) (2011) *Strafvordering: Tekst en Commentaar* (Deventer: Kluwer).

Cochran, R.F. Jr., DiPippa, J. and Peters, M. (2014) *The Counselor-at-Law. A Collaborative Approach to Client Interviewing and Counseling* (3rd edn., Lexis Nexis).

Combrink-Kuiters, L., van Gammeren-Zoeteweij, M. and Peters, S.L. (2011) *MonitorGesubsidieerde rechtsbijstand 2010* (Den Haag: Boom Juridische Uitgevers).

Cordner, G. (2017) Police Culture: Individual and Organizational Differences in Police Officer Perspectives, *Policing: An International Journal of Police Strategies & Management*, 40(1), 11–25.

Corstens, G.J.M. (2018) *Het Nederlands Strafprocesrecht* (9th edn., Deventer: Kluwer).

Creutzfeldt, N., Kubal, A. and Pirie, F. (2016) Introduction: Exploring the Comparative in Socio-Legal Studies, *International Journal of Law in Context*, 12(4), 377–389.

Crijns, J.H. (2017) 'Modernisering van het Wetboek van Strafvordering: Fundamentele Herijking of Grote Voorjaarsschoonmaak?', in: Leeuw, B.J.G., Ölçer, F.P. and ten Voorde, J.M. (eds.), *Leidse Gedachten voor een Modern Straf(proces)recht*, Meijers-reeks no. 279 (Den Haag: Boom Juridisch), pp. 1–19.

Crown Prosecution Service (2018) 'Charging and Charging Direct', available at: <www.cps.gov.uk/basic-page/charging-and-cps-direct> (last accessed on 30 March 2018).

Damaška, M. (1973) Evidentiary Barriers to Conviction and Two Models of Criminal Procedure: A Comparative Study, *University of Pennsylvania Law Review*, 121(3), 506–589.

Damaška, M. (1986) *The Faces of Justice and State Authority* (New Haven and London: Yale University Press).

Danermark, B., Karlsson, J.C., Jakobsen, L. and Ekström, M. (2002) *Explaining Society: An Introduction to Critical Realism in the Social Sciences* (London: Routledge).

Darbyshire, P. (2014) Judicial Case Management in Ten Crown Courts, *Criminal Law Review*, 1, 30–50.

Dehaghani, R. (2016) He's Just Not That Vulnerable: Exploring the Implementation of the Appropriate Adult Safeguard in Police Custody, *The Howard Journal of Crime and Justice*, 55, 396–413.

Dehaghani, R. and Newman, D. (2019) Can – and Should – Lawyers be Considered 'Appropriate' Appropriate Adults?, *Howard Journal of Crime and Justice*, 58(1), 3–24.

Delanty, G. (2005) *Social Science. Philosophical and Methodological Foundations* (2nd edn., Berkshire, England: Open University Press).

Delmas-Marty, M. and Spencer, J. (eds.) (2004) *European Criminal Procedures* (Cambridge: Cambridge University Press).

de Vocht, D.L.F. and Spronken, T.N.B.M. (2011) EU Policy to Guarantee Procedural Rights in Criminal Proceedings: 'Step by Step', *North Carolina Journal of International Law and Commercial Regulation*, 37, 436–488.

Dixon, D. (1991) Common Sense, Legal Advice and the Right to Silence, *Public Law*, 233–254.

Dixon, D. (1997) *Law in Policing* (Oxford: Oxford University Press).

Dixon, D. (2008) 'Can Coercive Powers Be Effectively Controlled and Regulated?', in Cape, E. and Young, R (eds.), *Regulating Policing. The Police and Criminal Evidence Act 1984: Past, Present and Future* (Oxford: Hart Publishing), pp. 21–44.

Dixon, D., Bottomley, K., Coleman, C., Gill, M. and Wall, D. (1990) Safeguarding the Rights of Suspects in Police Custody, *Policing and Society*, 1, 115–140.

Downes, D. and van Swaaningen, R. (2007) The Road to Dystopia? Changes in the Penal Climate of the Netherlands, *Crime and Justice*, 35(1), 31–71.

Drizin, S.A. and Leo, R.A. (2004) The Problem of False Confessions in the Post-DNA World, *North Carolina Law Review*, 82, 891–1007.

Duff, P.R. (2018) 'Scottish Criminal Law Adrift?', in: Duff, P.R. and Ferguson, P. (eds.), *Scottish Criminal Evidence Law: Current Developments and Future Trends* (Edinburgh: Edinburgh University Press), pp. 224–247.

Duve, T. (2018) Legal Traditions: A Dialogue between Comparative Law and Comparative Legal History, *Comparative Legal History*, 6(1), 15–33.

Ede, R. and Shepherd, E. (1997) *Active Defence: Lawyer's Guide to Police and Defence Investigation and Prosecution and Defence Disclosure in Criminal Cases* (1st edn., London: The Law Society).

Edwards, A. (2008) 'The Role of Defence Lawyers in a Re-Balanced System', in: Cape, E. and Young, R. (eds.), *Regulating Policing. The Police and Criminal Evidence Act 1984 Past, Present and Future Edited Regulating Policing* (Portland, OR: Hart Publishing), 221–255.

Edwards, D. and Stokoe, E. (2011) 'You Don't Have to Answer': Lawyers' Contributions in Police Interrogations of Suspects, *Research on Language & Social Interaction*, 44(1), 21–43.

Eisenstein, J. and Jacob, H. (1977) *Felony Justice: An Organisational Analysis of Criminal Courts* (Boston: Little Brown).

Feldman, S. and Wilson, K. (1981) The Value of Interpersonal Skills in Lawyering, *Law and Human Behavior*, 5(4), 311–324.

Field, S. (2009) Fair Trials and Procedural Tradition in Europe, *Oxford Journal of Legal Studies*, 29(2), 365–387.

Field, S. and Pelser, C. (eds.) (1998) *Invading the Private: State Accountability and New Investigative Methods in Europe* (Aldershot: Ashgate).

Field, S. and West, A. (2003) Dialogue and the Inquisitorial Tradition: French Defence Lawyers in the Pre-Trial Criminal Process, *Criminal Law Forum*, 14, 261–316.

Fielding, N. (1989) 'Police Culture and Police Practice', in: Weatheritt, M. (ed.), *Police Research: Some Future Prospects* (Aldershot: Avebury), 77–87.

Fionda, J. (2000) 'New Managerialism, Credibility and the Sanitisation of Criminal Justice', in: Green, P. and Rutherford, A. (eds.), *Criminal Policy in Transition* (Oxford,

U.K.: Hart Publishing), 109–130 (Oñati International Series in Law and Society), 240–257.

Fisher, H. (1977) *Report of an Inquiry by the Honourable Sir Henry Fisher into the Circumstances Leading to the Trial of Three Persons on Charges Arising out of the Death of Maxwell Confait and the Fire at 27 Doggett Road, London SE6* (London: HMSO).

Fletcher, A.J. (2016) Applying Critical Realism in Qualitative Research: Methodology Meets Method, *International Journal of Social Research Methodology*, 20(2), 181–194.

Follette, W.C., Davis, D. and Leo, R.A. (2007) Mental Health Status and Vulnerability to Interrogative Influence, *Journal of Criminal Justice*, 22(3), 42–49.

Foster, J., Richard, R., Rorher, R. and Sirkin, M. (2010) Understanding Lawyers: The Personality Traits of Successful Practitioners, Hildebrandt White Paper (Hildebrandt International).

Franken, A. (2012) 'The Judge in the Pre-Trial Investigation', in: Groenhuijsen, M. and Kooijmans, T. (eds.), *The Reform of the Dutch Code of Criminal Procedure in Comparative Perspective* (Leiden, Boston: Martinus Nijhoff Publishers), 31–45.

Franken, A. (2013) Het Geduldige Papier en de Weerbarstige Praktijk, *Delikt en Delinkwent*, 16, 157–165.

Freiberg, A. (2005) Managerialism in Australian criminal justice: RIP for KPIs?, *Monash University Law Review*, 31(1), 12–36.

Füglistaler, G. (2016) *The Principle of Subsidiarity and the Margin of Appreciation Doctrine in the European Court of Human Rights' Post-2011 Jurisprudence, Volume 295 of Cahier de l'IDHEAP* (Brussels: IDHEAP – Unité Droit Public).

Galanter, M. (1974) Why the 'Haves' Come out Ahead? Speculations on the Limits of Legal Change, *Law and Society Review*, 9(1), 95–160.

Garland, D. (2001) *The Culture of Control. Crime and Social Order in Contemporary Society* (Chicago: University of Chicago Press).

Giannoulopoulos, D. (2013) Custodial Legal Assistance and Notification of the Right to Silence in France: Legal Cosmopolitanism and Local Resistance, *Criminal Law Forum*, 24(3), 291–329.

Giannoulopoulos, D. (2016) Strasbourg Jurisprudence, Law Reform and Comparative Law: A Tale of the Right to Custodial Legal Assistance in Five Countries, *Human Rights Law Review*, 16, 103–129.

Glenn, P. (2014) *Legal Traditions of the World: Sustainable Diversity* (Oxford: Oxford University Press).

Goss, R. (2017) Out of Many, One? Strasbourg's Ibrahim Decision on Article 6, *The Modern Law Review*, 80, 1137–1150.

Grande, E. (2000) Italian Criminal Justice: Borrowing and Resistance, *American Journal of Comparative Law*, 48, 227–260.

Grande, E. (2008) 'Dances of Criminal Justice: Thoughts on Systemic Differences and the Search for the Truth', in: Jackson, J., Langer, M. and Tillers, P. (eds.), *Crime, Procedure and Evidence in a Comparative and International Context. Essays in Honour of Professor Mrjan Damaška* (Oxford and Portland, OR: Hart Publishing), 145–165.

Hannibal, M. and Mountford, L. (2016) *Criminal Litigation 2016–2017* (Oxford: Oxford University Press).

Hayward, R.M. and Tuckey, M.R. (2011) Emotions in Uniform: How Nurses Regulate Emotion at Work via Emotional Boundaries, *Human Relations*, 64(11), 1501–1523.

Healy, D., Hamilton, C., Daly, Y. and Butler, M. (2015) *The Routledge Handbook of Irish Criminology* (London and New York: Routledge).

Hermans, R.H. (2009) Kennisneming van Processtukken in het Voorbereidend Onderzoek in Strafzaken, *Delikt en Delinkwent*, 39(5), 494–526.

Heslop, R. (2011) The British Police Service: Professionalisation or "McDonaldization"?, *International Journal of Police Science & Management*, 13(4), 312–321.

Hessick, F.A. and Saujani, R. (2002) Plea Bargaining and Convicting the Innocent: The Role of the Prosecutor, the Defense Counsel, and the Judge, *Brigham Young University Journal of Public Law*, 16, 189–242.

Hillyard, P. and Gordon, D. (1999) Arresting Statistics: The Drift to Informal Justice in England and Wales, *Journal of Law and Society*, 26(4), 502–522.

Hodgson, J. (2005) *French Criminal Justice. A Comparative Account of the Investigation and Prosecution of Crime in France* (Oxford: Hart Publishing).

Hodgson, J. (2006) 'Conceptions of the Trial in Inquisitorial and Adversarial Procedure', in: Duff, A., Farmer, L., Marshall, S. and Tadros, V. (eds.), *Judgment and Calling to Account* (Oxford: Hart Publishing), 223–242.

Hodgson, J. (2011) Safeguarding Suspects' Rights in EU Criminal Justice: A Comparative Perspective, *New Criminal Law Review*, 14(4), 611–665.

Hodgson, J. and Bridges, L. (1995) Improving Custodial Legal Advice, *Criminal Law Review*, 101–113.

Hodgson, J and Mou, Y. (2019) 'Empirical Approaches to Criminal Procedure', in: Brown, D.K., Iontcheva Turner, J. and Weisser, B. (eds.), *The Handbook of Criminal Process* (Oxford: Oxford University Press), 43–66.

Horn, R. (1997) Not 'One of the Boys': Women Researching the Police, *Journal of Gender Studies*, 6(3), 297–308.

Irving, B.L. and McKenzie, M.K. (1989) *Regulating Custodial Interviews: The Effects of the Police and Criminal Evidence Act 1984. Vol II* (London: The Police Foundation).

Jackson, J. (2001) Silence and Proof: Extending the Boundaries of Criminal Proceedings in the United Kingdom, *International Journal of Evidence and Proof*, 5(3), 145–173.

Jackson, J. (2008) 'Police and Prosecutors after PACE: The Road from Case Construction to Case Disposal', in: Cape, E. and Young, R. (eds.), *Regulating Policing: The Police and Criminal Evidence Act 1984 Past, Present and Future* (Oxford: Hart Publishing), 255–277.

Jackson, J. (2016a) 'Cultural Barriers on the Road to Providing Suspects with Access to a Lawyer', in: Colson, R. and Field, S. (eds.), *EU Criminal Justice and the Challenges of Diversity. Legal Cultures in the Area of Freedom, Security and Justice* (Cambridge: Cambridge University Press), 181–199.

Jackson, J.D. (2016b) Responses to Salduz: Procedural Tradition, Change and the Need for Effective Defence, *The Modern Law Review*, 79, 987–1018.

Jackson, J.D. and Summers, S.J. (2012) *The Internationalisation of Criminal Evidence: Beyond the Common Law and Civil Law Traditions* (Cambridge: Cambridge University Press).

Jackson, J.D. and Summers, S.J. (2018a), 'Introduction', in: Jackson, J.D. and Summers, S.J. (eds.), *Obstacles to Fairness in Criminal Proceedings: Individual Rights and Institutional Forms* (Oxford, Portland, OR: Hart Publishing), 1–19.

Jackson, J.D. and Summers, S.J. (2018b), 'Seeking Core Fair Trial Standards across National Boundaries: Judicial Impartiality, the Prosecutorial Role and the Right to Counsel', in: Jackson, J.D. and Summers, S.J. (eds.), *Obstacles to Fairness in Criminal Proceedings: Individual Rights and Institutional Forms* (Oxford, Portland, OR: Hart Publishing), 99–127.

Johnston, T.E.S. (1966), Judges' Rules and Police Interrogations in England Today, *Journal of Criminal Law and Criminology*, 57(1), 85–92.

Johnston, E. and Smith, T. (2017) The Early Guilty Plea Scheme and the Rising Wave of Managerialism, *Criminal Law and Justice Weekly*, 181(13), 210–212.

Jones, C. (1993) Auditing Criminal Justice, *British Journal of Criminology*, 33(3), 187–202.

Jorg, N., Field, S. and Brants, C. (1995) 'Are Inquisitorial and Adversarial Systems Converging?', in: Harding, C., Fennell, P., Jörg, N. and Swart, B. (eds.), *Criminal Justice in Europe: A Comparative Study* (Oxford: Clarendon), 41–56.

Joyce, P. (2017) *Criminal Justice: An Introduction* (3rd edn., London and New York: Routledge).

Kadowaki, Joy (2015) Maintaining Professionalism: Emotional Labor among Lawyers as Client Advisors, *International Journal of the Legal Profession*, 22(3), 323–345.

Kassin, S.M., Drizin, S.A., Grisso, T., Gudjonsson, G.H., Leo, R.A. and Redlich, A.D. (2010) Police-Induced Confessions: Risk Factors and Recommendations, *Law and Human Behavior*, 34(1), 3–38.

Keller, H. and Stone Sweet, A. (2008) *A Europe of Rights: The Impact of the ECHR on National Legal Systems* (Oxford: Oxford University Press).

Kemp, V. (2010), *Transforming Legal Aid: Access to Criminal Defence Services* (London: Legal Services Research Centre, Legal Services Commission).

Kemp, V. (2012) *Bridewell Legal Advice Study – BLAST: An Innovation in Police Station Legal Advice*, Interim Report (London: Legal Services Research Centre, Legal Services Commission).

Kemp, V. (2013) *Bridewell Legal Advice Study. Adopting a 'Whole-Systems' Approach to Police Station Legal Advice*, BLAST II Final Report (London: Legal Services Research Centre, Legal Services Commission).

Kemp, V. and Balmer, N. (2008) *Criminal Defence Services: Users' Perspectives*, Interim Report (London: Legal Services Research Centre, Legal Services Commission).

Kemp, V., Balmer, N.J. and Pleasence, P. (2012) Whose Time Is It Anyway? Factors Associated with Duration in Police Custody, *Criminal Law Review*, 10, 736–752.

Kerasidou, A. and Horn, R. (2016) Making Space for Empathy: Supporting Doctors in the Emotional Labour of Clinical Care, *BMC Medical Ethics*, 178, 1–5.

Keulen, B.F. and Knigge, G. (2016) *Strafprocesrecht* (13th edn., Deventer: Kluwer).

Kirchengast, T. (2010) *The Criminal Trial in Law and Discourse* (Basingstoke: Palgrave Macmillan).

Kiser, R. (2015) The Emotionally Attentive Lawyer: Balancing the Rule of Law with the Realities of Human Behavior, *Nevada Law Journal*, 15(2), 442–463.

Klein Haarhuis, C.M., van Lierop, L., Aidala, R., Beenakkers, E., de Vroome, T., Damen, R., Maertens, G. and Burema, D. (2018) *Langetermijnmonitor 'Raadsman bij verhoor* (1st edn., Den Haag: WODC).

Krause-Jensen, J. (2010) *Flexible Firm: Design of Culture at Bang & Olufsen* (New York: Berghahn Books).

Kvalnes, Ø. (2019) *Moral Reasoning at Work: Rethinking Ethics in Organizations* (Cham: Palgrave Pilot).

Langer, M. (2004) From Legal Transplants to Legal Translations: The Globalisation of Plea Bargaining and the Americanization Thesis in Criminal Processes, *Harvard International Law Journal*, 45(1), 1–64.

Langer, M. (2014) The Long Shadow of the Adversarial and Inquisitorial Categories, in: Dubber, M.D. and Hoernle, T. (eds.), *Handbook on Criminal Law* (Oxford: Oxford University Press), 887–912.

Leng, R. (2001) Silence Pre-Trial, Reasonable Expectations and the Normative Distortion of Fact-Finding, *International Journal of Evidence and Proof*, 5(4), 240–257.

Leo, R.A. (2008) *Police Interrogations and American Justice* (Cambridge, MA: Harvard University Press).

Leubsdorf, J. (2001a) *Man in His Original Dignity: Legal Ethics in France* (Burlington: Ashgate).

Leubsdorf, J. (2001b) On the History of French Legal Ethics, *The University of Chicago Law School Roundtable*, 8(2), 341–352.

Licht, A.N. (2008) Social Norms and the Law: Why Peoples Obey the Law, *Review of Law and Economics*, 4(3), 715–749.

Lief, H.I. and Fox, R.C. (1963) 'The Medical Student's Training for "Detached Concern"', in: Lief, H.I., Lief, V.F. and Lief, N.R. (eds.) *The Psychological Basis of Medical Practice* (New York, Harper & Row), 12–35.

Lindeman, J.M.W. (2017) *Officieren van justitie in de 21e eeuw - Een verslag van participerend observatieonderzoek naar de taakopvatting en taakinvulling van officieren van justitie*, Pompe Reeks; 84 (den Haag: Boom Lemma Uitgevers).

Lively, K.J. and Powell, B. (2006) Emotional Expression at Work and at Home: Domain, Status, or Individual Characteristics?, *Social Psychology Quarterly*, 69(1), 17–38.

Loader, I. (2016) 'Changing Climates of Control: The Rise and Fall of Police Authority in England and Wales', in: Bosworth, M., Hoyle, C. and Zedner, L. (eds.) *Changing Contours of Criminal Justice* (Oxford: Oxford University Press).

Loftus, B. (2009) *Police Culture in a Changing World (Clarendon Studies in Criminology)* (Oxford: Oxford University Press).

Mahony, B.M., Milne, B. and Grant, T. (2012) To Challenge or Not to Challenge? Best Practices when Interviewing Vulnerable Suspects, *Policing*, 6(3), 301–313.

Manning, P.K. (1995) 'The Police Occupational Culture in Anglo-American Societies', in: Bailey, W. (ed.), *The Encyclopedia of Police Science* (New York: Garland Publishing), 472–475.

Maxwell, J.A. and Mittapalli, K. (2007) 'The Value of Critical Realism for Qualitative Research', Paper presented at the *Annual Conference of the International Association for Critical Realism*, Philadelphia, PA, 7–9 August 2007.

McAdams, R.H. (2009) An Attitudinal Theory of Expressive Law, *Oregon Law Review*, 79, 339–390.

McCambridge, J., Witton, J. and Elbourne, D.R. (2014) Systematic Review of the Hawthorne Effect: New Concepts are Needed to Study Research Participation Effects, *Journal of Clinical Epidemiology*, 67, 267–277.

McConville, M. (1992) Videotaping Interrogations: Police Behaviour On and Off Camera, *Criminal Law Review*, 532–548.

McConville, M. and Marsh, L. (2014) *Criminal Judges: Legitimacy, Courts and State-Induced Guilty Pleas in Britain* (Cheltenham, Northampton: Edward Elgar Publishing).

McConville, M. and Marsh, L. (2015) Adversarialism goes West: Case Management in Criminal Courts, *International Journal of Evidence and Proof*, 19(3), 172–189.

McConville, M. and Wilson, G. (eds.) (2002) *The Handbook of the Criminal Justice Process* (Oxford: Oxford University Press).

McConville, M., Hodgson, J., Bridges, L. and Pavlovic, A. (1994) *Standing Accused: The Organisation and Practices of Criminal Defence Lawyers in Britain* (New York: Oxford University Press).

McConville, M., Sanders, A. and Leng, R. (1991) *The Case for the Prosecution* (London: Routledge).

McEwan, J. (2011) From Adversarialism to Managerialism: Criminal Justice in Transition, *Legal Studies*, 31(4), 519–546.

McIntyre, L. (1987) *The Public Defender: The Practice of Law in the Shadows of Repute (Studies in Crime & Justice)* (Chicago: University of Chicago Press).

Meissner, C.A. and Kassin, S.M. (2002). 'He's Guilty!': Investigator Bias in Judgments of Truth and Deception, *Law and Human Behavior*, 26(5), 469–480.

Merryman, A. (1985) *The Civil Law Tradition* (Stanford: Stanford University Press).

Ministry of Justice (2013) Transforming Legal Aid: Delivering a More Credible and Efficient System, Consultation Paper CP14/2013, 38.

Ministry of Justice (2016) Criminal Justice Statistics Quarterly, England and Wales, available at: <www.gov.uk/government/statistics/criminal-justice-system-statistics-quarterly-december-2016> (last accessed on 16 July 2019).

Mols, G. (2009) 'Getuigen', in: Prakken, T. and Spronken, T. (eds.), *Handboek Verdediging* (Deventer: Kluwer), 297–327.

Mols, V. (2017) Bringing Directives on Procedural Rights of the EU to Police Stations: Practical Training for Criminal Defence Lawyers, *New Journal of European Criminal Law*, 8(3), 300–308.

Mols, V., Pivaty, A., Heemskerk, R., Horselenberg, R. and Vanderhallen, M. (2016) Bescherming van de Rechten van de Verdachte tijdens Politiedetentie en Politieverhoor: Naar een Effectieve Verdediging in de Praktijk, *Strafblad*, 369–374.

Montana, R. (2016) Procedural Tradition in the Italian Criminal Justice System. The Semi-Adversarial Reform in 1989 and the Inquisitorial Cultural Resistance to Adversarial Principles, *The International Journal of Evidence and Proof*, 20(4), 289–304.

Montana, R. and Nelken, D. (2011) 'Prosecution, Legal Culture and Resistance to Moral Panics in Italy', in: Smith, C.J., Zhang, S.X. and Barberet, R. (eds.), *Routledge Handbook of International Criminology* (New York: Routledge), 286–297.

Moston, S. and Stephenson, G. (1993) *The Questioning and Interviewing of Suspects Outside the Police Station, Royal Commission on Criminal Justice* (London: HSMO).

Motoc, I. and Ziemele, I. (eds.) (2016) *The Impact of the ECHR on Democratic Change in Central and Eastern Europe: Judicial Perspectives* (Cambridge: Cambridge University Press).

Muir, W.K. (1977) *Police: Streetcorner Politicians* (Chicago: University of Chicago Press).

Nelken, D. (2004) Using the Concept of Legal Culture, *Australian Journal of Legal Philosophy*, 29(1), 1–26.

Nelken, D. (2016) Comparative Legal Research and Legal Culture: Facts, Approaches and Values, *Annual Review of Law and Social Science*, 12(1), 45–62.

Newburn, T. (2007) 'Tough on Crime': Penal Policy in England and Wales, *Crime and Justice*, 36(1), 425–470.

Newman, D. (2012) Still Standing Accused: Addressing the Gap between Walk and Talk in Firms of Criminal Defence Lawyers, *International Journal of the Legal Profession*, 19(1), 3–27.

Newman, D. (2013) *Legal Aid Lawyers and the Quest for Justice* (Oxford: Hart Publishing).

Newman, D. (2016) Are Lawyers Alienated Workers?, *European Journal of Current Legal Issues*, 22(3), published online at: <http://webjcli.org/article/view/463/667> (last accessed on 16 July 2019).

Newman, D. and Welsh, L. (2019) The Practice of Modern Defence Lawyers: Alienation and Its Implications for Access to Justice, *Common Law World Review*, 48(1–2), 64–89.

Niks, I.M.W., de Jonge, J., Gevers, J.M.P. and Houtman, I.L.D. (2017) Divergent Effects of Detachment from Work: A Day-Level Study on Employee Creativity, *European Journal of Work and Organizational Psychology*, 26(2), 183–194.

Oakley, J. and Cocking, D. (2001) *Virtue Ethics and Professional Roles* (Cambridge: Cambridge University Press).

Oberlander, L.B., Goldstein, N.E. and Goldstein, A.M. (2013) 'Competence to Confess', in: Goldstein, A.M. (ed.), *Handbook of Psychology. Forensic Psychology* (New York: Wiley), 335–359.

Ogorodova, A. and Spronken, T.N.B.M. (2014) Legal Advice in Police Custody: From Europe to a Local Police Station, *Erasmus Law Review*, 4, 191–205.

Ölçer, F.P. (2013) 'The European Court of Human Rights: The Fair Trial Analysis Under Article 6 of the European Convention of Human Rights', in: Thaman, S.C. (ed.) *Exclusionary Rules in Comparative Law* (Dordrecht, Heidelberg, New York, London: Springer), 371–402.

Owusu-Bempah, A. (2013), Defence Participation through Pre-Trial Disclosure: Issues and Implications, *The International Journal of Proof*, 17(2), 183–201.

Packer, H.L. (1968) *The Limits of the Criminal Sanction* (Stanford: Stanford University Press).

Pakes, F. (1996) The Ebb and Flow of Criminal Justice in the Netherlands, *International Journal of the Sociology of Law*, 34(3), 141–156.

Pattenden, R and Skinns, L. (2010) Choice, Privacy and Publicly-Funded Legal Advice at Police Stations, *The Modern Law Review*, 73, 349–370.

Pearse, J. and Gudjohnsson, G. (1996) A Review of the Role of the Legal Adviser in Police Stations, *Criminal Behaviour and Mental Health*, 6, 231–239.

Pearse, J. and Gudjohnsson, G. (1997) Police Interviewing and Legal Representation: A Field Study, *The Journal of Forensic Psychiatry and Psychology*, 8(1), 200–208.

Peters, S.L., van Gammeren-Zoeteweij, M. and Combrink-Kuiters, L. (2014) *Monitor Gesubsidieerde Rechtsbijstand 2013* (Nijmegen: Wolf Legal Publishers).

Peterson-Badali, M., Care, S. and Broeking, J. (2007) Young People's Perceptions and Experiences of the Lawyer–Client Relationship, *Canadian Journal of Criminology and Criminal Justice*, 49(3), 375–401.

Phillips, C. and Brown, D. (1998) *Entry into the Criminal Justice System: A Survey of Police Arrests and their Outcomes, Home Office Research Studies, No. 185* (London: Home Office).

Phillips, S.P. and Dalgarno, N. (2017) Professionalism, Professionalization, Expertise and Compassion: A Qualitative Study of Medical Residents, *BMC Medical Education*, 17(1), 21.

Pini, B. (2005) Interviewing Men: Gender and the Collection and Interpretation of Qualitative Data, *Journal of Sociology*, 41(2), 201–216.

Pivaty, A. (2018) The Right to Custodial Legal Assistance in Europe: In Search for the Rationales, *European Journal of Crime, Criminal Law and Criminal Justice*, 26(1), 62–98.

Pivaty, A. and Soo, A. (2019) Article 7 of the Directive 2012/13/EU on the Right to Information in Criminal Proceedings: A Missed Opportunity to Ensure Equality of Arms in Pre-Trial Proceedings?, *European Journal of Crime, Criminal Law and Criminal Justice*, 27(2), 126–154.

Pizzi, W.T. (2000) *Trials without Truth: Why Our System of Criminal Trials Has Become an Expensive Failure and What We Need to Do to Rebuild It* (New York: New York University Press).

Plotnikoff, J. and Woolfson, R. (2001) *'A Fair Balance?' Evaluation of the Operation of the Disclosure Law, RDS Occasional Paper No. 76* (London: Home Office).

Prakken, T. and Spronken, T. (2007) 'The Investigative Stage of the Criminal Process in the Netherlands', in: Cape, E., Hodgson, J., Prakken, T. and Spronken, T. (eds.), *Suspects in Europe. Procedural Rights at the Investigative Stage of the Criminal Process in the European Union* (Antwerp, Oxford: Intersentia), 155–180.

Prakken, T. and Spronken, T. (eds.) (2009) *Handboek Verdediging* (Deventer: Kluwer).

Quinn, K. and Jackson, J. (2007) Of Rights and Roles: Police Interviews with Young Suspects in Northern Ireland, *British Journal of Criminology*, 47, 234–255.

Quirk, H. (2006) The Significance of Culture in Criminal Procedure Reform: Why the Revised Disclosure Scheme cannot Work?, *International Journal of Evidence and Proof*, 10(1), 42–59.

Quirk, H. (2017) *The Rise and Fall of the Right of Silence* (Abingdon: Routledge).

Raine, J.W. and Wilson, M.J. (1993) *Managing Criminal Justice* (Harvester Wheatsheaf, Hemel Hempstead)

Reijntjes, J.M. (2017) *A. Minkenshof's Nederlandse Strafvordering* (Deventer: Wolters Kluwer).

Reiner, R. (2010) *The Politics of the Police* (Oxford: Oxford University Press).

Reiner, R. (2017) Is Police Culture Cultural?, *Policing: A Journal of Policy and Practice*, 11(3), 236–241.

Rhode, D.L. (2004) *Access to Justice* (Oxford: Oxford University Press).

Ringnalda, A. (2010) Inquisitorial or Adversarial? The Role of the Scottish Prosecutor and Special Defences, *Utrecht Law Review*, 6(1), 119–140.

Ringnalda, A. (2014) Procedural Tradition and the Convergence of Criminal Procedure: The Case of the Investigation and Disclosure of Evidence in Scotland, *American Journal of Comparative Law*, 62(4), 1133–1166.

Roberts, R. (2015) 'Criminal Justice in Times of Austerity', Centre for Crime and Justice Studies, available at: <https://www.crimeandjustice.org.uk/resources/criminal-justice-times-austerity> (last accessed on 16 July 2019).

Rosenthal, D.E. (1974) *Lawyer and Client: Who's in Charge* (New York: Russel Sage Foundation).

Rotenberg, K.J. (2010) 'The Conceptualization of Interpersonal Trust: A Basis, Domain and Target Framework', in: Rotenberg, K.J. (ed.), *Interpersonal Trust during Childhood and Adolescence* (Cambridge: Cambridge University Press), 8–28.

Rowe, M. (2007) Rendering Visible the Invisible: Police Discretion, Professionalism and Decision-Making, *Policing & Society*, 17(3), 279–294.

Ruggeri, S. (2017) *Audi Alteram Partem in Criminal Proceedings: Towards a Participatory Understanding of Criminal Justice in Europe and Latin America* (Dordrecht: Springer).

Ryan, A. (2016) Comparative Procedural Traditions: Poland's Journey from Socialist to "Adversarial" System, *International Journal of Evidence and Proof*, 20(4), 305–325.

Ryan, J. (1989) Criminal Courts Revisited, *Law & Society Review*, 23(5), 933–938.

Sanders, A. and Bridges, L. (1990) Access to Legal Advice and Police Malpractice, *Criminal Law Review* 494–509.

Sanders, A. and Young, R. (2007) *Criminal Justice* (3rd edn., Oxford: Oxford University Press).

Sanders, A. and Young, R. (2008) 'Police Powers', in: Newburn, T. (ed.), *Handbook of Policing* (Cullompton, U.K.: Willan Publishers), 281–313.

Sanders, A., Bridges, L., Mulvaney, A and Crozier, G. (1989) *Advice and Assistance at Police Stations and the 24 Hour Duty Solicitor Scheme* (London: Lord Chancellor's Department).

Sanders, A., Young, R. and Burton, M. (2010), *Criminal Justice* (Oxford: Oxford University Press).

Saunders, B., Sim, J., Kingstone, T., Baker, S., Waterfield, J., Bartlam, B., Burroughs, H. and Jinks, C. (2018) Saturation in Qualitative Research: Exploring its Conceptualization and Operationalization, *Quality and Quantity*, 52(4), 1893–1907.

Sayer, R. (1992) *Method in Social Science: A Realist Approach* (2nd edn., London and New York: Routledge).

Sayer, R. (2010) *Realism and Social Science* (London, New Delhi, Thousand Oaks: SAGE Publications).

Schein, E. (2016) *Organisational Culture and Leadership* (5th edn., New York: John Wiley & Sons, Inc.).

Schön, D.A. (1984) *The Reflective Practitioner: How Professionals Think in Action* (New York: Basic Books).

Shaffer, T.L. (2005) *Shaffer and Elkins' Legal Interviewing and Counseling in a Nutshell* (4th edn., London: West Academic Publishing).

Siems, M. (2018) *Comparative Law* (Cambridge: Cambridge University Press).

Simon, W. (1978) The Ideology of Advocacy: Procedural Justice and Professional Ethics, *Wisconsin Law Review*, 29–145.

Skinns, L. (2009) 'Let's Get It Over with': Early Findings on the Factors Affecting Detainees' Access to Custodial Legal Advice, *Policing and Society*, 19(1), 58–87.

Skinns, L. (2010) *Police Custody: Governance, Legitimacy and Reform in the Criminal Justice Process* (London: Willan).

Skolnick, J. (1966) *Justice without Trial* (New York: John Wiley & Sons, Inc.).

Smith, T. (2013) The 'Quiet Revolution' in Criminal Defence: How the Zealous Advocate Slipped in the Shadow, *International Journal of the Legal Profession*, 20(1), 111–137.

Smith, T. and Cape, E. (2017) 'The Rise and Decline of Criminal Legal Aid in England and Wales', in: Flynn, A. and Hodgson, J. (eds.), *Access to Justice and Legal Aid: Comparative Perspectives on Unmet Legal Need* (Oxford: Hart Publishing), 63–86.

Sobh, R. and Perry, C. (2006) Research Design and Data Analysis in Realism Research, *European Journal of Marketing*, 4(11/12), 1194–1209.

Softley, P. (1980) *Police Detention: An Observational Study in Four Police Stations, Home Office Research Studies, No. 61* (London: Home Office).

Sommerlad, H. (1999) The Implementation of Quality Initiatives and the New Public Management in the Legal Aid Sector in England and Wales: Bureaucratisation, Stratification and Surveillance, *International Journal of the Legal Profession*, 6(3), 311–343.

Sommerlad, H. (2001) 'I've Lost the Plot': an Everyday Story of Legal Aid Lawyers, *Journal of Law and Society*, 28(3), 335–360.

Sommerlad, H. and Sanderson, P. (2013) Social Justice on the Margins: the Future of the Not for Profit Sector as Providers of Legal Advice in England and Wales, *Journal of Social Welfare and Family Law*, 35(3), 305–327.

Sommerlad, H and Wall, D. (1999) *Legally Aided Clients and Their Solicitors: Qualitative Perspectives on Quality and Legal Aid* (London: The Law Society).

Soo, A. (2017) How Are the Member States Progressing on Transposition of Directive 2013/48/EU on the Right of Access to a Lawyer?: An Inquiry Conducted among the Member States with the Special Focus on How Article 12 Is Transposed, *New Journal of European Criminal Law*, 8(1), 64–76.

Soubise, L. (2017) Prosecuting in the Magistrates' Courts in a Time of Austerity, *Criminal Law Review*, 11, 847–859.

Soubise, L. (2018) Guilty Pleas in an Inquisitorial Setting – An Empirical Study of France, *Journal of Law and Society*, 45(3), 398–426.

Soukara, S., Bull, R., Vrij, A., Turner, M. and Cherryman, J. (2009) What Really Happens in Police Interviews of Suspects? *Tactics and Confessions, Psychology, Crime and Law*, 15, 493–506.

Spencer, J.R. (2016) Adversarial vs Inquisitorial Systems: Is There Still Such a Difference?, *The International Journal of Human Rights*, 20(6), 601–616.

Spronken, T. (2001) *Verdediging: Een Onderzoek naar de Normering van het Optreden van Advocaten in Strafzaken* (Deventer: Gouda Quint).

Spronken, T. (2012) Het Strafrecht als Vergiet en het ZSM-Model als Snelkookpan, *Nieuwsbrief Strafrecht*, 4, 373–377.

Spronken, T. (2015) De Wasstraat, *Nederlands Juristenblad*, 5, 295–297.

Spronken, T. and de Vocht, D. (2011) EU Policy to Guarantee Procedural Rights in Criminal Proceedings: Step by Step, *North Carolina Journal of International Law and Commercial Regulation*, 37(2), 436–485.

Spronken, T., Vermeulen, G., De Vocht, D. and van Puyenbroeck, L. (2009) *EU Procedural Rights in Criminal Proceedings* (Brussels: European Commission, Directorate-General Justice, Freedom and Security).

Stevens, L. (2005) *Het Nemo-Teneturbeginsel in Strafzaken: van Zwijgrecht naar Containerbegrip* (Nijmegen: Wolf Legal Publishers).

Stevens, L. and Verhoeven, W.J. (2010) *Raadsman bij Politieverhoor. Invloed van Voorafgaande Consultatie en Aanwezigheid van Raadslieden, op de Organisatie en Wijze van Verhoren en de Proceshouding van de Verdachte* (Den Haag: Boom Juridische Uitgevers).

Stiansen, Ø. and Voeten, E. (2018) Backlash and Judicial Restraint: Evidence from the European Court of Human Rights, available from SSRN, <http://dx.doi.org/10.2139/ssrn.3166110> (last accessed on 16 July 2019).

Sukumar, D., Hodgson, J.S. and Wade, K.A. (2016) Behind Closed Doors: Live Observations of Current Police Station Disclosure Practices and Lawyer-Client Consultations, *Criminal Law Review*, 12, 900–914.

Summers, S. (2007) *Fair Trials: The European Criminal Procedural Tradition and the European Court of Human Rights* (Oxford and Portland, Oregon: Hart Publishing).

Sunstein, C.R. (1996) On the Expressive Function of Law, *University of Pennsylvania Law Review*, 144, 2021–2053.

Sykes, G.M. and Matza, D. (1957) Techniques of Neutralization: A Theory of Delinquency, *American Sociological Review*, 22, 664–670.

Tata, C. (2007) In the Interests of Clients or Commerce? Legal Aid, Supply, Demand, and 'Ethical Indeterminacy' in Criminal Defence Work, *Journal of Law and Society*, 34(4), 489–519.

Tata, C. and Stephen, F. (2007) 'When Paying the Piper Gets the 'Wrong' Tune: The Impact of Fixed Payments on Case Management, Case Trajectories and 'Quality' in Criminal Defence Work', in: *Transforming Lives* (London: The Stationery Office, U.K.), 186–210.

Tata, C., Goriely, T., McCrone, P., Duff, P., Knapp, M., Henry, A., Lancaster, B. and Sherr, A. (2002) Does Mode of Delivery Make a Difference to Criminal Case Outcomes and Clients' Satisfaction? The Public Defence Solicitor Experiment, *Criminal Law Review*, 120–135.

Thomas, M.S., van Kampen, P.T.C., van Lent, L., Schiffelers, M.J.W.A., Langbroek, P.M. and van Erp, J.G. (2016) *Snel, Betekenisvol en Zorgvuldig, Een Tussenevaluatie van de ZSM-Werkwijze* (WODC/Universiteit Utrecht).

Toney, R.J. (2001) English Criminal Procedure under Article 6 of the European Convention on Human Rights: Implications for Custodial Interrogation Practices, *Houston Journal of International Law*, 24(3), 411–475.

Townsley, L. (2014) Thinking Like a Lawyer Ethically: Narrative Intelligence and Emotion, *Legal Education Review*, 24(1&2), 68–92.

Travers, M. (1997) *The Reality of Law: Work and Talk in a Firm of Criminal Lawyers* (Aldershot: Dartmouth).

Twinning, W. (2009) *General Jurisprudence: Understanding Law from a Global Perspective* (Cambridge: Cambridge University Press).

Vähäsantanen, K. and Saarinen, J. (2012) The Power Dance in the Research Interview: Manifesting Power and Powerlessness, *Qualitative Research*, 13(5), 493–510.

Van Amelsvoort, A., Rispens, I. and Grolman, H. (2017) *Handleiding Verhoor* (7th edn., Den Haag: SDU Uitgevers).

Van den Brûle, I. (2014) Gezocht: Rol voor de Advocatuur bij ZSM, *Proces*, 1, 89–96.

Van der Meij, P. (2010) De Rechter-Commissaris als Onmisbare Schakel in het Strafrechtelijk Vooronderzoek?, *Trema*, 8, 331–338.

Van der Meij, P. (2014) De Andere Kant van de ZSM-Medaille: Het Gebrek aan Controle op Beleid en Beslissingen van het Openbaar Ministerie, *Nederlandse Juristenblad*, 25, 1666–1671.

Van der Meij, P. and Hartjes, L. (2015) 'Twijfels bij de Toekomstigheid van ZSM. Een Toets van het ZSM-Beleid aan Huidige en Voorzienbare Ontwikkelingen', in: Achterberg, N., Van Brandt, T., den Feiner, R., Van Heemst, B., Van Mathura, N. and Van Wijnbergen, L. (eds.), *Vrouwe Justitia zucht en steunt. Hoe houden we de rechtsstaat toekomstbestendig?* (Leiden: Stichting NJCM-Boekerij), 35–46.

Van Kampen, P.T.C. and Franken, A.A. (2013) 'Een Herbezinning op de Rol van de Raadsman in het Vooronderzoek', in: Groenhuijsen, M., Koooijmans, T. and Ouwerkerk, J. (eds.), *Roosachtig Strafrecht, Liber Amicorum Theo de Roos* (Deventer: Kluwer), 235–248.

Van Kampen, P.T.C. and Hein, D.W. (2013) Strijd om Stukken: de Wet Processtukken, *Nederlands Juristenblad*, 2, 72–78.

Van Kampen, P.T.C., Brouwer, D.V.A., van Lent, L. and van Wijk, M.C. (2018) *Mind the Gap. Modernisering Wetboek van Strafvordering: consequenties voor de verdediging* (Utrecht: Universiteit Utrecht – Montaigne Centrum voor Rechtspleging en Conflictoplossing).

Van Lent, L., Thomas, M.A.S. and van Kampen, P. (2016) De ZSM-Werkwijze in Praktijk – Op Zoek naar Balans, *Nederlands Juristenblad*, 37, 2753–2758.

van Puyenbroeck, L. and Vermeulen, G. (2011) Towards Minimum Procedural Guarantees for the Defence in Criminal Proceedings in the EU, *International & Comparative Law Quarterly*, 60(4), 1017–1038.

van Zanten, Peter, de Boer, A., Hoppe, T., van Rosmalen, F., Gemke, P. and de Bruijn, J.A. (2017) *Evaluatie van Prestaties van de Politie: Deel 2 van de Evaluatie van de Politiewet 2012* (Den Haag: WODC).

Vanderhallen, M. and Vervaeke, G. (2014) 'Between Investigator and Suspect: The Role of the Working Alliance in Investigative Interviewing', in: Bull, R. (ed.), *Investigative Interviewing* (New York: Springer), 63–91.

Vanderhallen, M., de Jong, A., Nelen, H. and Spronken, T. (2014) *Toga's in de Verhoorkamer. De Invloed van Rechtsbijstand op het Politieverhoor* (Den Haag: Boom Lemma).

Vanderhallen, M., van Oosterhout, M., Panzavolta, M. and de Vocht, D. (eds.) (2016) *Interrogating Young Suspects II: Procedural Safeguards from an Empirical Perspective* (Cambridge, Antwerp, Portland: Intersentia).

Varga, C. (1992) *Comparative Legal Cultures* (New York: New York University Press).

Vitkauskas, D. and Dikov, G. (2002) *Protecting the Right to a Fair Trial under the European Convention on Human Rights* (Strasbourg: Council of Europe).

Vrij, A. (2017) 'Het Verhoren van Verdachten', in: van Koppen, P.J., Horselenberg, R. and de Keijser, J.W. (eds.), *Routes van het Recht. Over de Rechtspsychologie* (Den Haag: Boom Juridisch), 643–669.

Waddington, P. (1999) Police (Canteen) Sub-Culture. An Appreciation. *British Journal of Criminology*, 39(2), 287–309.

Weigend, T. (2013) 'Germany', in: Ligeti, K. (ed.), *Towards a Prosecutor for the European Union Volume 1: Comparative Analysis* (Oxford and Portland, OR: Hart Publishing), 264–306.

Welsh, L. (2017) The Effects of Changes to Legal Aid on Lawyers' Professional Identity and Behavior in Summary Criminal Cases: A Case Study, *Journal of Law and Society*, 44(4), 559–585.

Westaby, C. (2010) 'Feeling Like a Sponge': the Emotional Labour Produced by Solicitors in Their Interactions with Clients Seeking Asylum, *International Journal of the Legal Profession*, 17(2), 153–174.

Westley, W.A. (1970) *Violence and the Police: A Sociological Study of Law, Custom, and Morality* (Cambridge, MA: MIT Press).

Willig, C. (2016) Constructivism and 'The Real World': Can They Co-Exist?, *QMiP Bulletin*, 21, 33–37.

Wooff, A. and Skinns, L. (2018) The Role of Emotion, Space and Place in Police Custody in England: Towards a Geography of Police Custody, *Punishment & Society*, 20(5), 562–579.

Yakren, S. (2008) Lawyer as Emotional Labourer, *University of Michigan Journal of Law Reform*, 42, 141–184.

Young, R. and Wall, D. (1996) 'Criminal Justice, Legal Aid and the Defence of Liberty', in: Young, R. and Wall, D. (eds.), *Access to Criminal Justice* (London: Blackstone Press Ltd.), 254–275.

Zander, M. (1972) Access to a Solicitor in the Police Station, *Criminal Law Review*, 342–350.

Index

Aanwijzing Rechtsbijstand Politieverhoor (Netherlands) 38, 52, 105
accreditation 64, 107, 117, 153, 180
accredited representative (England and Wales) 7, 64, 86, 185
active defence 13, 91, 106–107, 112–114, 153, 171–175
adverse inferences from silence: and CJPOA 1994 (England and Wales) 65, 72–73, 112, 119, 127–129, 145, 146; general 16, 64, 72–74, 80, 123, 125–130
advising client: advising silence 157–158, 159–162; and directive approach 72–75, 175; and England and Wales 72–75; gathering information 43–46, 102–103; general 18–20, 43–48, 67–75; during interrogation 21–25; and Netherlands 43–48; procedural strategy 19–20, 46–48, 72–75, 103–104; providing information 19, 46–48; and regulars 72, 158–159
'amoral' role (common law) 68–69, 101
appropriate adult (England and Wales) 85, 86
assistant prosecutor (Netherlands) 39, 52, 139
austerity 121, 145

Belgium 3, 7
Besluit inrichting en orde politieverhoor (Netherlands) 36, 38, 105
Bhaskar, R. 183, 189
Blackstock, J. 3, 7, 9, 18, 21, 25, 36, 39, 51, 52, 56, 62, 72, 78, 80, 81, 91, 108, 111, 113, 148, 153, 167, 172, 175
Brants, C. 6, 35, 36, 38, 93, 97, 98, 99, 115

canteen culture, police 150, 152
Can v. Austria 16, 26, 29
Cape, E. 4, 5, 23, 29, 33, 34, 63, 64, 65, 66, 73, 87, 92, 98, 100, 103, 113, 114, 122, 123, 130, 138, 147, 148, 152, 179
Cardiff Three (England and Wales) 107
Chan, J. 149, 150, 178
charge: and CPS role 139–141; England and Wales 33, 63, 67, 80, 92, 139–141
Charmaz, K. 183–184, 186, 187, 189
Charter of Core Principles 33
CIPA 1996 (England and Wales) 34, 65, 89, 98, 122–123
CJEU 15, 173–174
client-centred defence 107, 152
comparative approach 4, 5–6
Confait affair (England and Wales) 66, 106
confirmation bias 109
constructivist grounded theory 182–184, 189
contextual analysis 5–6
convergence thesis 97
cost-saving: fixed fees 107, 123, 137, 141–144, 163; legal aid 121, 123–124, 137, 141–144, 153
Council of Europe 9
Council Resolution 2009/C 295/01 9
crime control 97, 112, 118–119, 120; and lawyers 122–124
critical realism: actual level 183; causal mechanisms 5–6, 183–184; demi-regularity 183–184; empirical level 183; general 182–184, 189; theoretical redescription 184

culturalist approach 178
custody officer: England and Wales 66–67, 88, 92, 138–140; Netherlands 41, 49, 52

Damaška, M. 6, 98, 100–101
data coding 184
de auditu judgment (Netherlands) 37
Dev Sol judgment (Netherlands) 36
Directive 2016/800 22, 33, 34
Directive 2012/13/EU 19, 21, 26, 172
Directive 2013/48/EU 2–3, 10–11, 14–16, 22, 27, 32, 38; and implementation 38, 52; Wet Implementatie Richtlijn (Netherlands) 38
disclosure: access to case file 21, 36, 136–137, 172–173; and *Directive 2012/13/EU* 21; and England and Wales 111–114, 65–66, 80–81; general 21, 50–52, 65, 111–114; and Netherlands 50–52, 111–114, 136–137; obtaining (lawyers) 21, 50–52, 80–81, 111–114; and prosecutors 65–66; strategic 54
Dixon, D. 66, 106, 116, 178–179
dossier: general 99, 114, 153; and Netherlands 35–37, 44, 45, 47, 50–51, 135
due process 118–119, 179, 181
Dutch Bar Association (NOvA) 7, 52
Dutch Code of Criminal Procedure 34, 35–36, 120
duty lawyer 40, 59–60, 65–68, 153

early access, lawyer: and history (Netherlands) and history (England and Wales) 66; participatory rationales 16; protective rationales 16; and rates (England and Wales) 66; right 3, 16
ECHR 9, 14, 15, 22, 26, 29, 30, 31
ECtHR 3, 4, 9, 10, 11–14, 17–31, 32, 38
effective defence 11, 24–25
effective participation 15, 18, 22, 27–30, 173–174
emotional distancing: depersonalising clients 165; emotional labour 164–165; lawyers 162–165
examining magistrate (Netherlands) 35, 37, 42, 44, 50–51, 53, 58, 59, 133–134
expressive theory of law 179

fact-finding, participation: confrontation 28; defence investigation 29–30, 59–60, 64–65, 90, 109–111; and England and Wales 64–65, 89–90, 109–111; general 27–29, 59–60, 89–90, 109–111, 175; ID parade 27–29, 89–90; investigative act 27–29, 89; and Netherlands 37, 59–60, 109–111; and witnesses 59–60, 90, 109–111
false confession (risk of) 2, 3, 11, 22, 25, 34
Field, S. 4, 111, 115
'field' 168, 177–181
fitness for interview 22, 77, 86
France 3, 7, 9, 34, 116, 153, 172

Garland, D. 118
Gedragsregels (Netherlands) 37, 40, 110
Glenn, P. 95–96
guilty plea (England and Wales) 123, 128, 153

habeas corpus 26, 34
'habitus' 168, 177–181
Havana Declaration 16
Hodgson, J. 4, 6, 7, 9, 25, 65, 100, 109, 115, 148, 153

incommunicado detention (Netherlands) 24, 35, 110–111
independent agent (England and Wales) 144, 187
interrogation: and role lawyer 52–58, 81–84, 104–109, 173–174; countering pressure 56–58, 82–84; and England and Wales 81–84; and exclusion from 57–59; and Netherlands 52–58; and passivity lawyer 56–58, 82–84, 104–109; and police resistance (lawyers) 52; unfair questioning 23–25; and vulnerable suspects 22, 34, 86; written record 24–25
interrogation tactics: being friendly 54–55; and England and Wales 81–94; and lawfulness 56; manipulation 54–55, 57, 106; and Netherlands 34, 53–56; persuasion 34, 53–55, 83; police 34, 53–56, 83

investigative stage: general 2, 4–5, 36–37, 63–64; increasing shift towards 4–5, 171, 173; and participatory rights (England and Wales) 63–64; and participatory rights (Netherlands) 36–37; and procedural fairness 10–11; and role lawyer 1–2, 9–31, 64–66

Jackson, J. 2, 3, 4, 9, 10, 11, 29, 30, 32, 64, 80, 97, 98, 114, 122

Kemp, V. 4, 66, 80, 107, 123, 153
knowingly lying statement (Netherlands) 126–127, 158

Langer, M. 6, 29, 96, 97–98, 104, 112, 114, 115, 116, 176
lawyer-centred model 92, 103, 168
lawyer–client consultation: and England and Wales 66–68; general 17–20; and Netherlands 39–40
lawyer–client relationship: confidentiality 18; and England and Wales 68–75, 101–104; general 17–18, 40–43, 68–75, 101–104; loyalty to client 17; and Netherlands 40–43, 101–104; trust, general 17, 40–43, 102; trust, lack of 41–43, 70–72, 155–159; and truth 41, 42, 45, 47, 54, 62, 65, 69, 70, 126, 130–131, 155–159
lawyer–police relationship: and England and Wales 77–81; general 77–81, 165–168; non-confrontational 77–81, 165–168
Legal Aid Board (Netherlands) 39, 107
legalistic approach 178
Leidraad Politieverhoor (Netherlands) 52
Leng, R. 128
Loftus, B. 150, 151

managerialism: criminal justice 119–124, 177; and England and Wales 119–124; and lawyer role 121–124; and Netherlands 120–124
McConville, M. 4, 6, 23, 25, 66, 80, 89, 91, 106, 109, 112, 113, 118, 123, 152, 153, 155, 158, 165, 166, 167
medical assistance 20, 22, 49, 50, 77, 162

minor (age) 37–38, 53, 56, 57, 58, 108, 125, 143, 174
minor offence 39, 67, 135

Nelken, D. 6, 95
neutralisation technique 108
Newman, D. 4, 107, 118, 124, 152, 153, 155, 163, 177, 180, 186
new public management (England and Wales) 124

observation: fieldwork 184–188; going native 187–188; methodological self-consciousness 184; methodology 185–188
occupational cultures: enacted values 116, 154–155; espoused values 116, 148, 154; general 4, 148–155, 177; internal dispositions 115–116, 176; and lawyers 4, 150–168; and police 4, 148–150; and research 4, 149–150; Schein's model 148–149, 154; underlying assumptions 149, 155
out-of-court disposal: caution (England and Wales) 67, 75, 87–89, 137–138; general 30–31, 75, 135–138; and investigative stage 30–31, 135–138; and lawyer role 30–31, 75, 87–89; penal order (Netherlands) 34, 35, 120

PACE (England and Wales) 63–64, 72–73, 75–76, 84–87, 89, 92, 105–106, 112–113, 134–135, 179; Code of Practice C 72, 76, 92, 105, 106
Packer, J. 118, 145
participatory role 172–174
police detention: and bail (England and Wales) 33, 63, 67, 77, 80, 87–89, 138, 140, 144; and bureaucratisation 138–141, 145; and conditions 20, 163–165; general 20, 109; and release 26, 58–59, 132–133
post-*Salduz* judgment (Netherlands) 37–38
Prakken, T. 35, 36, 47, 48, 58, 59, 108
prepared statement (England and Wales) 72–74, 81, 104, 129–130, 147, 156–157
pre-trial detention: access to case file 26; general 26, 35, 43, 53, 133, 134, 147; release 16, 26, 173

procedural irregularities: and England and Wales 84–87, 134–135; general 34, 58–59, 84–87, 132–135; and Netherlands 58–59, 133
procedural tradition: adversarial 63, 69, 78–79, 94, 98–101, 102, 104, 107, 109, 111–116, 154, 166, 174; and behaviour 114–116; and occupational culture 154–155; dichotomy 97–98; and discourse 114–115; general 5–6, 93–101, 114–116, 174–175, 176–177; inquisitorial 29, 35, 37, 94, 98–101, 102, 104, 107, 108–109, 111–116, 154, 174; and legal culture 95–96; and legal tradition 95; normative information 96; rhetorical function 114–115; and role lawyer 99–101
professional ethics: and England and Wales 130–132; lawyers 37, 99–101, 126, 130–132; and Netherlands 37, 40–41
Protocol Raadsman Politieverhoor (Netherlands) 52

qualitative interviewing 186–187
quality assurance 180
Quirk, H. 65, 127, 129

Recommendation No. R (2000) 21, 33
Reiner, R. 120, 150, 151
repeat players: lawyers 161–162, 165–168, 175
research ethics 188
risk avoidance (lawyers) 159–162
Royal Commission on Criminal Procedure (England and Wales) 66

Salduz v. Turkey: *Beuze v. Belgium* 14; *Dayanan v. Turkey* 13; and *Directive 2013/48/EU* 14–16; general 3, 9, 11–12, 38; *Ibrahim and others v. UK* 13–14; post-*Salduz* 12–14

Schein, E. 148–189, 151, 154, 183
silence: improper compulsion 23–24; and informing about 46, 47, 72–73; and interrogation 23; right 23, 46, 47, 72–73
Skinns, L. 2, 18, 20, 66, 153, 164
Smith, T. 4, 107, 116, 123, 124, 177, 179
Sommerlad, H. 20, 124, 181
Spronken, T. 7, 9, 10, 15, 35, 36, 37, 38, 41, 47, 48, 58, 59, 108, 110, 120, 122, 135
SRA Code of Conduct 65–66, 68
Statuut Raadsman (Netherlands) 36, 37, 40, 102
Stevens, L. 46, 52, 127
structural approach 178–179
Summers, S. 4, 10, 11, 29, 30, 32, 97
support client: and detention 20, 48–50, 162–163; and England and Wales 75–77; and Netherlands 48–50

training 180
'trusted person' (Netherlands) 48–50
truth-finding 45, 97, 99–100, 109, 112, 114, 179

UN Guidelines and Principles 33

van Kampen, P. 8, 34, 51, 61, 108, 113
Verhoeven, W.J. 8, 46, 52
volunteer in custody (England and Wales) 86, 92

Waddington, B. 150, 152
Welsh, L. 4, 107, 124, 167, 177
West, A. 4, 111, 115
working personality, police 150, 155

ZSM procedure (Netherlands) 112, 120, 125–126, 135–137, 146, 177, 179; legal assistance pilots 135

Printed in the United States
By Bookmasters